Constitution Making in Eastern Europe

Constitution Making in Eastern Europe

edited by A. E. Dick Howard

 Published by The Woodrow Wilson Center Press

Distributed by The Johns Hopkins University Press

Woodrow Wilson Center Special Studies

The Woodrow Wilson Center Press
Editorial Offices
370 L'Enfant Promenade, S.W.
Suite 704
Washington, D.C. 20024-2518 U.S.A.
telephone 202-287-3000, ext. 218

Distributed by
The Johns Hopkins University Press
Hampden Station
Baltimore, Maryland 21211
order department telephone 1-800-537-5487

Printed in the United States of America

⊗ Printed on acid-free paper.

9 8 7 6 5 4 3 2 1

Library of Congress Cataloging-in-Publication Data

Constitution making in Eastern Europe / edited by A.E. Dick Howard.
     p.   cm.—(Woodrow Wilson Center special studies)
   Includes bibliographical references and index.
   ISBN 0-943875-48-X (paper : acid-free paper)
   1. Europe, Eastern—Constitutional law.   I. Howard, A. E. Dick.
II. Series
KJC4445.C66 1993
342.47' 02—dc20   93-4044
[344.7022]   CIP

The Woodrow Wilson International Center for Scholars

The Center is the "living memorial" of the United States of America to the nation's twenty-eighth president, Woodrow Wilson. The U.S. Congress established the Woodrow Wilson Center in 1968 as an international institute for advanced study, "symbolizing and strengthening the fruitful relationship between the world of learning and the world of public affairs." The Center opened in 1970 under its own presidentially appointed board of directors.

Woodrow Wilson Center Special Studies

The work of the Center's Fellows, Guest Scholars, and staff and presentations and discussions at the Center's conferences, seminars, and colloquia often deserve timely circulation as contributions to public understanding of issues of national and international importance. The Woodrow Wilson Center Special Studies series is intended to make such materials available by the Woodrow Wilson Center Press to interested scholars, practitioners, and other readers. In all its activities, the Woodrow Wilson Center is a nonprofit, nonpartisan organization, supported financially by annual appropriations from the U.S. Congress, and by the contributions of foundations, corporations, and individuals. Conclusions or opinions expressed in Center publications and programs are those of the authors and speakers and do not necessarily reflect the views of the Center's staff, Fellows, Trustees, advisory groups, or any individuals or organizations that provide financial support to the Center.

Contents

Acknowledgments

This book had its origins in a core seminar series on "East European Constitutions," held in the fall of 1991 and spring of 1992. The sessions were organized by East European Studies of the Woodrow Wilson International Center for Scholars in Washington, D.C. Funds supporting these seminars and the publication of this book came from a grant awarded to the Woodrow Wilson Center's East European Studies program by Congress under the terms of the Soviet and East European Research and Training Act of 1983.

The editor gratefully acknowledges Paula Bailey Smith, East European Studies program associate, and Traci Nagle, editorial assistant, who prepared the manuscript for publication, with help from East European Studies program assistant Kristin Hunter and program interns Sandra W. Smith, Steve Langmuir, and B. Susan White.

Introduction

A. E. Dick Howard

Writing a constitution is a symbolic event in the life of a people or country. A few countries, such as the United Kingdom and Israel, do without a written constitution. Most, however, see a constitution as a document in which the fundamentals of a polity are set down.

Constitutions serve many purposes. They ordain the uses of power by creating such institutions of government as a parliament, an executive, and courts. They channel government's power, for example, in specifying how a bill becomes a law. They put limits on power, for example, in bills of rights declaring fundamental rights.

Some constitutions live a long time. The United States Constitution was drafted in 1787 and, with its amendments, remains in force today. Other constitutions are short-lived; since 1789, the start of the French Revolution, France has had seventeen constitutions.

Great crises—revolution, civil war, political upheaval, fundamental changes in regime—tend to trigger the making of a constitution. The Belgian Constitution of 1830 and the constitution of France's Fifth Republic are examples.

The collapse of the Soviet Empire has brought just such a time of constitution making to the countries of Central and Eastern Europe. The dawn of a new era requires constitutions that reflect

1

the premises of a democratic society in which the rule of law replaces the rule of the party.

As the process of constitution making unfolds, it is fitting that the Woodrow Wilson International Center for Scholars should undertake to assess the lessons of that experience. Woodrow Wilson, himself a great student of constitutional government, took a personal interest in the kind of regimes that would emerge in Central and Eastern Europe after World War I. Indeed, on a recent trip to Albania, I was told by that country's president of the large number of Albanian children who have been named Wilson in honor of an American whose principles are still remembered there. I am sure that, were he to read these essays, Wilson would be pleased to see his namesake institution inquiring into the metes and bounds of constitutionalism in Central and Eastern Europe.

The Wilson Center's East European Studies program invited six scholars to its 1992–93 core seminar on constitution making in the countries of Central and Eastern Europe. The chapters that compose this volume are the fruits of those scholars' thinking. Anyone who reads these essays is bound to be struck by the difficulties that face the countries of the region as they attempt to write new constitutions. The euphoria that characterized Czechoslovakia's "velvet revolution" and similar events in neighboring countries has given way to a sober assessment of the hard political and economic decisions that must be made. As these authors make clear, it was easier to agree on ousting the ancien régime than it has been to chart a course for the future.

Andrzej Rapaczynski, who here writes about constitutional politics in Poland, points to the most fundamental problem facing the region's constitution makers—"the fact that the new constitution must be prepared at a time of profound and rapid changes in the political and economic structure of the country." Politics, of course, rears its head, and short-term goals are given greater attention. Rapaczynski paints a vivid picture of the way in which, after Solidarity's split into two factions, intellectuals of the "Warsaw" faction began to view the draft constitution as a means to prevent Lech Wałęsa, backed by the "Gdańsk" faction, from dominating Parliament and the government.

Similarly, Katarina Mathernova, who in her essay surveys the efforts to write a constitution for the Czech and Slovak Federal Republic, comments on the fact that, even while Slovak leaders in the Federal Assembly propelled the country toward separation by creating deadlock, public opinion polls had consistently shown that a majority of the population in both the Czech and Slovak republics wanted to remain in a common state. She concludes that the struggle has been, in good part, a power struggle.

In these struggles, history and nationality play their part. Americans and other Western observers sometimes tend to lump the countries of Central and Eastern Europe together, as if the same generalizations might apply to all of them. Those countries do indeed have certain things in common, the most obvious their being brought within the sphere of Soviet domination after World War II.

Many factors, however, make each country distinctive. In ethnic terms, Poland and Hungary are more homogeneous than is Romania, with its large Hungarian minority, or Bulgaria, with its people of Turkish heritage. Even the Czechs and Slovaks are, as the term is used in Central Europe, two separate "nations" (the Slovaks especially view themselves that way). Bohemia, at one time an independent kingdom, was the most prosperous part of the Austro-Hungarian Empire, whereas until 1918 Slovakia, poorer than the Czech lands, was under Hungarian rule. It is small wonder that Mathernova comments on the "backpack full of history" that the peoples of Central Europe carry on their shoulders.

Custom and tradition have their effect on constitutional development. Even the repressions of the Communist years, during which party leaders sought to mold the local equivalent of the "Soviet man," could not wipe out centuries of traditional ideas about constitutionalism. Péter Paczolay, chief counselor to Hungary's Constitutional Court, stresses in his chapter the importance of customary law in Hungarian constitutional history.

The Hungarian notion of a "constitutional revolution" emphasizes the place of law, not only in mapping out a future political arrangement, but also in justifying the manner and mode of transition. Paczolay remarks on the similarities between the revolution of 1848 in Hungary and the way in which constitutional change unfolded beginning in 1989. Thus Hungary achieved a peaceful transition to a multiparty system without resorting to force or other extraconstitutional means.

Ideas, as well as politics, history, and custom, play their part when new constitutions are written (ideas, of course, are intertwined with those forces). The notion of popular sovereignty, intertwined with Jean-Jacques Rousseau's notion of the general will, is a powerful force in French political thought. Rapaczynski remarks on the strength of this view in Poland; it presents "the people" as the true sovereign, "endowed with a will of their own from which all legitimate political authority stems." A tendency to "take certain democratic clichés too literally," however, complicates any effort to create a viable balance between parliament, the government, and the president.

Bureaucratic habits—these will be familiar to students of government in the West—can make reforms tenuous. Joanna Regulska considers the prospects for local government in the constitutions of Central and Eastern Europe. She sees major barriers to establishing autonomous local self-government in the region. There are, to be sure, conceptual problems in laying the foundation for authentic local government, yet the problems extend beyond those of concept.

Whatever the relevant constitution and laws may say about the status and powers of local government, Regulska notes the tendency of central government's ministries to establish their own branch offices rather than allow self-government to emerge from the bottom up. Local governments often find themselves denied sufficient financial resources. Constitutional proclamations of local autonomy clash with tendencies of those at the center to retain power.

Existing governmental structures, especially those established at an earlier time when circumstances were different, can be important factors in the shape of constitutional revision. For example, a key element in the compromise hammered out during Poland's 1989 roundtable talks was the restoration of the Senate, which the Communists had abolished after World War II. The opposition could compete freely with the Communists for seats (65 percent of the seats in the lower house were assigned to the Communists and their allies). The 1989 elections dealt such a blow to the Communists, however, that Solidarity was able to form a government.

Under these circumstances the Senate had lost the essential reason for its having been reinstated. Yet the drafters of the new constitution were confronted with a dilemma. If the lower house was on its way to being a truly democratic institution, they could not leave the Senate as it was. Yet they could not move to abolish the Senate; it had to vote on a new constitution. A subcommittee of the constitutional drafting commission sought to resolve this problem by providing for the indirect election of senators and having the senators represent units of local government.

Structure can indeed be critical to the success or failure of constitutional drafting. Mathernova believes that one of the chief reasons for the failure of the effort to agree on a new constitution for the Czech and Slovak Federal Republic lay in the institutional structure created by a 1968 amendment to the Constitution. That document created a Federal Assembly with two houses: a Chamber of People, elected by Czechs and Slovaks on the basis of population, and a Chamber of Nations, with equal numbers of deputies from the Czech and Slovak lands. On important bills the 1968 amendment required the concurrence of a majority of the deputies from each of the two republics in the Chamber of Nations. During the efforts to write a new constitution, Slovak opposition party members were able to exercise a veto in what turned out to be, in effect, a Federal Assembly made up of three chambers.

In the face of such obstacles, one can begin to understand why the road to constitutional reform in Central and Eastern Europe has been so difficult. In the early months after the overthrow of the old order, it was natural to suppose that Poland, Hungary, and Czechoslovakia would be the first of the former Warsaw Pact countries to adopt new constitutions. It was Poland that had galvanized the forces of change with the emergence of Solidarity, and Poles had high hopes of having a new constitution in place in time to celebrate the bicentennial of the great constitution of 3 May 1791.

Czechoslovakia, too, gave cause for optimism. It cherished the legacy of a vibrant, functioning democracy in the years between the world wars. The "velvet revolution" had produced the most admired figure in all of the countries of the region, Václav Havel, a leader of great moral stature. Hungary also had made an auspicious start, having been the region's innovator in economic change. Who would have predicted, in 1990, that the first two countries in the region to adopt new constitutions would be Bulgaria and Romania?

It would be a mistake, however, to measure progress simply by the yardstick of the formal adoption of brand-new constitutions. Problems notwithstanding, there has been progress on important fronts. One should take note, in particular, of the establishment of constitutional courts and the decisions being handed down by those courts to enforce constitutional principles.

Judicial review—the power of a court to declare a legislative act invalid on the grounds of its unconstitutionality—is a familiar feature of the American constitutional landscape. It is a relative newcomer, however, to the European scene. After World War II, constitutional courts were established in various countries of Western Europe. But in the Communist countries, the idea of independent courts, like that of the rule of law, was antithetical to ideas of state and party. With the demise of Communist rule in Central and Eastern Europe, constitutional courts have appeared on the landscape of that region as well.

Herman Schwartz, a seasoned practitioner of human rights and constitutional law, writes about the constitutional courts of Central and Eastern Europe. The civil law tradition of judging, as Schwartz points out, produces "career judges" who see their job as simply carrying out the will of their country's parliament. Against this civil law background, and the regional legacy of courts as ciphers during the Communist period, Schwartz notes how the newly created constitutional courts of Central and Eastern Europe have operated "with surprising independence." Those who don a judge's robes in those countries "can become courageous and vigorous defenders of constitutional principles and human rights."

Will the countries of Central and Eastern Europe have their "constitutional moments"? Americans had such a moment with the adoption, in the 1780s, of their federal Constitution. Despite the opposition of the Anti-Federalists to ratification, and the close vote in some of the ratifying conventions, the Constitution became, in time, the nearest thing the United States has to an ark of the covenant. In the gropings of constitution makers in Central and Eastern Europe, it appears that such a "moment" has not occurred there yet.

One should recall, however, that before James Madison and his colleagues arrived at Philadelphia in 1787, Americans had lived through a decade of trial and error in establishing the foundations of an enduring constitutionalism. The first state constitutions, beginning with those adopted in 1776, were hardly flawless. They gave legislatures too much power, they tolerated a limited franchise and legislative malapportionment, and sometimes they were challenged as lacking authentic legitimacy. At the federal level, the Articles of Confederation were even more flawed; they created a central government so dependent on the states as to be unable to deal with economic problems at home and largely impotent in the face of foreign challenges abroad. From such unsteady beginnings came much of the insight that produced the 1787 Constitution.

Americans weathered the 1770s and 1780s, charting a course for their future. Two centuries later, citizens of the older democracies can hope that the peoples of Central and Eastern Europe will find a sure foundation for their constitutional aspirations. The problems are daunting: the raging fires of nationality and ethnicity, the dislocations of rebuilding enfeebled economies, the malaise and cynicism that accompany hard times, the need to inculcate civic values that will make democratic ideals part of the people's moral fiber. In their effort to build constitutional democracies, the peoples of Central and Eastern Europe have the affection and encouragement of all who search for the blessings of ordered liberty.

Chapter 1

How Ideas Travel:
Rights at Home and Abroad

A. E. Dick Howard

Neither time nor place can cabin ideas. In 1987 United States citizens celebrated the two hundredth anniversary of their Constitution, and in 1991 they marked the bicentennial of their Bill of Rights. At just the same time—as if history were a creative choreographer—the peoples of Central and Eastern Europe were proving the resilience of old ideas about freedom, human dignity, and democracy. After living for so many years under oppressive one-party regimes, people in Central and Eastern Europe and the Soviet sphere now find themselves questing for choices long denied them.

New times require new constitutions. Nearly every country, even the most repressive, has a "constitution." We are all too familiar with constitutions, such as the Soviet Union's 1936 Constitution, whose glowing promises of justice and human dignity have little relation to reality. Such documents must be discarded, and authentic constitutionalism planted in their place.

Thus, as the United States reflected on the two hundred–year odyssey of its Bill of Rights, Russians, Poles, Bulgarians, and others began to write new constitutions. At the core of each of these new documents lies a bill of rights. Indeed, in January 1991 the national assembly of the Czech and Slovak Federal Republic gave priority to the adoption of a new bill of rights; meanwhile debate continued on other constitutional provisions—in particular, those effecting a division of powers between the federal government and the two republics.

Those who draft a bill of rights must understand the history and traditions of the country for which the document is being created. One who sought to write a bill of rights for Hungary, for example, would need to know about the great Golden Bull of 1222 (which is to Hungarian history what Magna Carta is to that of England), the impact of Enlightenment thought on eighteenth-century Hungary, and the reformist thrust of the 1848 revolution. Likewise, a Polish drafter would wish to recall the legacy of Polish Constitutionalism, including the notable Constitution of 3 May 1791—the world's second national constitution (after the Philadelphia Constitution of 1787).

Stating a people's rights is not, however, a parochial exercise. Drafters of bills of rights look not only to their own country's experience but also to that of other countries. Professors and scholars who work with constitutional commissions in Central and Eastern Europe are well read; they know the Federalist Papers and the writings of Western theorists such as John Locke and Montesquieu. Drafting commissions invite experts from other countries to pore over drafts and offer comments and advice.

Traffic is heavy between the United States and the emerging democracies, as well as between those countries and the capitals of Western Europe. Americans who travel to consult on new constitutions are sometimes dubbed "constitutional Johnny Appleseeds." West European experts are equally in demand. The president of France's Conseil Constitutionnel, Robert Badinter, and Heidelberg professor Helmut Steinberger (formerly a justice of the West German Supreme Court) have been frequent guests in Prague and Bucharest.

This international traffic in discourse about rights and constitutions is nothing new. Drafters of the early American constitutions, like their modern counterparts in Central and Eastern Europe, looked to both homegrown and imported ideas for inspiration. Indeed, the colonies' original charters linked rights in the Old World to those in the New. Each charter had a provision like that of the Virginia Company's charter of 1606 guaranteeing settlers "all liberties, franchises, and immunities . . . as if they had been abiding and born within this our Realm of England."

America's heritage from the British Constitution traces back for centuries. Magna Carta (1215) carried a guarantee of proceedings according to the "law of the land"—the forerunner of the principle of due process of law. Magna Carta's assurance that there should be no sale, denial, or delay of justice anticipated modern constitutional guarantees of equality before the law.

The struggles between Parliament and the Stuart kings in seventeenth-century England produced other "liberty documents" that influenced American views on constitutional rights. Sometimes the precedents are exact. England's Bill of Rights (1689) includes the precise counterpart of the First Amendment's guarantee of the right to petition for redress of grievances, the Second Amendment's assurance of the right to bear arms, and the Eighth Amendment's ban on excessive bail, excessive fines, and cruel and unusual punishment.

The framers of early American documents were also influenced by the writings of the great European political theorists. James Madison drew upon Montesquieu in declaring, in the Federalist No. 47, that allowing legislative, executive, and judicial powers to fall into the same hands "may justly be pronounced the very definition of tyranny." From Locke the American founders gleaned notions of a social compact and citizens' retention in civil society of the inherent rights of life, liberty, and property.

American drafters during the colonial period also introduced the fruits of their own deliberations on rights. Responding to complaints about the lack of an established body of laws protecting rights in Massachusetts Bay, the colony's magistrates adopted, in 1648, the Laws and Liberties of Massachusetts. Pennsylvania's founder, William Penn, drafted that colony's Frame of Government (1682), containing such guarantees as open courts, jury trial, and moderate fines.

The year 1776 brought revolution, independence, and the opportunity for Americans to declare those rights they deemed fundamental to a free society. In May 1776 a convention, meeting in Williamsburg, instructed Virginia's delegates in Congress to move to declare the United Colonies free and independent states. At the same time, the convention appointed a committee to prepare a declaration of rights and a frame of government for Virginia.

The first state constitutions differed from each other in some specific provisions. For example, some states provided for a bicameral legislature, others for a single chamber. On many major issues, however, there was general agreement among the early state drafters. The state constitutions reflected the theme of republicanism, including a belief in limited government, the consent of the governed, and frequent elections.

How were rights to be protected? Not every state constitution had a bill of rights. Moreover, the courts' power to declare legislative acts unconstitutional—a powerful device for enforcing rights—was still embryonic in the states (Chief Justice John Marshall's decision in *Marbury v. Madison* still lay in the future).

The state drafters applied democratic modes of government to guard against incursions upon the people's rights. Associating tyranny with kings, governors, and courts, the drafters relied upon a Whig tradition that emphasized direct, active, continuing popular control over the legislature in particular and of government in general. Thus, despite declarations about the separation of powers, the early state constitutions in fact made the legislature the dominant branch of government. State governors were, by contrast, ciphers; only in New York and Massachusetts was the governor not elected by the legislature.

Americans' experiments with self-government, and their efforts to devise ways to articulate and protect rights, excited intense interest across the Atlantic. During his tenure as the American envoy in Paris, Thomas Jefferson took great delight in sharing with his French friends the latest political or constitutional idea from the United States. When the General Assembly of Virginia enacted that commonwealth's Statute for Religious Freedom, Jefferson had the statute translated into French, and it found its way into Denis Diderot's *Encyclopédie*.

Benjamin Franklin was an exceptionally popular figure in Paris (on Franklin's death, Count Mirabeau introduced a memorial resolution in the National Assembly). Franklin's personal wit and charm drew particular attention to the Constitution of Pennsylvania. Robert Badinter tells the story of how, during the mob's sacking of a palace during the French Revolution, a book flew out of a window and struck an American bystander on the head. The book was a bound copy of the Constitution of Pennsylvania—an uncommonly palpable example of the way constitutional ideas travel.

American ideas about rights proved a frame for much of the debate about rights in revolutionary France. George Mason's Declaration of Rights for Virginia (1776), which furnished a model for other American states and for the Bill of Rights of the United States Constitution, also influenced those who framed France's Declaration of Rights of Man and the Citizen in 1789.

Popular sovereignty—grounded in Jean-Jacques Rousseau's notion of the "general will"—was a powerful force in revolutionary France. Having stated a theory of rights in the declaration of 1789, the French then turned to drafting a new constitution. French intellectuals were divided over the extent to which democratic institutions should be checked by devices such as a bicameral legislature or an executive veto.

The Abbé Mably, a friend of John Adams, liked the American idea of the separation of powers, a principle embodied in the United States Constitution. In the debates in the National Assembly over a new constitution, J. J. Mounier argued for a balance of powers: two chambers and an executive veto. The Marquis de Condorcet wanted the nation to be represented in a single assembly. His formula for avoiding tyranny was to have frequent elections and to spell out the people's rights in a declaration of rights. Those who agreed with Condorcet could point, for precedent, to the American state constitutions.

Ultimately the National Assembly chose to have a single house and only a limited power of veto. Thus, in the early years of France and the United States, those countries chose divergent approaches to protecting rights. There was considerable common ground in the articulation of rights; one need only compare Mason's 1776 declaration and that adopted in France in 1789. The framers of the United States Constitution, however, sought structural means—separation of powers, checks and balances, and federalism—to protect rights by limiting government's power. By hewing closer to notions of popular sovereignty, the French chose quite a different path, as the unhappy course of events in France after 1789 made abundantly clear.

The United States Constitution inspired liberal reformers both in Europe and in Latin America. A Venezuelan who had traveled to Philadelphia translated the 1787 Constitution into Spanish in time for it to be available to the framers of Spain's Cádiz Constitution (1812). American constitutional ideas were especially strong in Central and South America during the era of liberation from Spanish rule. Examples include the Constitutions of Venezuela (1811), Mexico (1824), and Argentina (1826).

The United States Constitution and Bill of Rights, written in the eighteenth century, were shaped by men steeped in Enlightenment ideals. They lived in a time when reason was the avenue to understanding and when intellectuals in various lands could agree with Condorcet about the existence of a "common core of human happiness" that transcended differences of nationality and ethnicity. Thus liberal reformers in many lands could see American constitutional principles as proper models to emulate.

The nineteenth century brought a reaction that undermined common notions flowing from the Age of Reason. On the political front, reaction took the form of settlements like the Holy Alliance and the Congress of Vienna. Nationalism and nationality began to be the battle cry, as in the revolutions of 1848. European intellectuals looked increasingly to their own national roots—a tendency that German philosophers such as Friedrich Karl von Savigny called the *Volksgeist*.

As more and more constitutions were written for European states, the influence of American documents became less direct. More immediate models appeared on the scene. Especially influential was the Belgian Constitution of 1830, a font of much constitutional drafting in nineteenth-century Europe. American ideas hardly became irrelevant; they simply became one thread in a much richer constitutional tapestry.

In the years immediately following World War II, it was possible to speak of the "American century." With much of Europe in ashes, and Asia yet to become a major economic force, the United States enjoyed immense influence. In Japan, the staff of General Douglas MacArthur's headquarters drafted a new constitution in seven days for that defeated country. Similarly, the mark of American ideas on West Germany's postwar constitution is evident.

Even in the period after World War II, however, the influence of American constitutionalism was variable. In Africa, for example, British barristers and scholars were enlisted to work on constitutions for British colonies, such as Ghana, that were becoming independent nations.

The upheavals in Central and Eastern Europe since the winter of 1989 have brought a burst of attention to constitutions and bills of rights. An American who reads the draft of a bill of rights or constitution for one of the region's fledgling democracies will find much that is familiar but also much that is not.

Two hundred years after their drafting, the United States Constitution and the Bill of Rights are widely recognized as furnish-

ing paradigms of the fundamental principles that define constitutional democracy. These principles include:

(1) *Consent of the governed.* The first three words of the United
States Constitution—"We the People"—embody the principle of
consent of the governed. But American constitutionalism has also
worked out the modes by which genuinely representative government can exist, including freedom to form political parties,
fair apportionment of legislative seats, a liberal franchise, and
free and fair elections.

(2) *Limited government.* Constitutionalism pays special attention—through devices such as separation of powers and checks
and balances—to preventing power from being concentrated in
such a way that it becomes a threat to individual liberty.

(3) *The open society.* Central to American precepts of individual
liberty are the rights to believe what one will, to embrace what
religious beliefs one chooses, to engage in free and robust debate,
to oppose the orthodoxy of the moment. No part of the Constitution is a more powerful beacon than the First Amendment.

(4) *Human dignity and the sanctity of the individual.* It is no accident that the Bill of Rights accords such detailed attention to
criminal procedure. A good measure of the respect accorded
human rights is how the state treats those charged with or sus-
pected of criminal activity. The sanctity of the individual also
connotes aspects of personal privacy and autonomy, those zones
of private life into which the state may not intrude at all or only
for demonstrable and pressing public needs.

(5) *The rule of law.* The principle of due process of law, an idea
as old as Magna Carta, requires fairness and impartiality in both
criminal and civil proceedings. A corollary of fairness is equality.
Constitutionalism's moral fabric is put to special test by discrimination involving race, religion, or similar factors. Liberty and
equality may, at times, seem to be in tension with each other,
but by and large they go hand in hand.

Bills of rights being drafted in Central and Eastern Europe
parallel, in some respects, the principles flowing from the Bill of
Rights of the United States Constitution and from American constitutionalism. Every draft bill of rights contains, in one form or
another, assurances of free speech, freedom of conscience, and
the right to form political parties. No draft fails to include some
version of the antidiscrimination principle, which bans discrimination on the basis of nationality, ethnicity, religion, or other

enumerated grounds. Procedural protections for those accused of crime are invariably included.

Other provisions of bills of rights being proposed or adopted in Central and Eastern Europe, however, will strike the American observer as less familiar, and in some cases disturbing. There are respects in which the bills of rights in the region go beyond the requirements of American constitutional law. There are other ways in which they fall short.

The Bill of Rights of the United States Constitution declares what government may *not* do; it is what Justice Hugo L. Black once called a list of "thou shalt nots." The document reflects the view that the function of a bill of rights is to limit government's powers. Central and East European drafters have enlarged this meaning of "rights." A legacy of the twentieth-century notion of positive government, an age of entitlements, is bills of rights that declare affirmative rights. Such bills include, of course, the traditional, negative rights, but they also spell out claims upon government, such as the right to an education, the right to a job, or the benefits of care in one's old age.

It may well be that, notwithstanding the language of the United States Bill of Rights, judicial gloss on the Constitution has brought American jurisprudence closer to the idea of affirmative rights than theory might suggest. The United States Supreme Court has rejected the argument that education is a "fundamental" right under the Fourteenth Amendment. Yet one who reads the many cases (especially those in lower courts) regarding school desegregation, education for the children of illegal aliens, and other school cases may well conclude that, in many respects, education is indeed a protected constitutional right. Be that as it may, bills of rights in the newer nations make explicit rights (such as education) that are, at most, only implicit in American constitutional law.

Thus the Charter of Fundamental Rights and Freedoms of the Czech and Slovak Federal Republic, adopted in January 1991, declares that workers "are entitled to fair remuneration for work and to satisfactory working conditions." Other sections decree free medical care, material security in one's old age, maternity benefits, and assistance to assure the needy of "basic living conditions." At the same time, some new bills of rights promise less than they seem to. Free speech will enjoy only qualified protection. Although stating that one may speak freely, the typical draft bill of rights proceeds to list significant exceptions. Drafts commonly state that advocacy of "fascism" or "communism" is excepted from the constitution's protection, or that speech may be forbidden if it conflicts with "public morality" or with the "constitutional order." Such exceptions overshadow the rule, especially when a draft (as always seems the case) does not require some finding of "clear and present danger" or a similar standard to justify a restriction on speech.

For example, Romania's Constitution, adopted in 1991, declares the "freedom to express ideas, opinions, and beliefs" to be "inviolable." But the document then adds that the law "prohibits defamation of the country and the nation; provocation to war or aggression, and to ethnic, racial, class, or religious hatred; incitement to discrimination, territorial separatism, or public violence; and obscene acts, contrary to good morals." What ethnic Hungarian, inclined to complain about conditions in Transylvania, would care to rely on his or her right to speak freely as being "inviolable" in the face of such sweeping and malleable exceptions?

Draft bills of rights, in addition to banning various forms of discrimination, often declare affirmative rights of culture, language, and education. The Czech and Slovak charter, for example, guarantees national and ethnic minorities the right to education in their language, the right to use that language in official settings, and the right to participation (form unspecified) in the settlement of matters concerning those minorities. But left unaddressed in most drafts is the explosive question whether rights of national minorities are simply rights of the individuals who make up those minorities or take on the character of group rights—an issue of utmost gravity wherever, as in so much of Central and Eastern Europe, disparate racial and ethnic groups are involved.

A constitution must, of course, be planted in a country's own soil to take root. One should not expect that a Bulgarian or Pole drafting a constitution or bill of rights will copy the American model, or any other model. Moreover, one should not be surprised that Central and East Europeans will draft documents that, at least in their specific provisions, bear more resemblance to fundamental laws in Western Europe than to American documents.

Several forces pull Central and East European drafters and lawmakers into the European orbit. After decades of an Iron

Curtain, the people of the region yearn to rejoin the "family of Europe." Ties of tradition include the strong appeal of French ideas in some intellectual circles and the long-standing custom of legal scholars in many countries to view German scholarship as offering the highest and most rigorous standards.

New bills of rights also reflect the hope of the emerging democracies to be fully accepted as members of the civilized community of nations. Drafters thus study such documents as the Universal Declaration of Human Rights and the European Convention on Human Rights. Lofty aspirations are also coupled with more practical considerations: countries aspiring to membership in such regional arrangements as the European Community want to be seen as having fundamental laws in line with principles accepted in Western Europe.

Increasingly in this century, bills of rights have come to resemble political party platforms that appeal to this or that constituency, though in the poorest countries such rhetoric inevitably confronts the hard realities of poverty and privation. The revolutionaries who drafted Mexico's 1917 Constitution paid special attention to labor and social welfare, decreeing the rights to an eight-hour workday, a minimum wage, and workers' compensation—subjects on which constitutions are commonly silent. That document's Article 123 is considered so important that a street in Mexico City is named for it.

India's 1950 Constitution reflects the ethos of a Ghandian state. Its Directive Principles of State Policy point India toward the goal of a welfare state, the creation of a "casteless and classless society," and the promotion of world peace.

Perhaps the most baroque use of a bill of rights to legislate public policy is found in Brazil's 1988 Constitution. Rather than convene a constituent assembly, Brazil's leaders asked their Congress to draft a new constitution. All 559 members of Congress participated, dividing themselves into eight committees, each with three subcommittees. These twenty-four subcommittees worked without any master plan. The resulting document is unrivaled among constitutions for conferring favors on special-interest groups. There are, for example, thirty-seven sections dealing with just the rights of workers. Some rights, such as one day off in seven, derived from Brazil's 1946 Constitution; others, such as a forty-four–hour work week, had not been legally mandated before the adoption of the 1988 Constitution.

In South Africa, delegates to the drafting table will consider proposals to use the bill of rights to compensate for past inequalities. An African National Congress draft provides for diverting resources from richer to poorer areas "in order to achieve a common floor of rights for the whole country." The judiciary would be "transformed in such a way as to consist of men and women drawn from all sections of South African society." The nation's land, waters, and sky are declared to be the "common heritage" of the people of South Africa, and the state's agencies and organs are admonished to take measures against air and water pollution and other kinds of environmental harm.

The use of a bill of rights as an affirmative tool presents special problems. The traditional rights, such as expression or assembly, tell government what it *cannot* do and may be enforced through injunctions and other familiar judicial remedies. Affirmative rights tell government what it *must* do. Here enforcement is more problematic. Affirmative rights commonly entail legislative implementation or decisions about allocation of resources, tasks for which courts are often ill-suited. Anyone familiar with cases in which American judges have become administrators of school systems, prisons, or other public institutions will understand the skewing effect that decreeing affirmative rights has on public budgets.

The fortunes of Americans and peoples in the new democracies intertwine in many ways. Bills of rights—verbal declarations of fundamental aspirations—are a visible reflection of a shared legacy and common concerns. To flourish, however, constitutionalism requires skillful political leadership, viable political parties, a healthy press and media, an independent bench and bar, a sound economy, and a system of education in which young minds will prosper. A good constitution and bill of rights can foster these things but cannot assure them.

Ultimately, for rights to be respected there must be a mature civic spirit—an attitude in the minds of ordinary citizens. A nation of people who do not understand the basic precepts of free government are unlikely to keep it alive and vibrant. Describing his Bill for the More General Diffusion of Knowledge, Thomas Jefferson called for "rendering the people the safe, as they are the ultimate, guardians of their own liberty."[1]

This lesson is as cogent in Washington or Albany as it is in Moscow or Warsaw. Americans have good cause to celebrate two hundred years of the Bill of Rights. They likewise have every reason to hope for the principles of that document to take root in the lands now free of tyrannical rule.

Neither East nor West can take liberty for granted. Witnessing the making of constitutions in the emerging democracies is an occasion for probing the lessons implicit therein: the nature and meaning of rights, the means by which they are enforced, and the habits of mind that keep them alive.

Note

[1]Thomas Jefferson, *Notes on the State of Virginia*, William Peden, ed. (Chapel Hill, N.C.: University of North Carolina Press, 1954), 148.

Chapter 2

The New Hungarian Constitutional State: Challenges and Perspectives

Péter Paczolay

Drafting and adopting a new constitution for a society entering a new period of existence is grueling, but at the same time it is also a solemn and exceptional task. No one has expressed this feeling with greater enthusiasm than did John Adams in 1776: "You and I, my dear friend, have been sent into life at a time when the greatest lawgivers of antiquity would have wished to live. How few of the human race enjoyed an opportunity of making an election of government, more than of air, soil, or climate, for themselves or their children!"[1]

In 1989, certainly a more skeptical era, Hungary undertook its job of constitution writing well, but missed the solemnity of the moment. Citizens hardly realized how fundamentally everything had changed. They were far from sharing the kind of devotion that had been Thomas Paine's at the end of the eighteenth century: "Let a day be solemnly set apart for proclaiming the charter; let it be brought forth placed on the divine law, the Word of God; let a crown be placed thereon, by which the world may know, that so far as we approve of monarchy, that in America the law is king."[2]

In contrast to Paine's vision, the new Hungarian constitutional order was introduced as an amendment. How did this happen? What have been the experiences of the first two years of the new constitutional order? What are the consequences of this unique Hungarian transition? This chapter describes the evolution of the

21

constitutional system that has made possible Hungary's transition from authoritarian rule to democracy and the rule of law. It begins by outlining the historical and theoretical background of the transition and its constitutional change, and then focuses on some important problems faced by the new institutions.

Historical and Political Background

Hungary's Constitutional History

For many centuries the basic conditions of the constitutional order in Hungary were regulated by customs and a series of fundamental—so-called cardinal, or basic—laws stemming from different periods beginning with the thirteenth century. The first of these important laws was the Golden Bull (Aranybulla) of 1222, which included the nobles' right to resist the king.[3] For centuries, the political and constitutional system was shaped by this "historical constitution," which had several theoretical and practical consequences.

First, Hungarian constitutional theory developed a rather broad notion of constitution and constitutionalism. The historical constitution meant that the laws regarded as customarily basic laws formed the body of the constitution. These basic laws were enacted, written laws, but their "basic" character, with some rare exceptions,[4] was defined by customary law. Constitutional theory regarded basic law as a legislative act in that (1) legislation explicitly defined basic law, or (2) the basic law regulated the fundamental institutions and principles of the constitution.[5] Apart from legislative acts, a basic source of Hungarian public law was customary law. For instance, Act No. X of 1791 ordered that "Hungary should forever be governed according to its own laws and customs." The king would pledge at his coronation to maintain the laws and customs of Hungary.

The rule of this ancient constitutional and public law was interrupted for a short period by the regime of the Hungarian Soviet Republic. On 2 April 1919, its Governing Council passed the Preliminary Constitution of the Soviet Republic that outlined the institutional system of the councils (soviets) as well as the electoral system. On 23 June 1919, a comprehensive text of the constitution was passed, but little more than a month later, on 1

August, the Hungarian version of Soviet dictatorship collapsed. The first law of 1920 declared the "restoration of constitutionality," which indeed restored the former constitutional system with the exception of Hapsburg rule.[6] Customary constitutional law also played an important role in reinforcing the national identity of the Hungarians.

Second, the fact that Hungary had a historical constitution led to a substantive definition of the constitution as the organization of a community, instead of a formalistic definition as a written charter that establishes the organization of the state and guarantees fundamental rights.[7] In other words, the definition was sociological and political: "The Constitution is nothing other than the structure of the state in its own sovereignty."[8]

A third peculiarity is that, because the Hungarian historical constitution was not located in a single charter, it developed gradually, depriving the Hungarians of a real constitutional moment, a specific date to which the adoption of a written constitution could be attached. This gave a double character to the Hungarian constitutional process: it was both reformist and conservative. "The Hungarian public law had undergone changes from time to time, but progress was only one side of the changes, the other being always of a conservative character. All of our large-scale reform laws besides a new principle contained also the perpetualness of the ancient rights, the Hungarian reform being nothing other than the adjustment of ancient principles to new circumstances."[9] This quotation from the Hungarian constitutional scholar János Horváth resembles closely Edmund Burke's views on the British Constitution: "All the reformations we have hitherto made have proceeded upon the principle of reference to antiquity; and I hope, nay, I am persuaded, that all those which possibly may be made hereafter will be carefully formed upon analogical precedent, authority, and example."[10]

After World War II, the first real break in the continuity of the millennial historic constitution occurred with the introduction of the republican and parliamentary form of government. The fundamental document of this—unfortunately provisional—democratic order was Act No. I of 1946, which defined the powers of the president of the Republic and the Government[11] and listed the citizen's fundamental rights.[12]

In 1949, the first written constitution in the history of Hungary was adopted. This "Socialist" constitution, like all the other constitutional documents adopted in Eastern Europe after the Comof power, was strongly influenced by the Soviet ... of 1936. The arbitrary establishment of the new con-...nal system disregarded the constitutional traditions of ...ach country. Because the principle of legal continuity was interrupted by the Communist regime, the Hungarian Constitution of 1949 did not educate the population to respect a written constitution. The 1949 Constitution was subsequently amended several times, but these revisions, including the rather wide-ranging amendment of 1972, did not affect the essential features of the Communist system. Still, since 1949 Hungary has had a written constitution, even if it was a semantic one that did not provide for the realization of the rhetorically positive-sounding principles formulated in its text.[13]

The Constitutional Revision of 1989

Significant efforts to implement legal reforms in Hungary began in the 1980s. Among them were a reform of the electoral law[14] and the consolidation of very limited constitutional protection by the establishment of a Constitutional Law Council.[15] In the changing political climate of 1988, the first draft of a new constitution was prepared by the reformist Communist government. Yet during the roundtable negotiations between the government and the opposition in the following year, the governing Hungarian Socialist Workers' Party and the democratic opposition agreed for the time being to make some major amendments to the 1949 Constitution and to leave the drafting of a new constitution to the first freely elected parliament. The considerably revised 1949 Constitution was thus instituted on 23 October 1989, the thirty-third anniversary of the 1956 revolution.

In 1990, the constitution was further amended nine times. The most important changes were made in June.[16] Among the provisions that were cancelled were those parts of the October 1989 text that had resulted from the compromise between the Communist party and the opposition; thus all references to the values of socialism were eliminated. The protection of fundamental rights was strengthened. The president of the republic was to be elected by a parliament, and not by the people. As the result of a compromise between the two largest parliamentary parties, the MDF (Hungarian Democratic Forum, the leading force in the government coalition) and the SZDSZ (Alliance of Free Democrats, the opposition),[17] the power of the cabinet was considerably expanded through the establishment of the so-called constructive vote of no-confidence. The amended constitution defined three categories of legislative acts: (1) ordinary laws, which can be passed by an absolute majority, by a "yes" vote of more than half of the deputies present, or by a quorum of half of the members of Parliament; (2) laws that need to be passed by two-thirds of the deputies present, such as those affecting fundamental rights, local government, or the armed forces; and (3) major laws, for which a two-thirds vote of all the parliamentarians is needed, for instance, constitutional amendments or election of certain high officials of the state (justices of the Constitutional Court, the chief justice of the Supreme Court).

THE CONSTITUTIONAL REVOLUTION

In the post-Communist era, the Hungarians have consciously opted for a constitutional revolution, choosing law over power not only for the future political system but also for the transition itself. This follows the Hungarian tradition of lawful and constitutional revolution, which was evident even in the revolution of 1848. The 1848 spring of nations was a significant event in the history of modern Hungary as the first grand attempt to create a proper constitution. Under the rule of a great power, the Hapsburg monarchy, Hungarian lawmakers approved a series of bills that formally conformed to the existing constitutional order but, in fact, shaped a fundamentally new political and social system: "As the Hungarian liberals saw it, theirs had not been a revolution at all, but a peaceful adjustment to the times and the legal reconquest of Hungary's historical freedoms."[18] This philosophy was based on the avoidance of conflict and division, aiming to restore fundamental freedom to the Hungarian nation. The ancient rights of the monarch were preserved, and the following principles were instituted: the government's answerability to Parliament, equality of all before the law, proportional and general taxation, abrogation of privileges, termination of arbitrary arrest and detention, and the guarantee of fundamental rights.

History sometimes repeats itself, and so turning to the revolution of 1989 we can see a series of similarities. As was previously mentioned, the basic concern of Hungarians has long been peaceful change, the shaping of a constitutional state, and the avoidance of any possible conflict with the Soviet Union. There were also certain likenesses in the behavior of the ruling classes:

in 1848, the nobility voluntarily renounced its privileges in order to lay the foundations of a constitutional state and a free society, which would promote the further development and prosperity of the ruling class. The governing Communists of the late 1980s must have had something similar in mind. By voluntarily renouncing some of their privileges inherent in single-party rule and by promoting some features of a constitutional state, they hoped to find a modus vivendi with the other Socialist countries. This aimed to fulfill public expectations and at the same time to keep the Communists in power. They miscalculated, however, as did the Polish and Czechoslovak leaderships: in none of these countries could the system be reformed except at the expense of the ruling party's monopoly of power. What the Communists failed to foresee was that if they gave up their monopoly, they would indeed lose most of their power, even though they could still remain actors on the political scene. Many Western scholars shared their illusion that socialism could be reformed with constitutional changes.[19]

All the political forces in Hungary cooperated to guarantee peaceful political change and harmony with the Soviet Union. They ensured that changes would be carried out within the constitutional and legal framework. Hence the term "constitutional revolution": the changes were not only lawfully prepared but also based on the existing constitution, with emphasis on the continuity of the existing legal system. The bargaining between the ruling party and the opposition resulted in the creation of a multiparty system by peaceful transition, based on what is basically a new—although technically speaking only an amended—constitution, without resort to force or other extraconstitutional means. Following a series of further amendments to the constitution, the constitutional order of the new Hungary has been assured.

The victory of law over power in Hungary is now both a fact and an ideal. It includes the legal protection of human rights, the limitation by law of government and all other factors of political life, the banning of force from political life, the regulation by law of all political processes, and the proscription of ex post facto application of rules governing the resolution and arbitration of conflicts of interests.

Hungary's constitutional document resulting from this process was very similar to the post–World War II constitutional changes made in France, Italy, and Germany. Such changes were termed negative revolutions by Carl Friedrich: "These constitutions are not the result of any positive enthusiasm for the wonderful future; they flow rather from the negative distaste for a dismal past."[20] The process of regime-change appeared to be similar to the post-Franco transition in Spain—the exclusion of political extremes and a strictly legal breakout of the authoritarian system.[21]

REVOLUTION AND LEGAL CONTINUITY

The peculiar way in which the post-1989 Hungarian constitutional system was created may be viewed as a de facto acknowledgment of continuity with the Communist legal system. This standpoint, obviously, is not tantamount to the acknowledgment of the legitimacy of the Communist power's right to govern; it is only an acceptance of the formal lawfulness and validity of the old legal system.

According to a definition by Ralf Dahrendorf, the change of regime in Hungary was a transition: the controlled transformation of illiberal states into liberal ones. Transitions are initiated from above. They may be a response to more or less popular pressure, but they are carried out by the government of the day. Such governments generally undergo great changes as transitions continue. Although the effects of transitions may be revolutionary, the thread of continuity is never broken completely.[22]

From the legal point of view, there are different ways in which the constitutional system can change. The theory of legal continuity states that every illegal change in a constitution is revolution. This theory, first elaborated by Hans Kelsen, has been accepted by social scientists; still, their references to the constitutional and legal background of revolutions are surprisingly rare. For example, Paul Schrecker, in his essay "Revolution as a Problem in the Philosophy of History," establishes a definition that clearly follows the theory of legal discontinuity. Schrecker sets up two essential preconditions for revolution: first, the change must affect the fundamental laws of a state or a nation and, second, the change must be illegal under the very law that it abolishes.[23] He also warns that even a despotic regime can be transformed legally, without revolution.[24]

The legal nature of revolution has been widely discussed in the philosophy of law, but a persuasive consensus has not yet been reached. Kelsen himself is clear on this question, however.

For him, a revolution in the most general sense "occurs whenever the legal order of a community is nullified and replaced by a new order in an illegitimate way, that is in a way not prescribed by the first order itself."[25]

Kelsen stresses the importance of the so-called rules of succession, which regulate the legitimate process of succession or change in the regime. In accordance with international law, if the territory and population of a state remain identical, no new state has come into existence. On the one hand, a revolution in the broad sense establishes a new government. On the other hand, a new government established by revolution by violating the existing constitution and the rule of succession creates a new legal order. International law thus recognizes the continuity of legal order even in the case of a revolution. But if we ignore or go beyond this interpretation of international law, we must acknowledge the break in the legal system created by a revolution. Kelsen develops a peculiar test for this continuity: if the constitution is changed according to its own provision, the state and its legal order remain the same. It does not matter how fundamental these changes in the contents of the legal norms are, since, if they conform to the provisions of the constitution, the continuity of the legal system is not interrupted.[26]

Contrary to Kelsen's formal approach, Alf Ross emphasizes the necessary discontinuity of a new constitutional order. According to Ross, the new constitution is brought into effect by a political ideology. During the final exchange of competencies there exists an authority not enacted by another authority, but which is simply presupposed.[27] Unlike Kelsen, whose purely legal explanation pertains to the nature of changes, Ross explains the way in which the legitimacy of a constitutional order goes beyond the legal system.

In accordance with the purely formalistic approach presented by Kelsen, it is unquestionable that the Hungarian transition was only a constitutional amendment, because the state and its legal order remained the same. In other words, the old legal order remains valid within the framework of the amended constitution while its legitimacy rests on the old constitution as well as the old legal order. This creates a serious problem since, if the legitimacy of the new order is founded upon the previous constitution, this is tantamount to the acknowledgment of the legality of the former constitutional system and its legal order. This specific case reveals the discrepancy inherent in the form and substance of a legal order as the difference between the continuity of the previous formal laws and the basic change in the underlying social reality. Therefore, it can be argued that "a constitution, or at least an ultimate rule of succession of rules, cannot be wholly replaced in accordance with its own stipulations; purported replacements are really 'legal camouflage' for a 'peaceful revolution' in which the replacement is a break with the past."[28]

The Hungarian transition undermines Kelsen's formalistic approach, laying bare the sociological reality that displays the fundamental changes and obvious divisions. These changes were determined to be constitutionally protected since the actual circumstances of the transition involved a fundamental compromise with the former regime. Peaceful transition, undeniably a supreme value compared to violent revolt, was highly desirable in the Hungarian case. One may only hope that all future changes will be made within the framework of the constitution, even if such a transition is challenged by some political groups attempting to accelerate the transition.

Discussions of transitions from communism to constitutionalism often invoke lessons learned from the breakdown of national Socialist and other totalitarian regimes. There is a great difference between these two forms in the continuity of the law: the totalitarian regimes of Nazi Germany, Fascist Italy, and Francoist Spain did not try to make basic changes in property relations, social stratification, or the entire body of law. These governments did not attempt to create an explicit discontinuity in the legal system. On the contrary, they exploited the body of law and judicial system they inherited for their own purposes.[29] In the Hungarian transition, the revised and amended constitution has nonetheless required the comprehensive transformation of the legal system. Even gradual changes at a certain point become revolutionary, in the sense of fundamental social change. This stage of the transition results in the inevitable transformation of the entire legal system. Although constitutions usually create the legal framework around social and political changes that preceded them, in Hungary the opposite happened.

THE LEGITIMACY OF THE CONSTITUTION

The commonly accepted theoretical reason for not adopting a new constitution in 1989 was the illegitimacy of the Parliament elected in 1985. The preliminary draft of the 1989 amendment was prepared by expert commissions under government direction. Different sections of the draft were then discussed in the working groups and subcommittees of the roundtable talks, when the democratic opposition thoroughly modified its final text. Then the Parliament passed the constitutional amendment with no serious debate, effectively rubber-stamping the outcome of the roundtable talks.

Although the legitimacy of the constitutional revision was based on extraparliamentary negotiations, it was conducted by strictly constitutional provisions. Obviously, the legality of the opposition-government roundtable is also questionable, at least in strictly legal terms, since the parties in the roundtable talks had not been elected. In fact, in the wake of the elections some of them remained outside the Parliament, while others lost significance and eventually disappeared from the political stage. These uneven negotiations between the Communist party still fully in power and groups whose real influence remained uncertain nonetheless produced an agreement that Hungary needed a normative ("valid, fully activated, and effective")[30] constitution. But no provision was made for a constitutional convention.

There is no single universal method of adopting a constitution; indeed, the ways of drafting and adopting constitutions vary greatly. A constitution can be enacted as a single document, but it can also consist of a body of basic laws and customs. It is also extremely difficult to define the exceptional moments when a just constitution can be drafted. A just constitution, in the definition of John Rawls, "would be a just procedure arranged to insure a just outcome."[31] He suggests a four-stage sequence, modeled mostly on the history of the U.S. Constitution, to achieve it. But Rawls himself points out that his idea "is a part of moral theory, and does not belong to an account of the working of actual constitutions."[32] In practice, such constitutional moments rarely exist. In Hungary's case, the transition based on legal continuity prevented such a moment from happening. The first freely elected Parliament was not created to become a constituent assembly, and its members consequently refused to act as a constituent body. Moreover, the adoption of a constitution is rarely fully legitimized from a sociological point of view as the will of the people. Even the legitimacy of the first modern constitution has often been questioned.[33]

Even though the basic revision had been passed by Hungary's previous Parliament in 1989, the further amendments made by the new, freely elected legislature serve as the express acknowledgment of those revisions and legitimation of the Constitution.[34] The Constitutional Court's several hundred decisions interpreting the Constitution have not only contributed to its acceptance, but also enriched its content. Now that principles regarding legislative work and the Constitutional Court's decisions are contained in the text of a "transitory" constitution, the drafting of a new constitution which would restructure the state's institutions, redefine their rights, and rewrite the Bill of Rights would lead to new discontinuity in the constitutional and legal system. Thus the new constitution must be adjusted to encompass the existing institutions. It should include the more exact circumscription of their responsibilities and eliminate the vague provisions and vestiges of the Socialist constitution, as well as providing a clear formulation of basic rights. The exact date of the framing and adoption of an entirely new constitution has not been set.[35]

The winner of the first free parliamentary elections, the Democratic Forum, accepted and thus implicitly legitimized the 1989 Constitution by amending it. Subsequently the idea of writing a completely new constitution took a back seat, as it was obvious that the 1989 text is a new, democratic document creating the constitutional base for the transition. The legislature, rightly, concentrated on more urgent tasks. Thus Hungary missed the moment when it could have adopted an entirely new constitution and chose instead to reform its constitution step by step. But it challenged the document's legitimacy when it became clear that the Constitution restrains some of the powers of the parliamentary majority. Hungary again passed up the opportunity to adopt, at least in the procedural or ceremonial act, a completely new fundamental law; the constitutional amendment without a doubt poured new wine into an old bottle, but it may be hoped that, contrary to the scriptural text, both of them can be preserved.

Respect for a written constitution is not deeply rooted in the Hungarian political culture, because there was the tradition of the "millennial historical constitution" and the first written constitution was unfortunately enacted by the Communist regime. Thus, since 1989, controversial feelings have prevailed toward the provisional character of the democratic Constitution.

And yet both Czechoslovakia and Poland missed their constitutional moments even more dramatically. Both countries want to adopt wholly new constitutions, but political reasons hinder such an action, and now both are muddling through with amended versions of their old Socialist constitutions. By comparison, Hungary's seemingly worse solution of adopting a provisional constitution has so far been the best.[36] Such a gradual approach can be equally successful over the long term as it resolves specific problems one by one. A constitutional state needs to meet two requirements: first, a relatively stable constitution, also a prerequisite for judicial review; and, second, a large consensus for the adoption of constitutional amendments. The most definite legitimation of a constituent act stems from the ratification by popular referendum. But a popular referendum is desirable only to ratify a new constitution; in the case of narrow corrections and modifications, the consensus of political leaders and parliamentary parties should be sufficient.

The Hungarian Parliament is not only the highest legislative organ of the state but also its constituent assembly. This investment of both functions in the same body reflects, in part, the great importance attached to the Parliament in the Communist era. The relative smoothness of the process of amending the Constitution creates a further problem, since a vote of two-thirds of the members of the single-chamber Parliament is required to pass an amendment. It is thus not surprising that the Constitution was amended a number of times after October 1989, the last time on 2 August 1990. The present, relatively long break in amendment-writing is due only to the self-restraint of the legislators. The ease with which the supreme law of the land can be amended could deprive the Constituton of its prestige and turn it into a political pawn. Obviously, in cases when the parliamentary parties are divided on an amendment, the two-thirds majority can be a very tough requirement.

The everyday practice of amending the Constitution has provided the advantage of demonstrating its shortcomings. The Hungarian Constitution is basically a democratic constitution in that it enables the functioning of the constitutional state, and yet from a technical point of view, it is far from perfect. The speed with which the proposed text was prepared by the experts of the Ministry of Justice, the short time made available for political negotiations and its final drafting (from 13 June to 18 September 1989), the series of political compromises incorporated into the final version, and the misunderstandings and oversight of some constitutional problems have all created difficulties for those applying and interpreting certain of its provisions. The placement of completely new institutions and provisions amid vestiges of the 1949 Constitution introduces additional incoherence into the Constitution.

Recent voices in the press, shared by representatives of the Democratic Forum and the Smallholders' Party, have challenged the legitimacy of the Constitution by claiming that it is still a Stalinist document. This argument is repeated frequently, although even a superficial comparison of the current and the pre-1989 texts reveals that only a few sentences have remained the same (including the sentence stating that the capital of the country is Budapest).[37] The attacks on the legitimacy of the Constitution stem from some political forces that in 1989 saw constitutionalism and the rule of law as a means to limiting, perhaps even overthrowing, the Communist party. Now in power, these same people consider any restrictions on the will of the parliamentary majority as "mines laid by the Communists," "rope used to tie up the government's hands," "protection for the privileges and wealth of the leaders of the former regime, hampering the government in the effective operation," and "an obstacle to the people in doing justice."[38] The targets of these claims are the provisions that restrain the absolute power of the parliamentary majority and establish elements of consensual democracy. They include the two-thirds majority requirement for passing the most important laws, constitutional review by the Constitutional Court, and the limited power of the president to protect constitutionality.

THE DOCTRINE OF LEGAL CONTINUITY IN THE JURISDICTION OF THE CONSTITUTIONAL COURT

The doctrine of legal continuity as the basis of the constitutional transition in Hungary was finally formulated in a judgment of the Constitutional Court. The court also outlined its philosophy of the rule of law in a decision turning down a parliamentary bill. The legislature passed a law on 4 November 1991 on the prosecutability of serious crimes committed between 21 December 1944 and 2 May 1990 and left unpunished for political reasons. This law aimed to lift the statute of limitations on treason, murder, and other grievous crimes, and would have been a mild Hungarian version of the "decommunization" laws in other countries of Eastern Europe. The president of the republic, who had doubts about the constitutionality of this law, refused to sign it and asked the Constitutional Court to examine its constitutionality. A unanimous court ruled the bill unconstitutional and repealed it, explaining their decision by citing the bill's contradiction with the provision in the penal law that defines the statute of limitations for crimes committed under the laws in effect at that time. The lifting of the statute of limitations would be unconstitutional since it would create ex post facto, or retroactive, legislation. The court further ruled that the fact that certain crimes remained unpunished for political reasons does not create a constitutional justification for discrimination. The inclusion of treason among these crimes led to further unconstitutionality because the substantial meaning of treason has changed several times over the decades. In the significant philosophical part of the court's argument are five basic statements on the change of regime in Hungary and on legal continuity:

(1) The 23 October 1989 constitutional amendment "brought into effect a practically new constitution."[39] The rule of law means the "real and absolute prevalence of the Constitution." For the legal system the change of regime means nothing other than that the entire legal system must be brought, and the new legislation must be kept, in conformity with the Constitution.

(2) In accordance with the first principle, there is no substantive distinction between legal rules enacted under the Communist regime and since the promulgation of the new Constitution.

(3) Consequently, there is no double standard in adjudicating the constitutionality of legal norms. The new constitutional state has been shaped according to the principles of legality and legal continuity. The change of regime took place on the basis of legality. The principle of legality requires a constitutional state to give absolute effect to the rules governing the legal system. The Constitution and the basic laws that introduced revolutionary changes from a political point of view were enacted without formal defects according to the rules of lawmaking of the old regime and deriving their binding force from them.[40]

(4) The importance of legal certainty in the constitutional state is great. There is a distinction between the validity of legal norms and the legal relationships built on them. The latter have a separate life of their own, and do not automatically share the fate of the underlying norms. Therefore, even if a law is declared unconstitutional, the legal consequences of that law—with rare exceptions—remain valid.

(5) The "specific historical circumstances of the change of regime" can be taken into account by recognizing that the fundamental guarantees of the rule of law cannot be put aside by invoking a historical situation or justice. A constitutional state cannot be built by acting against it. Legal certainty based on objective and formal principles takes precedence over justice, which is generally partial and subjective.[41]

This formalistic approach of the court implies also the choice of a specific interpretative method, namely that of objective standards and neutral principles.[42] This philosophy was not elaborated for the first time during the decision on the lifting of the statute of limitations, but rather has been developed by a series of consistent opinions.[43] The court gave an unconditional priority to the formalistic and procedural requirement of the rule of law as the only possible "objective" interpretative method in the midst of the changes, even if the Constitutional Court cannot ignore history, and it "has always borne in mind essential historical circumstances in dealing with different issues."[44]

Controversies Concerning the New Institutions

THE HUNGARIAN CONSTITUTIONAL SYSTEM

The text of the Constitution is moderately long with seventy-eight articles; it leaves the detailed regulation of many fundamental constitutional questions to separate laws enacted by a qualified parliamentary majority. According to the present Constitution, Hungary is a republic,[45] an independent, democratic, constitutional state. The Constitution does not regulate in detail the role of the political parties in the constitutional system but only guarantees that political parties may be freely formed and operated, as they express the will of the people.[46] This provision is of major historical relevance since it puts an end to the Communist single-party system. The Constitution also provides for the defense of the democratic and pluralist character of the state by limiting the powers of the political parties and preventing the political participation of unconstitutional political forces: none of the parties or other organizations of citizens may direct its activities toward acquiring, violently exercising, or exclusively wielding power. Anyone has the right and the duty to take action against such endeavors in any lawful way.[47] Also, in reaction to the single-party state, the Constitution restricts the potential role of the parties in power, ruling that parties may not exercise public power directly and that no party may control or direct any state organ. In order to ensure the effective separation of political parties from state power, specific related laws determine the public offices that cannot be filled by a member or officer of any party (for example, judges[48] and public prosecutors[49] cannot belong to any party, and civil servants cannot hold office in political parties[50]).

The constitutions of several different Western democracies have had an indelible impact on the current text of the Hungarian Constitution. The objective of the Constitution was to create a document in conformity with European constitutional standards, in order to establish a framework for "Europeanism," or thinking analogous to the ideals of the post-Franco Spanish Constitution.[51] Thus the influence of international human rights documents can be seen in the Hungarian Constitution as some of their provisions appear literally translated in its text. For example, the influence of the German *Grundgesetz* (basic law) and of the Italian Constitution was very strong, and from among the constitutions of more recent democracies those of Spain and Portugal had a clear impact. The U.S. Constitution, because of its unique character, had no direct influence on particular Hungarian provisions, only a more general effect on the basic constitutional principles (for example, constitutional government, separation of powers, guarantees against majority tyranny, judicial review, supremacy of the constitution, and limited government).[52]

POWERS OF THE PARLIAMENT

Socialist ideology and constitutional law viewed the Parliament as the supreme organ of the state and as having a monopoly on power. The principle of the supremacy of Parliament prevailed only in the state organization and did not affect the leading role of the Communist party. Otherwise, the Socialist state organization was based on the principle of the indivisibility and unity of power. This was realized in the primacy of the supreme representative body, which exercised its power uncontrolled, since there was no state organ that could counterbalance its power. Naturally, this body served to guarantee the leading role of the

Marxist-Leninist party (in 1972 this principle was included in the Constitution).

According to the new regulations, the constitutional power of the Parliament is concentrated in three main areas: legislation, the determination of the basic orientation of governmental policy, and the election of top state officials. These three competences invest the Parliament with great power, clearly reflecting that Hungary is a parliamentary democracy. All important powers are concentrated in the hands of the Parliament, although the will of the parliamentary majority is restricted by several means: qualified majority requirements for the enactment of the most important laws and the election of high state officials; constitutional control by the president of the republic over some aspects of its legislative work; and judicial review by the Constitutional Court.

The pact between the Hungarian Democratic Forum (MDF) and the Alliance of Free Democrats (SZDSZ) and the consequent constitutional amendments strengthened the power of the government. The idea behind these changes was to avoid a continuous governmental crisis and to give the country a strong executive capable of managing the difficulties of the transition. The power of the government is protected by two constitutional provisions, both of them close to the German model. First, only the prime minister must be elected by the Parliament. The candidate is proposed by the president of the republic but, clearly, needs to be the candidate also of the parliamentary majority. Parliament approves the candidate after hearing his or her government program. The cabinet is then proposed by the prime minister and appointed by the president of the republic, without parliamentary approval.[53] Second, the Constitution adopted the solution of constructive no-confidence: when a motion of no-confidence is promoted by at least one-fifth of members of Parliament, it must include the name of the new candidate for prime minister.[54] Following another constitutional provision, the Parliament then decides on the new prime minister and on the new government's program at the same time.[55] These provisions make it extremely difficult, if not impossible, to oust a government, and the prime minister remains virtually unremovable during his or her term, except when the governmental coalition breaks. This solution strictly follows the German and Spanish models, but departs radically from the French and Italian Constitutions. Yet this provision rests on a misconception that identifies the strength of a government with its stability. It guarantees only the stability of the government, and especially that of the prime minister,[56] though the durability of a government does not necessarily imply its effectiveness.

To sum up, the powers of the Parliament, despite the implementation of the separation-of-powers principle, are great, and the new constitutional system has preserved many features of the Communist system, which was based on the supremacy of Parliament. This influence is reflected also in the fact that Parliament has a wide range of exclusive legislative competences, though no subject is excluded from its competence. However, the new Constitution has severely restricted the "archdemocratic" pattern of the omnipotence of the popularly elected assembly, which in the Communist countries conformed perfectly with single-party rule.[57] This historical experience in Eastern Europe discredited the idea of parliamentary omnipotence just as Fascism did in Western Europe.

The rhetoric used by the parliamentary majority in the first two years of the young Hungarian democracy often recalls the majoritarian principle as a basic characteristic of democracy. The everyday practice of politics favors majoritarian over consensual rule. Majoritarian rule simply provides almost unlimited possibilities for the implementation of the will of the parliamentary majority; its counterpart, the consensus model, formulated by Arend Lijphart, presupposes an explicit consensus among the major social groups and political forces of a country.[58] However, the wide range of laws requiring a two-thirds super majority introduces the consensual principle. The opposition has the opportunity to block legislation on certain fundamental issues or to force the majority to accept consensual solutions. This arrangement without doubt makes the implementation of the will of the government difficult, but the Hungarian parliamentary system is not identical to the Westminster model, as some people erroneously refer to it. The Westminster system, as a pure majoritarian system, presupposes a majority electoral system (the dominance of majoritarian vote in single constituencies), a two-party system, and other features. The Hungarian solution is a mixed system, containing elements of both majority and consensus government. Since the language of the Hungarian Constitution is quite literally the same as that of the German, we can refer to the German experience, which clearly shows that this executive system can work also as a chancellor democracy (*Kanzlerdemokratie*) with a definite predominance of the head of the government or as a great coalition, as it functioned between 1966 and 1969. Therefore, theoretically the Hungarian solution is compatible with both practical arrangements.

PRESIDENTIAL POWERS

The Hungarian head of state is elected by the Parliament. One of the signs of the great power of Parliament is its right to elect all the high state officials. As for the election of president, a long debate preceded the decision on how to choose that official. The options included amendments to the Constitution and a popular referendum on the ratification of that provision of the Constitution that regulates the way of electing the president. The compromise was modeled on a historical precedent, Act No. I of 1946 on the Form of Government of Hungary. The president is elected by the Parliament, and in the final, third round an absolute majority is sufficient for his or her election. The election by the Parliament reflects the limited powers of the president who is not legitimized by direct popular vote. Actually, President Arpád Göncz was elected for five years in August 1990. His nomination was a component of the compromise between the two major parties that made it possible for a member of the opposition to be elected president of the republic.

The Parliament holds the right to initiate the procedure of impeachment against the president; it requires a decision by a two-thirds majority. Thus the election of the president lies in the hands of the absolute parliamentary majority, but his or her impeachment requires a supermajoritarian consensus.

Although the president is Hungary's highest-ranking public official—its formal head of state—his or her real political power is limited, although it is not purely symbolic. For historical reasons, the powers of the president were expanded during the political negotiations of 1989, in circumstances when Hungary was surrounded by countries governed by hard-line Communist governments. Many Hungarians believed that a Communist president could serve as a guarantee of loyalty to the Warsaw Pact and the Soviet Union. The president was thus invested with powers primarily in the areas of foreign and military relations. The result was a vague definition of presidential powers and the division of some jurisdictions between the president and the prime minister.

The president of the republic has important functions vis-à-vis the Parliament. The president may dissolve the Parliament in certain clearly defined conditions: (1) if Parliament withdraws confidence from the government at least four times within twelve months, or (2) if, in case of the termination of the term of the government, the Parliament does not elect the person proposed by the president as prime minister within forty days from the first nomination.[59]

The president of the republic also has political control of constitutionality over legislation.[60] He or she signs and promulgates the acts of the Parliament, and has the right in two cases to delay the promulgation of an act by exercising political control. Political review by the president under the Hungarian Constitution is broader in scope but more limited in means than judicial review. Judicial review protects the constitutionality of laws. Therefore, if the president deems that any provision of a law is unconstitutional, he or she may send it to the Constitutional Court. If the president disagrees with the act or any of its provisions, he or she may return it to the Parliament for another round of debate, but must sign it upon its return, even if the act remains unchanged.[61]

The inconsistencies and gaps in the current text of the Constitution regarding presidential powers has led to constitutional dispute between the president and the prime minister. President Göncz claimed that the existing gaps in the Constitution should be filled by arrangements establishing customary constitutional practices. The conflict of competences between the president and the government covers a variety of issues: Who represents Hungary in foreign affairs? What are the powers of the president as commander-in-chief of the army? What are the rights of the president in appointing the heads of state radio and television? The latter two issues came before the Constitutional Court. The president's written argument stated that there are gaps in the Constitution regarding the separation of powers between the president and the government. His statement promoted the writing of a new constitution to resolve this problem, but until its adoption he proposed that "these collisions should be mitigated through arrangements between the president and the prime minister establishing customary constitutional practices."[62] By "customary constitutional practice" the president meant consensus-based arrangements between him and the prime minister. In other words, the gaps in the Constitution would be filled by this arrangement as a result of political negotiation. To the president, customary law meant political deals that are not part of the Constitution or of legislation.

Despite the fact that the prevalence of customary constitutional law was a feature of medieval or feudal systems, in the age of written constitutions, it retains some importance. The most obvious reference to it is Britain, where a group of documents is customarily deemed to have constitutional importance. A recently founded state, Israel has no written constitution either, but instead a series of basic laws regulating the constitutional framework. Constitutional customs can survive parallel to a written constitution as in France, where the constitutional laws of 1875 were complemented by customs.[63]

Thus the question of customary constitutional law did not remain a subject of Hungary's legal history but instead became a prominent public issue in 1991 that has been taken seriously. The Constitutional Court's ruling did not explicitly answer the president's argument, but a concurring opinion signed by two justices (András Szabó and János Zlinszky) provided a detailed answer to it.

In Hungary, constitutional customs have a long tradition. To obtain normative character, that is to become law, these customs need to prevail peacefully over a long period of time, their content must be obvious, and they must be in harmony with the general principles of the legal system. Custom can become law after having been accepted by the state; it should be accepted and enforced by either the legislator or the executive body.[64] The concurring opinion accepts the traditional doctrine of customary law, emphasizing that customary behavior becomes a legal norm only through recognition by the state, and referring to the generally accepted characteristics of custom developed by the Roman-Canonist theory (it has been followed for a long time, it has been exercised peaceably, it must be consistent with the fundamental principles of the legal system).[65]

Thus there are three different positions regarding the problem of legal gaps in the Constitution. The majority opinion of the Constitutional Court that is binding on all its members[66] reflects the conviction, which is expressly formulated by the concurring opinions, that the Constitution is a unity without internal contradictions:[67] The Constitutional Court's jurisdiction to interpret the Constitution is aimed at ensuring the unity of the constitutional system. Public power shall always be based on law. In this field gaps cannot exist. The court is obliged to clarify the methods of exercising public power and its limits in accordance with the constitution in force; should the legislature disagree with this interpretation, it can give new meaning to the provisions in question by amending that constitution.[68]

The dissenting opinion of three justices took up the opposite position, stating that the lack of a precise regulation of presidential powers does in effect create a gap in the Constitution. Filling these gaps lies in the exclusive jurisdiction of the constituent body, the Parliament, which is solely responsible for adopting the constitution. The Constitutional Court does not have constituent power.[69]

The third position in the dispute, adopted by President Göncz, perceives a clear gap in the Constitution but wants to fill it with customary constitutional law, that is, with individual agreements made by political actors. All three positions can be justified. The majority opinion of the justices draws upon the unity of the Constitution.[70] Its reasoning alludes to the constitutional duty of the Constitutional Court to decide all cases pertaining to its jurisdiction. The gap in the Constitution can and must be filled by judicial interpretation. The dissenting opinion, on the other hand, represents the standpoint of judicial restraint. The president's position reflects a sociological, or realist, view of constitutional politics.

The Constitutional Court decided that the president as commander-in-chief "is outside the structure of the armed forces, he is the leader of the army but not its chief commanding officer. Therefore, the commander-in-chief does not act as a superior officer in respect of any of the armed forces."[71]

As for the more burning issue, regarding appointments, the court pointed out that all appointments made by the president, with the exception of judges, are subject to countersigning. The countersignature (usually by a member of the cabinet) is necessary to validate a presidential act. The countersignature ensures that the president's action does not contradict the government's policy, and at the same time that the government takes over the political responsibility for the act. The right of nomination is not the president's but that of other organs or officers of the state. A presidential appointment following the nomination by another body, usually the government, serves as the confirmation of the nomination. The president can and must reject the appointment for formal reasons if the candidate does not meet the necessary legal preconditions, such as Hungarian citizenship or professional qualifications. The president may reject the appointment for substantial reasons only if he or she has well-founded reservations that the appointment might seriously endanger the "democratic functioning of the state organization" (Article 29, Paragraph 1 of the Constitution).

By rejecting a formally correct nomination, the president definitively intervenes in the merits of the functioning of the state and prevents the politically responsible body from fulfilling its duties without taking over this responsibility from that organ. The president's refusal that is based on substantial argument serves as final guarantee; it is an extraordinary means to be applied only to avert serious functional disorders in the state organization.[72] The practice of countersigning is derived from constitutional monarchies. As the king could not be held politically or legally responsible, that responsibility was taken over by his ministers. For example, in the Austro-Hungarian monarchy, "all royal nominations, all special ordinances and the like, had to be assented to by the appropriate minister or ministers."[73]

The conflict was not ended by the Constitutional Court's decision of September 1991. When the prime minister asked for the dismissal of the heads of state radio and television, President Göncz refused, stating that these dismissals would endanger the democratic functioning of the state. The case returned to the Constitutional Court, which, in its new decision of June 1992, reaffirmed its previous position, further pointing out that the president had only a very limited power to reject the appointment of the nominees.[74]

Leaving aside the complexity of the issues involved in the dispute (such as the opposition's concerns that a dismissal of the officials threatened the freedom of the press), one must admit that presidential powers in the European democracies are quite limited. The division of executive power between the president and the cabinet in the French Third Republic as well as under the Weimar Constitution left sad memories among European constitution makers. The constitutional trends after World War II consequently led to the stabilization of the cabinet system and the strengthening of executive power.[75]

JUDICIAL REVIEW

Certainly the most unexpected new feature of Hungary's democratic constitutional system is the outstanding importance of its Constitutional Court. The court and the very idea of judicial review were previously unknown in the Hungarian constitutional tradition. The unwritten constitution also excluded the principle of the supremacy of a written constitution. The Constitutional Court, a completely new institution in Hungary, began to function in January 1990. It is considered a safeguard of human rights and an institutional guarantee of the separation of powers. The most important areas of the court's jurisdiction are the judicial review of acts and other sublegislative legal rules, the review of unconstitutional omissions by the legislature, and so-called constitutional complaint (for the violation of an individual's constitutional rights as a result of the application of an unconstitutional law), which may be initiated by anybody. The last category results in the great, perhaps too great, likelihood of popular action. The decision of the Constitutional Court is final and without appeal, binding on everyone. If the court finds a legal norm unconstitutional, it declares it wholly or partly null and void. Although the institution of judicial review clearly belongs to the heritage of American constitutionalism, in Europe it has been implemented in a completely different legal context. Judicial review by an independent judiciary as a mechanism for constitutional enforcement has a different role in the American constitutional system, where courts since *Marbury v. Madison* have controlled the acts of legislatures. During the twentieth century, and mainly after World War II, European democracies (Austria, Germany, Italy, Spain, and Portugal) set up constitutional courts to promote emerging constitutionalism, to help frame a new legal system to replace the former authoritarian one. These European courts, unlike the Supreme Court of the United States, represent the centralized type of judicial review where one single judicial organ has the jurisdiction to adjudicate the constitutionality of laws.[76]

The main missions of the Constitutional Court in Hungary are to protect human rights and to adjudicate the constitutionality of legal norms. The basic problem is that the overwhelming part of the legal norms date from a time before the enactment of the new Constitution. Therefore, it is a basic dilemma in defining the role of the Constitutional Court whether the primary task of the court is to guarantee the abstract constitutional order (and correct the legal system) or to remedy individual injuries affecting fundamental human rights. The court has taken an activist position in both reshaping the legal system and balancing the conflicts of political powers. The latter function, so characteristic of the European constitutional courts, is realized in the jurisdiction of ruling on conflicts between state bodies, the constitutional control of bills before enactment, protection of the rights of local self-governments, or, in the case of the German Constitutional Court, even electoral supervision and the adjudication of the unconstitutionality of political parties. This jurisdiction expressly proves that judicial review by European constitutional courts, has, unlike judicial review in the United States, a political character. The development by which political conflicts are solved by the judiciary and according to legal rationality can be called the judicialization of political power.[77]

In its interpretation of the Constitution, the Hungarian Constitutional Court follows the principle of the unity of the Constitution and under this principle tries to develop a coherent system through interpretation. Chief Justice László Sólyom elaborated this philosophical basis of the constitutional interpretation in his concurring opinion in the case of the death penalty: the Constitutional Court must continue its effort to explain the theoretical foundations of the Constitution and the rights included in it, and to form a coherent system with its judgments in order to provide a reliable standard of constitutionality, an "invisible constitution," which does not change according to transient political interests. This invisible constitution would not come into conflict with any constitutions that may take written form.[78]

During the first two-and-a-half years of its operations, the court made decisions on several important issues, including the death penalty,[79] compensation, abortion, and the previously discussed presidential powers and the lifting of the statute of limitations. Other important judgments addressed the interpretation of human dignity, privacy, and equal protection. Although the Constitutional Court enjoys great prestige among both politicians and the public, it has also been criticized. Some of these attacks are based on the incorrect argument that the court is protecting the Stalinist constitution. Other criticism makes the argument, familiar also in the United States, that it is counter-majoritarian and, consequently, antidemocratic.[80] The Constitutional Court does have, even by international comparison, broad jurisdiction to abrogate norms enacted by the Parliament. But what are the powers of the Parliament over the Constitutional Court?

First, the Parliament, being not only a legislative assembly but also a constituent body, may, by a single two-thirds vote, amend the Constitution or terminate constitutional institutions (for instance, limit the jurisdiction of the Constitutional Court or—absurdly—abolish it). Second, the Parliament may reverse a decision of the Constitutional Court by passing new legislation. A shocking example of this parliamentary power occurred in the last sessions of the former Parliament. On 27 February 1990, the Constitutional Court declared unconstitutional a provision of the Election Act, according to which persons temporarily abroad on election day are not allowed to vote. The Constitutional Court ruled this an unconstitutional limitation of the right to vote and appealed to the Parliament to fill the gap in the Election Act on the question of absentee ballots. Parliament did not heed the appeal but instead, due to the fast-approaching election day, amended the Constitution by adding the unconstitutional provision to its text.[81] Third, as the foregoing example shows, the Constitutional Court has no means to enforce its decisions against the will of the Parliament. Fourth, all members of the Constitutional Court are elected by the Parliament. An ad hoc nominations committee composed of representatives of each parliamentary party nominates candidates. The candidates then appear at a hearing of the Legal Committee of the Parliament, and are elected by a two-thirds vote in the Parliament. There are ten members of the court, who serve nine-year terms and may be reelected once.

The Parliament's formal control over the court ends with the election of its judges. But the Parliament's powers over the court give enough democratic legitimation to the institution.[82] Arguments over the countermajoritarian character of the court's activism can be easily justified because the court is not obliged to adhere to the views of the majority. Still, the critics misinterpret the nature of the Constitution. The current Hungarian Constitution is not based exclusively on majoritarian rule but also embodies the principle of constitutionalism. And constitutionalism limits the powers of the democratic majority by setting up a limited government. In the case of the Hungarian Constitution, this is expressed in the supermajoritarian requirement, judicial review, and, to a limited extent, the political control by the president of the republic. The Constitutional Court's decisions and legal philosophy have realized the ideal of liberal constitutionalism: they have made the rule of law into an absolute value.[83]

POLITICAL LIBERTIES AND SOCIAL RIGHTS

The revised Constitution contains a new chapter on fundamental rights. The most important provision of the new Constitution in the area of human rights is an article declaring that laws "must not impose any limitations on the essential contents and meaning of fundamental rights."[84] The ban on the encroachment of the essential content of a basic right is of outstanding importance, because it is the peculiarity of continental constitutions, as A. V. Dicey had remarked,[85] that they restrict the content of certain basic rights or, in a state of emergency, suspend them altogether.

As is the case in other emerging East European democracies, now that Hungary has a new and real bill of rights in its Constitution, the overwhelming majority of its citizens are interested not in political liberties but instead in social rights. Socialist constitutions listed a great number of social rights, and, despite their poor record of implementation, the populations grew accustomed to a wide range of virtually free welfare services. As a result of the current economic crisis across the region, the unpleasant consequences of developing a market economy, including rising unemployment and cost of living, the public is becoming increasingly sensitive to social rights. Most people cannot tolerate the growing differences among the diverse social groups or accept the reduction of the real value of their pensions and social services. Unfortunately, the drafters of the amended Constitution were not aware of the importance of including a precise and theoretically well-founded regulation explaining the scope of social and economic rights. Similarly, the participants in the political negotiations also neglected this question. Consequently, the Constitution contains an ambitious but at the same time vague section on that subject: (1) The citizens of the Republic of Hungary have the right to social security; they are entitled to provisions necessary for subsistence in old age, illness, disability, widowhood, orphanhood, and unemployment owing to circumstances beyond their control; (2) the Republic of Hungary shall realize the right to this provision through social insurance and social services.[86]

The language of this section of the Constitution is misleading in suggesting that the right to welfare services is identical to basic political rights and liberties, ones enforceable by judicial means. The Constitution fails to distinguish clearly between political and socioeconomic rights, the latter not being innate, inalienable rights but challenges to the government within its economic limitations. It is the burdensome duty of the Constitutional Court to interpret these unclear provisions of the Constitution. The first attempt to outline the content of the social rights was made by Chief Justice Sólyom in a concurring opinion. He judged that the provision in Article 70/E stating the citizen's right to social security does not entitle anyone to "social security and safety"; legal claims on such a general level cannot even be defined. Considering Article 70/E along with Article 17, which states that the Hungarian Republic takes extensive care of those in need, it may be said that social rights are not inherent rights but state tasks. Neither the extent nor the criterion of social care is specified by the Constitution; this and the related practical implementation are the responsibility and duty of the legislative and executive branches.[87] Thus the interpretation by Chief Justice Sólyom clearly states that social and economic rights are not raised to the rank of rights that can be enforced by the judiciary against the state.

Conclusions

The constitutional revision of 1989 and the further amendments made in 1990 created a new constitutional system without adopting a completely new single charter. In fact, a new constitution was adopted under the cover of revision. This text became the constitution of Hungary's transition to democracy and constitutionalism. With this unique, and at the time justified, solution, Hungary returned to its old traditions of developing its constitution gradually. As a consequence, however, it again missed the opportunity of a solemn constitutional moment. The adoption of a new constitution would be desirable for at least four reasons: first, the Constitution itself prescribes the necessity of adopting a new one. Second, the full respect for a constitution would be better grounded on a ceremoniously promulgated document. Third, the ratification of a constitution by popular vote would give it unchallenged legitimacy. Finally, the new document could eliminate the inconsistencies of the current text. Despite these reasons in favor of drafting a new charter, there is currently little chance that this will happen. The legislature has other urgent tasks, and there is a lack of consensus between the majority and opposition parties.

The stabilization of the present situation will lead to the growth of the importance of the Constitutional Court in its role of interpreter of the Constitution. The court, while bearing responsibility for the shaping of the new constitutional and legal system, must leave room for the free interplay of the political forces and cannot paralyze the decisions of the political branches. The court can also thereby avoid the accusation of "government by the judiciary."

One of the greatest achievements of the new Hungarian regime has been its ability to develop in a short time unconditional respect for the rule of law. The public in general has come to accept the rule of law and constitutionalism as the only possible framework for political argument and action.

Finally, constitutionalism is an important aspect of the new social order. But the country must still make fundamental changes in public morality and the economy. The constitutional, political, moral, and economic systems of a country cannot diverge for too long. It may be hoped that these changes in Hungary will proceed further with the strict observance of the rule of law and the continuing supremacy of law over power as guarantor of the constitutionality of the transition. Otherwise, if the constitutional and legal system collapses, forces that have often emerged in Eastern Europe in the past will regain power. As Jean-Jacques Rousseau warned the citizens of Geneva, "No one of you is so little enlightened as not to realize that where the vigor of the law and the authority of its defenders end, there can be no safety or freedom for anyone."[88]

Notes

[1]John Adams, "Thoughts on Government," in Charles S. Hyneman and Donald S. Lutz, eds., *American Political Writing During the Founding Era, 1760–1805* (Indianapolis: Liberty Press, 1983), vol. 1, 408.

[2]Thomas Paine, "Common Sense," in Philip S. Foner, ed., *The Complete Writings of Thomas Paine* (New York: Citadel Press, 1945), vol. 1, 29.

[3]See for details "The Historical Forerunners of the Hungarian Constitution," in Antal Adám and Hans-Georg Heinrich, eds., *Society, Politics and Constitutions* (Vienna: Böhlau Verlag, 1987), 150–57.

[4]In some cases the legislation explicitly declared certain laws as "basic laws": Act No. III of 1868 and Act No. III of 1827.

[5]János Horváth, *A magyar királyság közjoga* (The public law of the kingdom of Hungary) (Budapest: Dobrowski és Franke, 1894), 51.

[6]Adám and Heinrich, *Society*, 153.

[7]Giuseppe de Vergottini, *Diritto costituzionale comparato* (Padua: CEDAM, 1981), 66–69.

[8]Móric Tomcsányi, *Magyarország közjoga* (The public law of Hungary) (Budapest: Királyi Magyar Egyetemi Nyomda, 1942), 47, quoted in Adám and Heinrich, *Society*, 150.

[9]Horváth, *A magyar királyság közjoga*, 26.

[10]Edmund Burke, "Reflections on the Revolution in France," in the Beaconsfield edition, *The Writings and Speeches of Edmund Burke* (Boston: Little, Brown, 1901), vol. 3, 271.

[11]In this chapter, I capitalize the word "Government" to indicate the sense commonly used in parliamentary systems, in which it refers to the prime minister and the cabinet ministers, whereas "government" in lowercase is the American usage, referring to an established system of political administration by which a nation is governed.

[12]Adám and Heinrich, *Society*, 153.

[13]According to the classification of Karl Loewenstein, a constitution is only a semantic camouflage if "it is merely the formalization of the existing location and exercise of political power." Karl Loewenstein, "The Value of Constitutions in Our Revolutionary Age," in Arnold Zurcher, ed., *Constitutions and Constitutional Trends Since World War II* (New York: New York University Press, 1951), 204. On the constitutional history of Hungary, see Rett R. Ludwikowski, "Searching for a New Constitutional Model for East-Central Europe," *Syracuse Journal of International Law and Commerce* 17 (1991): 119ff.

[14]The new electoral law (Act No. III of 1983) required at least two candidates in every constituency.

[15]The provisions of the constitutional amendment (Act No. II of 1983) were specified in detail by Act No. I of 1984. The Constitutional Law Council had a very limited jurisdiction (e.g., it had no competence to revise legislative acts).

[16]Act No. XXIX of 1990 and Act No. XL of 1990.

[17]As a result of the elections held on 25 March and 8 April 1990, there are six parties in the Hungarian Parliament. The percentage of votes and the distribution of the 386 seats at the time of the formation of the Parliament were as follows: Hungarian Democratic Forum (MDF), 42.8 percent, 165 seats; Alliance of Free Democrats (SZDSZ), 23.6 percent, 91 seats; Independent Smallholders' Party (FKGP), 11.4 percent, 44 seats; Hungarian Socialist Party (MSZP), 8.6 percent, 33 seats; Christian Democratic People's Party (KDNP), 5.4 percent, 21 seats; Alliance of Young Democrats (FIDESZ), 5.4 percent, 21 seats; Others (independents, etc.), 2.8 percent, 11 seats. For further details see Kenneth C. Martis, Zoltán Kovács, Dezsö Kovács, and Sándor Péter, "The Geography of the 1990 Hungarian Parliamentary Elections," *Political Geography* 283, no. 11 (1992): 289. Since May 1990 several members of the Parliament have changed their party affiliation (the most dramatic shift was created by a split in the Smallholders' party when twelve

members quitted the faction) but the balance of power within the Parliament has remained basically the same.

[18]Istvan Deak, *The Lawful Revolution: Louis Kossuth and the Hungarians, 1848–1849* (New York: Columbia University Press, 1979), 99. See also A. E. Dick Howard, *The Road to Constitutionalism* (Charlottesville, Va.: Virginia Commission on the Bicentennial of the United States Constitution, 1992), 1–2.

[19]Jon Elster, "Arguments for Constitutional Choice," in Jon Elster and Rune Slagstad, eds., *Constitutionalism and Democracy* (Cambridge: Cambridge University Press, 1988), 303.

[20]Carl J. Friedrich, "Political Theory of New Democratic Constitutions," in Zurcher, *Constitutions*, 15.

[21]Andrea Bonime-Blanc, *Spain's Transition to Democracy: The Politics of Constitution-making* (Boulder, Colo., and London: Westview Press, 1987), 25.

[22]Ralf Dahrendorf, "Transitions: Politics, Economics, and Liberty," *Washington Quarterly* 13, no. 3 (1990): 134.

[23]Paul Schrecker, "Revolution as a Problem in the Philosophy of History," in Carl J. Friedrich, ed., *Revolution (Nomos VIII)* (New York: Atherton Press, 1966), 37. G. S. Pettee uses a common definition: "A revolution is a change in the constitution by illegal means," in Clifford T. Paynton and Robert Blackley, eds., *Why Revolution?* (Rochester, Vt.: Schenkman, 1971), 35.

[24]Schrecker, "Revolution," 38.

[25]Hans Kelsen, *General Theory of Law and State* (Cambridge, Mass.: Harvard University Press, 1945), 117.

[26]Kelsen, *General Theory*, 219.

[27]Alf Ross, *On Law and Justice* (Berkeley: University of California Press, 1959), 117.

[28]J. M. Finnis, "Revolutions and Continuity of Law," in *Oxford Essays in Jurisprudence*, 2d ser. (Oxford: Clarendon, 1973), 53. For a comprehensive analysis of the continuity of law principle in Hungary, see Ethan Klingsberg, "Judicial Review and Hungary's Transition from Communism to Democracy: The Constitutional Court, the Continuity of Law, and the Redefinition of Property Rights," *Brigham Young University Law Review*, no. 1 (1992): 41–144.

[29]Otto Kirchheimer, *Political Justice* (Princeton, N.J.: Princeton University Press, 1961), 300–302.

[30]Loewenstein, "Value," 204.

[31]John Rawls, *A Theory of Justice* (Oxford: Oxford University Press, 1971), 197.

[32]Rawls, *A Theory of Justice*, 197.

[33]Bruce Ackerman, *We the People* (Cambridge, Mass., and London: Harvard University Press, 1991), 41.

[34]Nevertheless, the preamble of the Constitution illustrates the need to adopt a new constitution: "In order to facilitate a peaceful political transition to a constitutional state implementing a multiparty system, parliamentary democracy, and social market economy, the National Assembly, until the adoption of the new Constitution of the country, establishes the text of the Constitution of Hungary as follows." "A Magyar Köztársaság Alkotmánya"

(The Constitution of the Republic of Hungary), in *Hungarian Rules of Law in Force* (trilingual edition), no. 26 (Budapest, 1991), 1625–61 [hereinafter Constitution].

[35]There are two "unofficial" drafts for a completely new constitutional text: one made by the staff of the former Minister of Justice, Kálmán Kulcsár, and another drawn as a private initiative by Professor András Sajó.

[36]Edward McWhinney, *Constitution-making: Principles, Process, Practice* (Toronto: University of Toronto Press, 1981), 42.

[37]Unlike some members of the Democratic Forum, Prime Minister József Antall clearly and definitely stated that "those who call the Constitution a Stalinist constitution commit a grave error against the truth. Hardly anything is left from the original constitution. This constitution, in eastern-central European terms, is among the best ones." Interview with Prime Minister József Antall, Budapest, Kossuth Radio, 24 May 1992, *Foreign Broadcast Information Service—Daily Report*, East Europe (Washington, D.C.), 27 May 1992, p. 16.

[38]These quotations are some random examples of the criticism that can be read in the papers and heard among politically involved Hungarians.

[39]Decision No. 11/1992. (III.5.) AB h. of the Constitutional Court, *Magyar Közlöny* (Official gazette), no. 23 (1992): 934.

[40]Decision No. 11/1992. (III.5.) AB h. of the Constitutional Court, *Magyar Közlöny*, no. 23 (1992): 935.

[41]Decision No. 11/1992. (III.5.) AB h. of the Constitutional Court, *Magyar Közlöny*, no. 23 (1992): 935.

[42]On a debate concerning objectivity in legal interpretation, see Ronald Dworkin, "My Reply to Stanley Fish (and Walter Benn Michaels): Please Don't Talk About Objectivity Any More," in W. J. T. Mitchell, ed., *The Politics of Interpretation* (Chicago: University of Chicago Press, 1983), 287–313; Owen Fiss, "Objectivity and Interpretation," *Stanford Law Review* 34 (1982): 739–63; Robert Bennett, "Objectivity in Constitutional Law," *University of Pennsylvania Law Review* 132 (1984): 445–96.

[43]See Péter Paczolay, "Judicial Review of the Compensation Law in Hungary," *Michigan Journal of International Law* 13 (1992): 401, 413ff.

[44]Decision No. 11/1992. (III.5.) AB h. of the Constitutional Court, *Magyar Közlöny*, no. 23 (1992): 935.

[45]Article 1 of the Constitution.

[46]Article 3, Paragraphs 2 and 3 of the Constitution.

[47]Article 2, Paragraph 3 of the Constitution.

[48]Article 50, Paragraph 3 of the Constitution.

[49]Article 53, Paragraph 2 of the Constitution.

[50]Act No. XXIII of 1992 on the Public Servants, Article 21.

[51]Francisco Rubio Llorente, "The Writing of the Constitution of Spain," in Robert A. Goldwin and Art Kaufman, eds., *Constitution Makers on Constitution Making: The Experience of Eight Nations* (Washington, D.C.: American Enterprise Institute, 1988), 257.

[52]On the limited impact of American constitutional institutions in general, see Klaus von Beyme, *America as a Model* (New York: St. Martin's Press, 1987);

Louis Henkin and Albert J. Rosenthal, eds., *Constitutionalism and Rights: The Influence of the United States Constitution Abroad* (New York: Columbia University Press, 1990), especially the comprehensive bibliographical essay by Andrzej Rapaczynski, 405–62.

[53] Article 33 of the Constitution.

[54] Article 39/A of the Constitution.

[55] Article 33, Paragraph 3 of the Constitution.

[56] Rubio Llorente, "Writing," 262. A commentator designated the German variation of parliamentary government as "demo-authoritarian," in Loewenstein, "Value," 195, 202.

[57] Loewenstein, "Value," 203.

[58] Arend Lijphart, *Democracies* (New Haven, Conn.: Yale University Press, 1984), 6–36; Robert A. Dahl, *Democracy and Its Critics* (New Haven, Conn.: Yale University Press, 1989), 156–60.

[59] Article 28, Paragraph 3 of the Constitution.

[60] Mauro Cappelletti, *Judicial Review in the Contemporary World* (Indianapolis: Bobbs-Merrill, 1971), 2–3 (on the distinction of judicial review and political review).

[61] Article 26, Paragraphs 2 and 3 of the Constitution.

[62] Decision No. 48/1991. (IX.26.) AB h. of the Constitutional Court, *Magyar Közlöny*, no. 103 (1991): 2111ff.

[63] Customs in constitutional law in general have different characteristics from those in private law: the progress of time does not have such great importance as in private law (e.g., it took more than one and a half centuries to adopt the cabinet government in England, whereas it took only twenty-five years to affirm the ministerial responsibility toward the Senate under the 1875 Constitution of France); the repeatedness of the precedent also has only limited significance; and the subjects of the constitutional customs are limited to certain constitutional organs—therefore, the requirement of generality is irrelevant. See Vergottini, *Diritto costituzionale comparato*, 81 n. 7, and Norberto Bobbio, "Consuetudine (teoria generale)," in *Enciclopedia del Diritto* (Milan: Giuffre, 1961), 428–29.

[64] Decision No. 48/1991. (IX.26.) AB h. of the Constitutional Court, *Magyar Közlöny*, no. 103 (1991): 2111ff.

[65] See Carleton Kemp Allen, *Law in the Making*, 6th ed. (Oxford: Oxford University Press, 1958), 127ff. Allen also mentions other conditions, as certainty and opinion necessitates (the belief that the acts constituting the custom ought to take place).

[66] Act No. XXXII of 1989 on the Constitutional Court.

[67] Decision No. 48/1991. (IX.26.) AB h. of the Constitutional Court, *Magyar Közlöny*, no. 103 (1991): 2111, p. 2123 (Justices Adám, Herczegh, Lábady, Tersztyánszky, concurring).

[68] Decision No. 48/1991. (IX.26.) AB h. of the Constitutional Court, *Magyar Közlöny*, no. 103 (1991): 2111, p. 2124 (Justices Szabó and Zlinszky, concurring).

[69]Decision No. 48/1991. (IX.26.) AB h. of the Constitutional Court, *Magyar Közlöny*, no. 103 (1991): 2111, p. 2123 (Justices Kilényi, Schmidt, and Vörös, dissenting).

[70]For a similar view in the jurisdiction of the German Constitutional Court, see eighteen *Southwest State Case* BVerfGE 14, 32 (1951).

[71]Decision No. 48/1991. (IX.26.) AB h. of the Constitutional Court, *Magyar Közlöny*, no. 103 (1991): 2111ff.

[72]Decision No. 48/1991. (IX.26.) AB h. of the Constitutional Court, *Magyar Közlöny*, no. 103 (1991): 2111, p. 2120.

[73]Arthur J. May, *The Hapsburg Monarchy 1867–1914* (Cambridge, Mass.: Harvard University Press, 1951), 42.

[74]Decision No. 36/1992. (VI.10.) AB h. of the Constitutional Court, *Magyar Közlöny*, no. 59 (1992): 2025. Both decisions of the court were advisory opinions: the Hungarian Constitutional Court is obliged to give abstract interpretation of constitutional provisions on the request of certain state organs and officers. This kind of jurisdiction is impossible in the United States, and it is also considered controversial with the European constitutional courts. For the Hungarian case, see Klingsberg, "Judicial Review and Hungary's Transition," 58–59; Paczolay, "Judicial Review of Compensation Law," 407–8. In general see Edward McWhinney, *Supreme Courts and Judicial Law-making: Constitutional Tribunals and Constitutional Review* (Dordrecht: Nijhoff, 1986), 16ff.

[75]Joseph Dunner, "Stabilization of the Cabinet System in Western Europe," in Zurcher, *Constitutions*, 81–94. For a broader perspective, see Juan J. Linz, "The Perils of Presidentialism," *Journal of Democracy* 1 (Winter 1990): 51–69.

[76]Cappelletti, *Judicial Review*, 46–65.

[77]Cappelletti, *Judicial Review*, 53; Loewenstein, "Value," 216–17.

[78]Decision No. 23/1990. (X.31.) AB h. of the Constitutional Court, *Magyar Közlöny*, no. 107 (1990): 37.

[79]The death penalty case was analyzed by George P. Fletcher, "Searching for the Rule of Law in the Wake of Communism," *Brigham Young University Law Review*, no. 1 (1992): 145–64.

[80]On the countermajoritarian difficulty of the U.S. Supreme Court, see Ackerman, *We the People*, 8–10, reviewing the basic standpoints; Alexander Bickel, *The Least Dangerous Branch*, 2d ed. (New Haven, Conn.: Yale University Press, 1986), 16–23, on the chief doubts concerning judicial review; Jesse H. Choper, *Judicial Review and the National Political Process: A Functional Reconsideration of the Role of the Supreme Court* (Chicago: University of Chicago Press, 1980), 10, arguing that "the process of judicial review is not democratic because the Court is not a politically responsible institution"; Charles L. Black, *The People and the Court* (New York: Macmillan, 1960), 183–222, rejecting attacks on judicial review.

[81]Article 70, Paragraph 1 of the Constitution: "Every Hungarian citizen . . . shall have the right, if he is within the territory of the country on the day of the elections, to vote."

[82]For a similar argument on the democratic legitimacy of the German Constitutional Court, see Donald P. Kommers, *The Constitutional Jurisprudence*

of the Federal Republic of Germany (Durham, N.C., and London: Duke University Press, 1989), 64.

[83]For that characterization of liberal constitutionalism, see Loewenstein, "Value," 224.

[84]Article 8, Paragraph 2 of the Constitution.

[85]"The general rights guaranteed by the constitution may be, and in foreign countries constantly are, suspended." A. V. Dicey, *Introduction to the Study of the Law of the Constitution*, reprint ed. (Indianapolis: Liberty Classics, 1982), 119.

[86]Article 70/E of the Constitution.

[87]Decision No. 31/1990. (XII.18.) AB h. of the Constitutional Court, *Az Alkotmánybíróság határozatai 1990* (Decisions of the Constitutional Court 1990) (Budapest, 1991), 142 (Justice Sólyom, concurring).

[88]Jean-Jacques Rousseau, *Discourse on the Origin of Inequality*, translated by Donald A. Cress (Indianapolis: Hackett Publishing, 1983), 109–10.

Chapter 3

Czecho? Slovakia: Constitutional Disappointments

Katarina Mathernova

People often view the Czech and Slovak Federal Republic, Hungary, and Poland jointly as being countries of the former Eastern bloc most likely to achieve democratic political and market economic reform. The recent constitutional developments of these three countries do possess some similar traits—all three have striven to reinstate the rule of law, to create new democratic structures, to protect fundamental rights and freedoms, to create a system of reliable checks and balances, and to introduce a genuine judicial review. It is important to realize, however, that despite these similarities, constitutional debate in Czechoslovakia, which has since divided (see Addendum, p. 78), has been quite different from the debate in the other countries.

The most fundamental difference is that Czechoslovakia is not ethnically homogeneous, whereas both Hungary and Poland are more or less ethnically homogeneous societies.[1] In Poland, the Poles constitute approximately 95 percent of the population; in Hungary, the Hungarians form approximately 93 percent.[2] Consequently, debate concerning the future of Czechoslovakia and the constitutional framework of the Czechoslovakian state centers on "national"[3] friction between the Czechs and the Slovaks, at the expense of other pressing, vital issues. The myopic focus of this debate casts into doubt the ability of the current Czechoslovakian state to surmount the obstacles it must confront.

The first section of this chapter briefly outlines the history of the relationship between the Czechs and the Slovaks and points out some of the origins of the current conflict. The second section focuses on post-1989 constitutional developments, including an outline of the institutional framework of the present governmental power and an explanation of its crucial impact on the ongoing attempts to draft a new constitution. Finally, I attempt to explain the factors contributing to the failure to adopt a new constitution by the original deadline of June 1992, and outline possible scenarios for the future.

Historical Background

Understanding the historical development of Czechoslovakia is a prerequisite for understanding the current constitutional debate. Peoples of Central Europe characteristically pay much attention to historical events; they carry a "backpack full of history" on their shoulders. In Czechoslovakia, one still hears references not only to World War II, the prewar years, and the revolution of 1848, but also to the Empire of Samo, allegedly founded on the territory of modern Czechoslovakia in the year A.D. 623.

Compared to Samo's Empire, the coexistence of the Czech and Slovak peoples is a fairly new circumstance, dating back to the year 1918. The Czechs and Slovaks, despite their similar ethnic and cultural heritage,[4] experienced rather different histories.[5] Before 1918, the Slovaks belonged to the Hungarian kingdom for almost a thousand years. The Czechs, by contrast, governed an independent kingdom for the first half of this millennium, before being annexed by the Austrian Empire in 1627 for the next three hundred years. In 1918, after the fall of the Austro-Hungarian Empire, the first Czechoslovak Republic ("the First Republic"),[6] the home for both Czechs and Slovaks, came into being. The Treaty of Versailles confirmed its creation in 1919.

The First Republic was a relatively well-functioning democracy.[7] Its basic document, the Declaration of Independence, promulgated by the Czechoslovak National Council in Paris in 1918,[8] spelled out the basic principles of Czechoslovak constitutionalism: parliamentarianism; governmental legitimacy based on a broad national consensus; proportional representation; and protection of fundamental rights and freedoms, including the rights of national minorities.[9] The first Czechoslovak constitution of 29 February 1920 incorporated these principles.

Despite the largely positive democratic characteristics of the First Republic, the Slovaks felt that they had merely traded Hungarian domination for that of the Czechs. They lacked an administrative and political expression of self-governance. During World War I, future Czechoslovakian President Tomáš Masaryk first agreed with Slovak representatives in the United States,[10] in the Cleveland Agreement in 1916,[11] that the future Czechoslovakia would be a federation. Later, the Slovaks obtained a further confirmation of their goal of autonomy in the Pittsburgh Agreement.[12] This agreement between Masaryk and the American Slovaks, formed in May 1918, without explicitly referring to a federation, formulated institutional safeguards of Slovak self-governance: a Slovak administration, assembly, and courts.[13] The interpretation of the Pittsburgh Agreement and its validity has not been consistent.[14] By the end of the war, the founding fathers opposed having a federation composed of two separate sovereign republics, and, as a result, the First Republic became a unitary state. The idea of a federation currently dominates the drafting of the new constitution.[15] The official ideology of the First Republic was the existence of a single "Czechoslovak nation," bound by one government and cemented by one language.[16] The Slovaks never accepted this concept, and it remains the aspect of President Masaryk's political views most criticized by Slovaks.[17]

The Slovak feelings of oppression and resentment caused by the lack of self-governance and self-determination continued throughout the existence of the First Republic. The unfulfilled promise of a federal structure or autonomy aggravated these negative feelings, which ultimately led to the creation of a putatively "independent" Slovak Republic in 1939.[18] In reality, this republic was merely a puppet of Hitler's Germany, a stigma against which Slovak nationalism today still struggles.[19] The republic, however, gained enough momentum to cause the postwar transitional democratic government to adopt a plan in 1945, the so-called Košice governmental program, which granted Slovaks some degree of self-determination within Czechoslovakia. It created a unitary state with a special position for Slovak bodies and their exclusive jurisdiction in certain areas.[20] Unfortunately, when the Communists seized power in February 1948, Czechoslovakia's democratic existence was terminated for over forty years, but not Slovakia's hopes for greater autonomy.

The Constitution of 9 May 1948 retreated from the idea of a single Czechoslovak nation. In its preamble, the Constitution defined Czechoslovakia as a state composed of "two equal Slavic nations, Czechs and Slovaks."[21] It also provided for a Slovak National Council and a Committee of Delegates (Zbor Povereníkov) in Slovakia.[22] These bodies did not have equivalents in the Czech lands and presumably were partial compensation for having the center of power and the capital located in Czech Prague. This unusual asymmetry even survived the new Constitution of 11 July 1960,[23] which broadened the power of the Slovak National Council.

Slovak yearnings for substantiation of their "national" identity came to the forefront of constitutional policies again in the aftermath of the 1968 Prague Spring. The Law on Czechoslovak Federation, adopted after the Soviet occupation in 1968 as an amendment to the 1960 Constitution,[24] established a federal structure with a bicameral Parliament in a country with twice as many people living in the Czech lands as in Slovakia. It failed to resolve the real issue, however—Slovak self-governance. Also important, the absolute rule of the Communist party's Central Committee effectively thwarted the implementation of the 1968 Federation amendment.[25] In other words, the federal structure set up by the 1968 amendment was never tested in practice, since the bicameral Federal Assembly was reduced to a rubber-stamping organ. Referring to 1968, Václav Havel—before 1989 a prominent dissident, and now the president of Czechoslovakia—said that history stopped and the country was put to sleep for twenty years.

Post-1989 Constitutional Developments

Disintegration of the Anti-Communist Coalition After the Revolution of 1989

In late 1989 Czechoslovakia woke up again. Following the successful attempts of people in other Eastern bloc countries to rid themselves of Communist rule, Czechoslovak citizens forced the resignation of their Communist leaders. This overthrow, or "revolution," started on 17 November 1989, when the police in Prague clamped down on a peaceful student demonstration commemorating the 1938 Nazi execution of a student. It culminated on 29

December 1989, when Havel, who led the coalition against the former regime, became president.

The revolution, which acquired the adjective "velvet" for its bloodless character, however, did not offer any solution to the Czech-Slovak seemingly ethnic dispute. During the revolution itself, the Slovaks fought their common enemy, the Communist establishment, hand in hand with the Czechs. The broad anti-Communist coalition in Czechoslovakia had not required elaboration of any other concrete political goals or development of a unified vision of the future democratic institutions.[26] Following the overthrow of their common enemy, however, the Czechs and the Slovaks started to fight among themselves.[27]

Like many coalitions against a common enemy, the members of the anti-Communist coalition in Czechoslovakia disregarded obvious ideological discrepancies and adverse political agendas to achieve their paramount goal of overthrowing the prior regime. Once the totalitarian regime was defeated, and the broad national consensus that transcended the revolution and the immediate "postrevolutionary" period in Czechoslovakia eroded, it became evident that the two "nations" living in the country were at very different and, arguably, incompatible stages of development.[28] It transpired that the different histories of the two "nations" dictated that they possess divergent aspirations for the future. The Czechs, after conquering the communist totality, aspire to become part of transnational institutions, a development that would necessarily require them to give up some of the prerogatives of a sovereign nation. Some Slovaks, on the other hand, are still striving for their own sovereign state—either openly through achieving outright independence, or more subtly through limiting their ties to the Czechs to those of a confederation.[29]

Another aspect that tends to be underestimated in characterizing the current political dynamics in Czechoslovakia is the disparate religious background of the Czech and Slovak societies. The Czechs, originally Protestant and now largely secular with some Catholic population, cherish the democratic ideals of a civil society, liberalism, and individual rights. In contrast, one of the dominant factors in the Slovak society is a traditional, socially conservative form of Catholicism.[30] In addition, the political spectrum in each republic seems to be developing in a different direction on economic issues. People in the Czech lands have largely enthusiastically embraced the ambitious and aggressive plan for profound transformation of the centrally planned economy into a market economy. In Slovakia, most of the politicians, apart from some members of the current fragile government coalition, advocate a slow transformation with a goal of establishing a "social-market economy."[31] This approach, due to the grim economic situation in Slovakia,[32] has broad support among the population.[33]

It is beyond the scope and aspiration of this chapter to identify and analyze the entire spectrum of disparities and frictions between the Czechs and the Slovaks. These few examples indicate that the gap between the two "nations" exists on several levels, including religious, political, economic, and ethnic. This gap, disguised behind the mask of unity mandated and controlled by the Central Committee of the Communist party throughout the last decades, seems to be widening further. It is not beyond imagination that the gulf may soon be so wide that no bridge of a common state would be able to stand.[34]

Slovak concerns and yearnings, with their historical basis in the period of domination by Hungary and a complex relationship with the Czechs, and the unfulfilled expectations of autonomy and self-governance, had periodically surfaced when the country was undergoing transitions and crises.[35] History repeats itself now, and the Slovaks are again calling for more sovereignty. The call of the Slovaks for self-governance is not surprising under the circumstances. In today's world, with pleas arising for self-determination on almost all continents, it can hardly be considered anachronistic. Such a call represents in essence a political struggle of a "nation" that is trying to define itself, including its own political structures, vis-à-vis the rest of the world, rather than an ethnically driven hatred directed against the Czechs.

The right to self-determination, however, need not necessarily lead to secession. Indeed, only a small portion of Slovaks favors secession.[36] For others, the desired amount of self-governance is possible in a country shared with the Czechs. Their desire is more for a future institutional structure to reflect the *equality* of the two "nations." Consequently, it is important to distinguish in Slovakia the still rather limited nationalistic groups and parties demanding secession,[37] and a much broader-based appeal for a greater degree of self-governance.

Regardless of whether it is justified or not, this appeal is a real one. It draws people by the thousands for meetings in the streets. The call needs to be dealt with in a proper institutional manner. Unless the government adequately addresses it, the Czech and

Slovak Federal Republic (CSFR) cannot emerge from its present situation with the requisite constitutional stability necessary for economic transformation and growth, protection of human rights and the rights of minorities, and the nurturing of democratic values and institutions.

ECONOMIC VERSUS CONSTITUTIONAL PROCESSES

In the first postrevolution elections on 8 and 9 June 1990, three parliaments—the Federal Assembly and the Czech and Slovak National Councils—were elected for two years, half the normal term, with a mandate to adopt a new constitution. Apart from its practical legal implications, the new democratic constitution would fulfill a paramount symbolic role: the old Constitution, the pinnacle of the Communist legal system, would be replaced by a document embodying the visions and aspirations of the people together with their concepts of a democratic state, thus formally breaking away from their totalitarian past. Since such a document cannot be drafted overnight, the federal Parliament decided to leave the 1960 Constitution operational until a new one is adopted, and amend only the necessary parts.[38]

An important characteristic of Czechoslovakia in this transitional period is the existence of two parallel but distinct attempts to restructure the country. First, to solidify the newly created democratic institutions and build the trust of the people in them. This undertaking, while difficult in its own right, is complicated by the second task—the necessity to carry out simultaneous fundamental structural economic changes designed to break away from the decades-long Communist legacy of centrally planned shortages and inefficiency.

The first concept, which entails the constitutional process, is plagued by bitter disputes over the future framework of the country. In contrast, the economic concept, unlike the constitutional one, has been comparatively successful given the state of the economy after the overthrow of the Communists. After June 1990, the Federal Assembly managed to pass many significant pieces of economic legislation,[39] as well as other important acts, such as the civil and penal substantive and procedural codes.

The reasons for the different results in the constitutional and economic legislations can likely be found in the initial continuance of the national consensus after the June 1990 elections, and the first goodwill efforts of the main political parties to find solutions to common problems and the ability and willingness to compromise, before the deep fragmentation of the country's political spectrum took place. This was, however, only possible thanks to the absence of the institutional barriers to compromise, which will be discussed in the next section.

Of course, any economic achievements realized to date may be short-lived; the success of any economic regime necessarily depends on a solid constitutional underpinning and stability. Also, the economic transformation that is taking place requires, for its success, a stable and strong government that is able to make unpopular and difficult decisions necessary for the reform.

REASONS FOR THE FAILURE OF THE CONSTITUTIONAL PROCESS

One of the main reasons for the failure of the constitutional process we witness in Czechoslovakia today lies in the institutional structure created by the 1968 Federation amendment.[40] This document introduced a federal structure with exceptional protections and safeguards for the Slovaks, who constitute, together with all the minorities living in Slovakia, one-third of the population. These protections include the principle of parity in one chamber of the federal Parliament and in high executive positions, and supermajority voting requirements in certain instances. Most important, however, the 1968 Federation amendment established a concept referred to as the "prohibition of majoritarian rule" (zákaz majorizácie), which now, after the 1990 first post-Communist free elections, has turned into the single most important institutional roadblock preventing the lawmakers in Czechoslovakia from proceeding with constitutional reform.

Prohibition of Majoritarian Rule

Both the Czech and the Slovak republics have their own separate legislative bodies, the National Councils, and both republics are represented on the federal level by the Federal Assembly. The Federal Assembly consists of two chambers: the Chamber of People, which consists of deputies elected directly by the entire population on a proportional basis; and the Chamber of Nations, which consists of seventy-five deputies elected in the Czech republic and seventy-five deputies elected in Slovakia. For each piece of important legislation,[41] the Czech and Slovak components in the Chamber of Nations vote separately. A bill is approved only if adopted by a majority of not the present, but the elected deputies representing each republic.[42] Consequently, thirty-eight votes in the Czech part—or thirty-eight votes in the Slovak part—of the Chamber of Nations can block any ordinary legislation. In addition, only thirty-one votes in either part are sufficient to block constitutional acts or amendments that need a three-fifths majority of the elected deputies for approval.

Although the composition of the Chamber of Nations favoring the smaller republic (Slovakia) is not dissimilar to other federal states,[43] the consequences of the voting procedure in the Chamber of Nations are quite unique. These voting procedures result in a de facto creation of a three-chamber Federal Assembly consisting of the Chamber of People and the Czech and the Slovak parts of the Chamber of Nations. Since both chambers must approve each legislative act, the structure grants an effective veto power to a small minority of Czech or Slovak deputies. Obviously this type of voting mechanism in a country with only two constituent parts is bound to create impasses.

The situation in the Federal Assembly in the past year and a half demonstrates its structural problems. The nationalistic Slovak opposition parties in the assembly[44] have regularly exercised the broad veto power in the Chamber of Nations. Whereas originally, after the elections, the Slovak parties arguably functioned as a "constructive opposition," they shifted gears and now paralyze the Parliament on any constitutional issue. This destructive role serves at least two important functions: it magnifies the inability of the government coalition parties to create a new constitution; and it maintains the institutional status quo until after the elections.

Supermajority Voting Requirements

Pursuant to the 1968 Federation amendment, all constitutional acts and amendments, the declaration of war, and the election of the president need to be approved by a three-fifths majority of all elected deputies in all three parts of the Federal Assembly.[45] Considering the fragmented political spectrum in Czechoslovakia today,[46] this requirement makes it extremely difficult to reach political consensus on any of the major issues.

Two-Member Federation

The complexity of the institutional structure set up by the 1968 Federation amendment is elevated by the "dual" nature of the Czechoslovak federation. The CSFR consists of only two constituent republics; the Czechs live in one, the Slovaks in the other. In this respect, Czechoslovakia differs from other "federal" systems, for example, India, Spain, Switzerland, the United States, and Canada.[47] Belgium provides the closest analogy to Czechoslovakia's ethnic division, with its dominant Walloon and Flemish parts. Belgium, however, maintains a unitary form of government, granting the ethnic groups a greater say only in matters of language and culture. Belgium also has a bicameral Parliament, but neither of the chambers de jure represents the regions or ethnic groups; the deputies in both chambers are elected on a representative basis by the entire Belgian population.[48]

In contrast to Belgium, Czechoslovakia has a tension already built into its institutional structure. As a result, two constituent units with divergent aspirations and political cultures are unable to find a compromise on fundamental issues of the future form of a common country. The existence of only two partners in the federation causes each constitutional issue to become overpoliticized. Consequently, all issues are typically solved at a negotiating table rather than by a rational search of optimal constitutional solutions. When discussion between the republics reaches a deadlock, there is no swing vote, no third force to break the impasse.

It is in this respect that one needs to look at the history of the country in order to understand the current Czech-Slovak conflict. The bad memories the Slovaks retained from the periods of Magyar (Hungarian) domination, the lack of sovereignty they perceive, their unfulfilled hopes for a federation in 1918, and the nonfunctional institutional framework all combine to hinder any constructive constitutional discourse. It is important to keep in mind that the unworkable 1968 amendment was drafted during the Communist period, when the Constitution was simply a meaningless piece of paper, and when typically all parliamentary decisions were unanimous, regardless of any voting structure or mechanism. At its inception, the amendment was not intended to function without the authoritarian Communist rule, in a democratic pluralistic Parliament. This ill-conceived structure gives inordinate power to a small number of deputies of the assembly who, as a result, possess the ability to block any important legislation proposed by a majority.[49]

The constitutional process in the CSFR is further complicated by a sociocultural phenomenon under which heightened emotions characterize all discussions and negotiations between the Czechs and Slovaks. Both sides juggle undefined and imprecise terms.[50] Descriptions of the future framework of the country range from a federation, true federation, authentic federation, confederation, union, to a loose union. Recently, commentators started using a peculiar term, a "unitary form of federation."[51] Efforts to define the terms to facilitate discourse are lacking; the politicians even seem to thrive on the confusion and lack of precision.[52] It enables them to maneuver. Most of the terms used to qualify "federation," however, merely disguise the omnipresent political striving for greater autonomy and sovereignty.[53] This seemingly innocuous semantic battle is, unfortunately, a reflection of deeper, more fundamental dissimilarities between the two "nations."

CONSTITUTIONAL AMENDMENTS DURING 1990–91

Despite the inability of the Czechs and Slovaks to resolve their relationship, the two "nations" have already dealt with some issues in an institutional manner. Soon after the parliamentary elections in January 1991, popular feelings induced the lawmakers to adopt a bill of rights.[54] This was an understandable move, considering the Communist regime's numerous violations of civil and political rights, although the Communist regime's 1948 and 1960 Constitutions were supposed to make the U.S. Bill of Rights "pale by comparison."[55]

In December 1990, the Federal Assembly adopted a controversial constitutional act on power-sharing between the federation and the republics.[56] In March 1991, it adopted a constitutional act on the Constitutional Court[57] and in July 1991 a constitutional act on the judiciary.[58] In addition, Parliament enacted a constitutional act on the holding of popular referenda in August 1991.[59]

Despite these significant successes, the lawmakers concentrate too heavily on the issues of federalism and the future institutional structure. By doing so, constitutional drafters risk losing sight of the long-term interests and problems that a constitution should address.[60]

One example of an issue not sufficiently addressed due to the attention paid to the federalism debate arises in the Charter of January 1991. That Charter contains a provision establishing the supremacy of international treaties on human rights and fundamental freedoms, such as the International Covenant on Civil and Political Rights, ratified and promulgated by Czechoslovakia over domestic legislation. Such treaties directly apply to Czechoslovakian territory.[61] A provision to this effect is new and unique within the Czechoslovakian legal order. Neither Czechoslovak legal theory nor its practice agree on the issue of the hierarchy of norms of international law within the Czechoslovakian domestic legal order. The existence of this unusual provision in Section 2 of the Charter should signal lawmakers to pay sufficient attention to an issue as significant as the applicability and status of international law in the domestic legal order when they draft a new constitution.

Another example of an issue not sufficiently addressed is the treatment of the many national minorities living in Czechoslovakia. The preambles to the 1948 and 1960 Constitutions and the 1968 Federation amendment spoke of the "equal" or "fraternal" nations" of the Czechs and Slovaks.[62] The Constitution, however, does not mention other nationalities such as Hungarians, Poles, Romanies, Ukrainians, and Ruthenians who constitute about 20 percent of the population of Slovakia. In 1968, the Parliament enacted a separate constitutional act dealing with minorities.[63] It remains to be seen how this issue will be dealt with in a future constitution.[64]

PLAYERS IN THE CONSTITUTIONAL ARENA

Federal Assembly

From a constitutional point of view, an unusual situation developed in the CSFR. The federation still exists, but its supreme legislative body, the Federal Assembly, lost most of its ability to influence the Constitution's development to the republics' bodies, the Czech and Slovak National Councils and Czech and Slovak governments.[65] The main reason for this development is the paralysis of the federal Parliament in the constitutional arena. Many politicians, including President Havel himself, criticized the absence of federal bodies from the constitution-making process. At the beginning of 1992, the Federal Assembly made an attempt to enact three chapters of a federal constitution newly arranging the relations between the president, the federal Parliament, and the federal government.[66] This move was doomed from its inception thanks to the institutional structure of the Federal Assembly. It follows that the amendment, though securing approval of the Chamber of People, failed to get the approval of the Slovak opposition parties in the Slovak part of the Chamber of Nations.[67]

Czech and Slovak National Councils

The Federal Assembly, ineffective on constitutional matters, has been effectively replaced by the republics' governing bodies. In the past twenty months, the representatives of the National Councils and the republics' governments met approximately twenty times to discuss the future of the CSFR. Interestingly, these discussions were initiated by President Havel as consultations in search of an optimal solution for the future set-up of the country that would be based on a broad national consensus. The discussions, initially involving representatives of federal institutions as well as political parties, gradually evolved into negotiations between the National Councils. The main topics on their agendas included the creation of republic constitutions and a new redistribution of the respective powers ("competencies") between the federation and the republics.

Since the 1990 constitutional act on power-sharing, both the Czechs and the Slovaks expressed dissatisfaction with the status quo in the division of powers, although for contradictory reasons. Whereas many people in the Czech Republic consider the power of the federal government and Parliament inadequate, many Slovak politicians believe that too many powers remain at the federal level. In November 1991, the Slovak government adopted a conciliatory declaration[68] on the power-sharing dispute and its economic and social consequences.[69] The declaration signified a more rational attitude by the Slovak executive toward the complex relationship with the Czechs. Many deputies of the Slovak Parliament, however, do not share the executive's viewpoint.

State Treaty   The discussion of the National Councils on the division of powers became intertwined with negotiations over the so-called state treaty.[70] This controversial concept best reflects the different aspirations and visions of the two republics.[71] The history of the negotiations over the treaty presents us with an interesting list of issues and concepts over which the two "nations" differ. Although the treaty is not going to be adopted (at least not before the elections), it is useful to outline the events that led to this result, as an illustration of the Czech-Slovak conflict.

Theoretically, the state treaty was supposed to define the relationship between the two republics in a future common state and work in concert with a new constitution.[72] Initially, the Czech National Council firmly opposed the state treaty concept, but later the council agreed to it in principle, though controversies over the treaty remained. At first, there was contention based on the division of powers.[73] Afterward, no agreement could be found on a more conceptual level. The Czech and Slovak politicians differed on the way in which the treaty should be adopted and on its legal status and significance.[74]

In principle, the parties struggled with the question of whether to build a federation from "below," in which the republics delegate power to the federation, or from "above," in which the federation grants power to the republics. The Slovak politicians advocated building from "below." They argued this position by asserting that the treaty should contractually oblige two *independent* republics to live in a common state, to which each of the republics would delegate certain powers. The Czechs, on the other hand, supported the concept of building the federation from "above" and asserted that the legitimacy of the federation should derive directly from the people rather than from the republics.

Furthermore, nationalistic Slovak politicians claimed that each republic should be a subject of international law, like all sovereign states. This was unacceptable to the federal and Czech politicians, who asserted that as long as the federation existed it was the only body capable of being a subject of international law. Otherwise, one could not speak of a common state.[75]

In addition, the Slovak version of the treaty called for a permanently binding "state" treaty officially entitled "Treaty between the Czech and Slovak Republics." The treaty would include the Czech and Slovak republics as the only parties, thus implicitly recognizing Slovakia as an independent republic.[76] The Czech version called for a less formal, internal agreement between the two National Councils.

After months of negotiations over the power-sharing aspect of the treaty, the division of powers between the republics was more or less settled.[77] At the beginning of February, the joint commission appointed by both councils agreed on the text of the treaty.[78] The Czech National Council reacted to the agreement by a resolution approving the text.[79] In the words of the chairwoman of the Czech National Council: "[W]e have succeeded in really drawing up a draft treaty which truly corresponds to the requirements of both participating parties."[80] Ten deputies of the Slovak National Council's Presidium, however, did not share the chairwoman's perception. The Presidium failed to approve the treaty.[81]

The Slovak deputies had two principal objections to the text: (1) it did not define who was a party to the treaty,[82] that is, it was not an official treaty between two republics considered subjects of international law;[83] and (2) it was not contemplated as a permanent source of law, rather just a "legal initiative" to the Federal Assembly, which could either accept or disapprove the treaty.[84] Having failed to adopt the treaty, the two National Councils realized the futility of further negotiations, and agreed to suspend talks until after the June elections.[85]

There are two important aspects of the state treaty negotiations. First, this legally controversial concept and the issues raised in negotiations were just a pretense, a playground for political ping-pong among the politicians. A debate over the issues, such as whether to build an institution from "below" or "above," has approximately the same degree of precision and relevance as a debate over the difference between an "authentic" or "true" federation. The negotiations were, in fact, only another forum that highlighted the same differences between the two "nations" that paralyze the Federal Assembly.

Second, the real significance of the state treaty did not rest in its content or form. Its value was largely symbolic. A successfully concluded treaty would have been a preeminent symbol of national consensus, of the ability of the two peoples to compromise and reach agreement on overarching principles. The Czech disappointment with the failure to adopt a treaty, the concept they had originally opposed, best documents its symbolic importance.[86] The Slovak prime minister even commented that "if a treaty on the principles of a constitutional arrangement is not adopted, the breakup of the common Czechoslovak state is possible."[87]

Declaration of Sovereignty   The nationalistic parties have periodically brought another political tool into the negotiations between the National Councils—a threat to issue a "declaration of national sovereignty."[88] The threat of the Slovak National Council unilaterally presenting a declaration of sovereignty persists.[89] Such a declaration would, among other things, pronounce the supremacy of the Slovak National Council's laws over those of the Federal Assembly. This would, arguably, constitute a violation of the current federal Constitution. No declaration has been issued yet, and some say there is no danger of the declaration being issued before the elections.[90] What will happen afterward, however, remains to be seen. One reason for the hesitation over the declaration is that the Slovak National Council has been waiting for a Slovak constitution to be adopted. A draft of a constitution was presented in alternative forms in early January for public debate.[91] No action on it has taken place yet. The current options in the draft document cover a wide range of choices, from a functional federation to an independent state.[92] Depending on which alternative is adopted, the Slovak constitution itself, or certain provisions therein, may violate the federal Constitution.

CONSTITUTIONAL DEADLOCKS

The impasses, or some may say the constitutional crisis, that resulted from the failure of the Federal Assembly to adopt three chapters of a new constitution[93] as well as from the inconclusive treaty negotiations between the two National Councils, highlight another crucial deficiency of the 1968 Federation amendment. It does not provide for any effective safety valves or deadlock-breaking mechanisms.

During the past twenty years, following the Soviet occupation in 1968, deadlock-breaking mechanisms were unnecessary. Consequently, the magnitude of the Czech-Slovak conflict remained concealed due to the omnipotent Communist party, which, with its blessings from Moscow, effectively prevented people from getting involved in any highly emotional controversies.[94] Czechoslovakia's Communist party no longer has a dominant role in the society. Also, because the country does not belong to any defense alliance, it is left in a security vacuum. Thus the struggle between the two "nations" remains an internal matter.

With only two partners in this "dual" federation, and the built-in institutional tension, stalemates inevitably result. The country needs a third force, either internal or external, to provide balance in the volatile political situation. President Havel recently tried to introduce the missing role of a "third force" and, in an emotional television address to the people,[95] proposed several draft bills designed to combat the current impasses.[96] The politicians conducting the constitutional debate in Czechoslovakia have procrastinated for a relatively long time. One of the reasons is the fall-back position that the Parliaments created for themselves. While the 1960 Constitution remains valid, amendments implemented by Parliament may allow the political negotiations and "summitting" to continue indefinitely. How much time the country has, however, is impossible to estimate. In today's fast-moving world, the economic pressures may force Czechoslovakia to choose between speedily resolving the constitutional debate while simultaneously creating functioning democratic institutional structures in order to join European integrations, or continuing to squabble and leaving Czechoslovakia out of the integration processes.

PRESIDENT HAVEL'S LEGISLATIVE INITIATIVES

The CSFR is a parliamentary democracy, so the president is not elected by the people and is not the head of the executive branch. Czechoslovak constitutions traditionally gave little power to the presidents. President Havel's substantial influence in the country stems from his personal appeal and charisma—as was the case with President Masaryk—rather than from any particular constitutional provisions. The current Constitution and laws of Czechoslovakia give the president some limited powers[97] and implicitly include the rarely exercised right of legislative initiative. The Constitution, however, does not provide the president with any effective legal means to break deadlocks. The president cannot dissolve the Parliament (apart from the one instance when the Federal Assembly cannot agree on a budget), call for a referendum, or rule by decree.[98] In an attempt to abate the constitutional crisis and improve the ill-conceived institutional structure of the 1968 Federation amendment,[99] the president proposed several new laws to the federal Parliament.[100]

The president's first proposal called for a ratification of the new federal constitution by the Czech and Slovak National Councils, after its adoption by the Federal Assembly.[101] On 21 January 1992, even though President Havel's proposal met the demands of the radical Slovak politicians, the Slovak opposition parties in the Federal Assembly exercised their veto power and blocked its adoption for ratification.[102]

Next, the president proposed an amendment to the Referendum Law that would allow him to initiate a referendum in the entire country or in only one of the republics with the consent of the federal government. He would not have to secure consent of the Federal Assembly.[103] This proposal also obligated the president to call for a referendum if five hundred thousand people in the Czech republic or two hundred fifty thousand people in the Slovak republic sought one.[104] At present, two-and-a-half million signatures calling for a referendum have been collected in Czechoslovakia,[105] but to no avail. Current law[106] requires the initiation of a referendum no later than five months before the end of the election terms of the Federal Assembly and the National Councils. With the next election scheduled for June, hopes for a referendum are futile.[107] The Federal Assembly voted down the proposed bill on 21 January 1992.[108]

Another of Havel's proposals would give him the ability to dissolve the Parliament when the two chambers are unable to agree on a draft bill. It would further enable him to rule by presidential decree after dissolving the Parliament and before a new one would be elected.[109] This bill was rejected by both chambers of the Federal Assembly on 28 January 1992.[110]

Yet another of the president's proposals concerned a new Federal Assembly structure.[111] First, the proposal would transform the assembly into a unicameral body consisting of two hundred deputies. Second, the proposal would create a new entity, consisting of thirty members, called the Federal Council.[112] After the Federal Assembly failed to pass Havel's drafts on the ratification procedure and the amendment to the Referendum Law, he withdrew his Federal Council proposal.[113]

The president's final proposal concerned a new election law based on a mixture of the majoritarian and proportional election systems.[114] A group of eleven deputies of the Federal Assembly (from eight different political parties) proposed an alternative to Havel's proposal—an amendment to the current election law based on proportional representation.[115] The Federal Assembly declined the president's proposal and adopted the one presented by the deputies.[116] One reason for the refusal was that the Slovak opposition parties simply seem to resist any proposals from the president. But there was also a much more pragmatic reason for the preservation of the proportional election system: self-interest.

The deputies in the fragmented Parliament resisted a change in the election system that would endanger their prospects for re-election in the June elections. The mixed election system would prevent many small parties from getting seats in the parliament.

The fate of Havel's proposals in the Federal Assembly came as no surprise. The surprising part was the president's submission of the draft bills. Although all of the proposals, if adopted, would mean a valuable improvement to the constitutional framework of Czechoslovakia, they were destined to fail from the very outset. The veto power of thirty-one deputies in the Chamber of Nations and the track record of the "Slovak bloc"[117] in this chamber of successfully blocking any attempts to change the institutional order of the federal Parliament are well known. Therefore, it is not only surprising but indeed troubling to see the president launch a constitutional initiative that, albeit well-meant, cannot succeed under the circumstances. President Havel is one of the few integrating factors left in Czechoslovakia today. This unfortunate move only diminishes his prestige. If President Havel, a man of great vision and personal appeal, fails to make the politicians agree, it is doubtful that anything will.

POSSIBLE SCENARIOS FOR THE FUTURE

Czechoslovakia's future remains uncertain. At the time of this writing, one can only guess the results of the upcoming June elections and the developments they will bring. Indeed, the elections themselves may be problematic.

After the negotiations between the National Councils ended in failure, the political representatives decided not to make any further attempts to negotiate and instead have concentrated their hopes on the elections.[118] The elections, in principle, have no magic to them. Indeed, they might further destabilize the already volatile political scene, if their results create as fragmented a political spectrum as exists today. Since the institutional structure of the newly elected federal Parliament will be identical to the current one,[119] it might even prove impossible to elect any president by the necessary majority and form a federal cabinet.

Neither the 1968 Federation amendment nor any other applicable law dictates what happens if the Federal Assembly fails to elect a president.[120] The only applicable provision of the 1968 Federation amendment is Article 64, which gives presidential powers to the federal prime minister if the president, for various reasons, is not capable of executing his or her duties. But there is no provision on how to ultimately bring about a successful election, or any provision on who executes presidential functions if the Federal Assembly is unable to form a federal cabinet.

Some politicians, including President Havel himself, have recognized this danger. Voicing his concern while revealing his playwright's past, the president stated: "I am afraid that Jesus Christ combined with Winston Churchill would not be elected president in such an election. . . . It is possible to envisage that we will have neither a president nor a new government and, moreover, a non-functioning Parliament."[121] Aware of the small probability of electing a president with the currently valid provisions of the 1968 Federation amendment, the three parts of the Federal Assembly were, surprisingly, able to agree on a constitutional amendment that made the prospects of electing a president after the June parliamentary elections a little more plausible. The new amendment provides for a presidential election in two rounds. If a candidate is unable to obtain a three-fifths majority in all three parts of the Federal Assembly in the first round, an absolute (50 percent) majority will suffice in the second round.[122]

Despite the many unknowns, several likely scenarios for the future are possible. If the president is not elected and the federal government is not formed, the country may continue disintegrating to the point of a complete breakup.[123] Alternatively, Czechoslovakia may be trapped in a continual constitutional crisis and resulting long-term instability, reminiscent of postwar Italy.[124] This may take place even if the Federal Assembly ultimately does agree on the remainder of a new constitution, and creates a highly decentralized federal structure with minimal powers on the federal level or a confederation. Such a framework would furthermore cause the economic processes in the two republics to develop in different directions.

Although the post-1989 constitutional developments do not leave much room for excessive optimism, there are some grounds for a more optimistic outlook to counter this cynicism. Public opinion polls over time have consistently shown that a majority of the population in both republics wishes to remain in a common state. For these people, the struggle for self-governance and self-determination does not necessarily result in separatist tendencies or secession. If their wish is unequivocally demonstrated, for example, in a referendum, that expression of unity may contribute a great deal toward constitutional stability. A considerable

portion of the Czech-Slovak conflict is, in essence, a power struggle. There is some hope that if the most nationalistic politicians
assume posts in the federal structures, they might graduate into
"good citizens" of the common state.

Despite all of the foregoing scenarios, the economic realities,
together with international developments including the European integration processes, may induce the Czechoslovak lawmakers to move beyond the frictions and collisions and design a
functioning, common modus operandi.[125] If not, one must at least
trust that the country will muddle through these difficult times
in the hope that the two rival "nations" might come to terms
with each other in the near future.

Conclusion

Czechoslovakia is an example of how institutions are able to
frustrate people's hopes. At the outset, amid the postrevolution
and free election euphoria, few contemplated that the mandate
to replace the old Constitution with a new one before the June
1992 parliamentary elections would prove insurmountable. Now,
without a new constitution, the country is awaiting the elections
with mixed emotions—hope as well as fear of the fate of the
common state and the speed and shape of economic reform.

Initially, neither the population at large nor the politicians on
either side appreciated the significance of the factors that divide
the society. Two of the important factors considered in this chapter—the divergent aspirations of the two "nations" and the ill-
conceived institutional structure—have combined to produce an
unhappy result. If the aspirations alone differed, a positive institutional framework could have contributed toward satisfying
them. Conversely, if the structure were the only problem, and a
broad national consensus were to have continued, it could have
caused the structure to change. To combat both of these factors
simultaneously has proved impossible so far.

The Slovak call for self-determination and self-governance cannot be underestimated. Some argue it is a justified call, but regardless of any attempt to justify it by objective criteria, the demand is significant in its imminence and reality. The appeal has
to be dealt with in an appropriate institutional fashion, otherwise
it will remain a constant threat, a sword of Damocles hanging
over the Czech-Slovak relationship and coexistence. One must

make the distinction, however, between a broad-based self-determination call and populist secession demands reflecting the power struggle and ambitions of individual politicians. Perhaps the best distinguishing criterion between these two is how democratic are the means utilized by the politicians to achieve their goals.

Addendum

This chapter was written in January 1992 and was further edited during March and April of that year. Therefore, the dramatic developments after the June 1992 parliamentary elections leading to the eventual split of the country are reflected in the text only as predictions in the section entitled "Possible Scenarios for the Future."

During the summer of 1992, the leaders of the two victorious parties, the Movement for a Democratic Slovakia (MFDS) in the Slovak Republic and the Civic Democratic Party (CDP) in the Czech Republic, agreed on a breakup of the Czechoslovak federation as of 1 January 1993. In preparation for a separate existence, the Slovak National Council (renamed the National Council of the Slovak Republic) in July adopted a Declaration of Sovereignty, and on 1 September, it passed the Constitution of the Slovak Republic. The Czech National Council, after a complex and protracted debate, adopted the Constitution of the Czech Republic in December 1992.

The decision to break the country was carried out by the leadership of the MFDS and the CDP. No referendum was held, despite many public appeals coupled with consistent poll results against the breakup in both parts of the federation before the June elections. This lack of deference to the will of the public may in the future put in question the legitimacy of the creation of both independent states.

Thus 1 January 1993, the symbolic date of a closer integration of the twelve states of the European Communities, became the official date of the disintegration of the seventy-four-year-old state of the Czechs and Slovaks. Only a few weeks after the third anniversary of the celebrated "velvet revolution," the Czechs and Slovaks made the front page news again—this time with their civilized "velvet divorce." Considering the slaughters in the former Yugoslavia and the nontransparent chaos in the former Soviet Union, the peacefully negotiated breakup of Czechoslovakia was, undoubtedly, an achievement in its own right. Despite the absence of bloodshed, however, the breakup brought further instability to the already volatile situation in Central and Eastern Europe. Also, the events that occurred during the first months of the existence of the two independent republics have shown how illusory is the concept of a "velvet divorce." They confirmed the skeptic's point of view.

History is the best judge is an old saying. Therefore it will be a matter for the future to determine whether the split of the former Czechoslovakia only satisfied political ambitions of its protagonists, or whether it will be beneficial for the population at large.

Notes

The author wishes to thank the cochairs, as well as Sophie H. Pirie and Milan Lovíšek, for invaluable comments on earlier drafts. This chapter is adapted from a speech the author gave at the Woodrow Wilson International Center for Scholars in Washington, D.C., on 6 January 1992. At the time the author gave the speech and conceived this chapter, many of the events that subsequently took place were merely the author's predictions. Therefore, some of the items discussed are given greater prominence than the current status quo merits.

[1] Jon Elster defines a "homogeneous" entity as one containing only one people and having negligibly few members of that people live outside the entity, in "Constitutionalism in Eastern Europe: An Introduction," *University of Chicago Law Review* 58 (1991): 447, 450, discussing the commonalities and differences of the constitutional processes in the countries of Eastern Europe. With regard to "heterogeneous" entities, Elster distinguishes between an "internally heterogeneous" entity that has a large number of members of several peoples, and an "externally heterogeneous" entity that consists of one dominant people, a large number of which live outside the entity's borders. I use the term "heterogeneous" in the sense of internal heterogeneity.

[2] Elster, "Constitutionalism in Eastern Europe," 450.

[3] The word "nation," as used in Czechoslovakia and other parts of Central and Eastern Europe, exemplifies the semantic and conceptual problems of cross-cultural exchanges. The term "nation" has a different meaning in Czech, Slovak, and German languages from that in English and French. The Anglo-Saxon and French traditions define "nation" politically. The term "nation" means citizens of a state, members of a state entity. See Svetozár Bombík, "Národ v európskych súradniciach" (Nation in European Axis), Kultúrny Život 51/52 (1991): 9, analyzing the different conception of the terms "nation" and "self-determination" in the Anglo-Saxon and French tradition vis-à-vis the Central European understanding. In Central Europe, however, the understanding of the term "nation" is based on the linguistic and cultural-historic characteristics. This definition was conceived by the German

Romantic philosopher J. G. Herder. According to Herder, a community defined as a "nation" contains several attributes: common history, customs, culture, territory, and language. Consequently, the Czechs and Slovaks consider themselves distinct "nations."

English does not have a one-word expression that would adequately convey the same meaning as the term "nation" in the Central European linguistic and cultural-historic environment. The closest translation is probably the word "people." This term is used, for example, by Elster, who defines "people" as "a community with common traditions, common language, common religion, and—perhaps most important—common enemies." Elster, "Constitutionalism in Eastern Europe," 450. This chapter will refer to the Czechs and Slovaks as two *nations*, and for clarity will use quotation marks whenever the term "nation" contextually differs from its normal English connotation.

[4]Both Czechs and Slovaks descend from old Slavic tribes that settled roughly the territory of modern Czechoslovakia in the sixth century A.D. In the ninth century, they allegedly created an early feudal state, the Great Moravian Empire, which lasted only a short time. Thereafter, eastern tribes, later conquered by the strongest among them, the Magyars, penetrated the Danube lowland and separated the Slovak tribes from the Czech tribes for a thousand years. The historical paths of Czechs and Slovaks crossed several times during those thousand years. From the sixteenth century they both lived under the Hapsburg monarchs. Each "nation," however, remained so separate and distinct that the creation and development of national consciousness and self-awareness during the eighteenth and nineteenth centuries differed considerably in each "nation." See Podiven, "Národ Československý" (Czechoslovak nation), *Revue pro Střední Evropu* 17 (1990): 82, explaining the history of the Czechs and the Slovaks, and the history of their relationship; Kováč, "Slováci a Česi: Pohľad v spätnom zrkadle" (Slovaks and Czechs: Look into a rearview mirror), Kultúrny Život 5 (1992): 1, explaining the differences in understanding the concept of a common state between the Slovaks and the Czechs. See also Lloyd Cutler and Herman Schwartz, "Constitutional Reform in Czechoslovakia: E Duobus Unum?" *University of Chicago Law Review* 58 (1991): 511, discussing the approach of the newly renamed Czech and Slovak Federal Republic (CSFR) to each of four major constitutional issues: federalism; the bill of rights; an independent judiciary; and the separation of powers among the president, the cabinet, and the federal legislature.

[5]Rather few "commonalities" exist in the cultural profiles of Czechs and Slovaks. Consistent with tradition, Slovakia's cultural heritage revolved around Roman Catholic religion and rural living conditions prior to the Communist postwar industrialization. The Czech Republic has a mixture of Roman Catholic and Protestant religions. On the whole, however, many Czechs are secular and "religiously lukewarm," with a long tradition of town culture and a comparatively strong industrial base. See Petr, "Česko(-)Slovensko není samozřejmostí" (Czecho(-)Slovakia is not given), *Respekt* 42 (1991): 4, describing some of the differences between the Czechs and the Slovaks at the time the First Republic came into being; Sunstein, "Constitutionalism and Secession," *University of Chicago Law Review* 58 (1991): 633, 664, discussing how cultural integrity and self-determination frequently fuel secession

movements in Eastern Europe and elsewhere; Příhoda, "České dilema: Slováci" (Czech dilemma: Slovaks), *Přítomnost* 10 (1991): 1, discussing the various differences between the two "nations" and suggesting that a gradual and negotiated disintegration of the country may be the only way to settle the Czech-Slovak conflict.

[6]The Czechoslovak Republic was one of a number of small, culturally, religiously, and ethnically diverse states that came into being after the fall of the Hapsburg, Ottoman, and Czarist Empires from 1917 to 1921.

[7]See Cutler and Schwartz, "Constitutional Reform," 513, discussing how, in their first constitution, the Czechs and Slovaks looked to the West for inspiration and example, in particular to the French parliamentary and the American systems.

[8]Tomáš Garrique Masaryk, the founder of Czechoslovakia and its first president, headed this body.

[9]See generally, Jiří Grospič and Miloš Matula, "K Demokratické Tradici Československého Konstitucionalismu" (On the democratic tradition of Czechoslovak constitutionalism), *Právník, Teoretický Časopis pro Otázky Státu a Práva* (The lawyer, scientific review for problems of state and law) 130 (1991): 608, 611, detailing Czechoslovakia's constitutional history and democratic tradition.

[10]At the beginning of the century, a fairly well-organized Slovak community, formed by Slovaks who had emigrated for economic reasons, existed in the United States.

[11]See generally Doležel, "Česko ? Slovensko, Prostor slovenské politiky" (Czecho ? Slovakia, the space of Slovak politics), *Příloha Lidových Novin*, 15 October 1991, p. IV.

[12]Doležel, "Česko ? Slovensko," IV.

[13]Doležel, "Česko ? Slovensko," IV. See also Petr, "Česko(-)Slovensko," 4.

[14]Doležel, "Česko ? Slovensko," IV.

[15]Cutler and Schwartz, "Constitutional Reform," 514.

[16]See Podiven, "Národ," 82, noting that some declare the Slovak language a dialect of the Czech language, whereas others consider them "two branches of the same tree"; Doležel, "Česko ? Slovensko," I–IV.

[17] Podiven, "Národ," 82; Kováč, "Slováci a Česi," 1. Rather than trying to identify every reason why the Slovaks appeal for greater autonomy and sovereignty, this chapter focuses on the effect of these appeals on the constitutional processes in Czechoslovakia today.

[18]The Slovak Republic came into existence by a declaration of the Slovak Snem (assembly) on 14 March 1939, several months after the Munich dictate and the Viennese "arbitrage," pursuant to which Czechoslovakia lost its western territory, the Sudetenland, and southern Slovakia to Germany and Hungary, respectively. In November 1938, the Slovak Snem passed law No. 299 declaring the autonomy of Slovakia. The Slovak declaration of autonomy, and later the proclamation of an independent Slovak state, were unconstitutional acts under the Constitution of 1920, which did not allow territorial division of Czechoslovakia. Ján Mlynárik, "Pro Přesnost, Vyhlášení Slov-

enského Státu byl Protiústavní Čin" (For accuracy, proclamation of the Slovak state was an unconstitutional act), *Respekt*, 29 September–6 October 1991, p. 6. See also Doležel, "Česko ? Slovensko," I–IV.

[19] See Špaňár, "Slovensko: Ide o dušu" (Slovakia: The soul is at stake), *Kultúrny Život* 7 (1992): 1, discussing the necessity of the Slovak nation coming to terms with its Fascist period during World War II.

[20] See Doležel, "Česko ? Slovensko," I–IV. The plan was named after a city in Eastern Slovakia, Košice, where it was executed.

[21] Vratislav Pechota, "Československé Ústavní Dějiny" (Czechoslovak Constitutional History), *Právník, Teoretický Časopis pro Otázky Státu a Práva* 130 (1991): 273.

[22] Doležel, "Česko ? Slovensko," I–IV.

[23] Úst. zák. č. 100/1960 Zb., Czechoslovakian Constitution of 1960, reprinted in Albert P. Blaustein and Gisbert H. Flanz, eds., *Constitutions of the Countries of the World: Czechoslovakia* (Oceana: Dobbs Ferry, New York, 1974).

[24] Úst. zák. č. 143/1968 Zb., o československej federácii (Czech. Const. Act No. 143/1968 Collection of Laws [hereinafter Coll. of Laws], concerning the Czechoslovak Federation) [hereinafter 1968 Federation amendment], reprinted in Blaustein and Flanz, *Constitutions: Czechoslovakia*.

[25] "The administrative directive implementation of the leading role of the Communist party of Czechoslovakia distorted the entire political system, including the federal structure," Aleš Gerloch, "Nad Variantami Nového Státoprávního Uspořádání Československého Státu (On the alternatives of constitutional set-up of the Czechoslovak state), *Právník, Teoretický Časopis pro Otázky Státu a Práva* 130 (1991): 503–4.

[26] Andrzej Rapaczynski, "Constitutional Politics in Poland: A Report on the Constitutional Committee of the Polish Parliament," *University of Chicago Law Review* 58 (1991): 595, discussing the institutional aspects of the Polish constitutional process. The process of disintegration is also typical of conflicts other than the Czech-Slovak conflict. The political differentiation that occurred in Czechoslovakia after the revolution was a natural result of the diversity of the anti-Communist coalition formed in the first days of the 1989 revolution. For example, Civic Forum, the leading political force in the Czech lands, initially led by President Havel, won a sweeping victory in the June 1990 parliamentary elections. Within six months, however, Civic Forum broke into two large groups and one small grouping. Several months later, a similar disintegration took place in Public Against Violence, the Slovak equivalent of Civic Forum. Since then, most of the large movements or parties, including the Communist party and the Christian Democratic Movement, have weathered similar processes. This process is not unique to Czechoslovakia. Poland, for example, serves as a textbook illustration of the fragmentation of a political coalition following a successful overthrow of a totalitarian regime. The October 1991 elections brought over twenty-five parties to the Polish Parliament.

[27] The first significant open conflict between the two "nations" was over the official name of the country. In March 1990, the federal Parliament adopted a new name—Czechoslovak Federative Republic, dropping the word "Socialist." A month later, following a controversial debate that became

known as the "hyphen war," the federal Parliament adopted the name Czech and Slovak Federal Republic. Slovak deputies in the federal Parliament demanded the use of a hyphen between the words "Czech" and "Slovakia" in the shortened name of the country, Czechoslovakia, hence the term "hyphen war."

[28] Příhoda, "České dilema," 1.

[29] At the time of this writing, however, the Slovak governmental coalition still supports coexistence with the Czechs in a federation.

[30] This distinction between the republics is apparent in the efforts of the politicians of the Christian Democratic Movement, who are members of the government coalition to abolish the principle of separation of the church and state. Also, at the time of this writing, a bill pending in the Slovak Parliament would severely restrict the currently valid liberal law on abortions. These efforts are not paralleled, at least not to such an extent, in the Czech lands.

[31] For example, the Slovak Christian Democratic Movement, which demands a declaration of sovereignty and an adoption of a constitution of the Slovak Republic, also "favors a social market economy." "Klepac Party Favors Confederation, Social Economy," *Foreign Broadcast Information Service* [hereinafter *FBIS]-EEU-92-052*, 17 March 1992, p. 7 (citing *Československá Haćová kancelária* (*CSTK*) [hereinafter *Prague CSTK*], 16 March 1992).

[32] According to the Slovak premier, "Slovakia's economy is in worse shape than expected, with last year's gross domestic product having dropped by about 15 percent and industrial production by 25 percent." "Carnogursky Reviews Slovakia's 1991 Economy," *FBIS-EEU-92-020*, 30 January 1992, p. 7 (citing *Prague CSTK*, 28 January 1992). According to the same source, unemployment rapidly increased to approximately 300,000 by the end of 1991. This represents 11.8 percent of the total labor force. See also "Preliminary Slovak Statistical Data for 1991," *FBIS-EEU-92-025*, 6 February 1992, p. 4 (citing *Pravda*, 1 February 1992), giving statistics demonstrating Slovakia's 1991 economic decline.

[33] According to a survey conducted by the Group for Independent Social Analysis (AISA) in November and December 1991, "[a]dditional data reveal an interesting attitude toward the market economy, which is supported by 52 percent of respondents in the Czech Republic and 33 percent in the Slovak Republic, while 39 percent in the Czech Republic and 53 percent in the Slovak Republic favor a mixed economy." "Poll Shows Several Groups Have Key Influence," *FBIS-EEU-92-020*, 30 January 1992, p. 8 (citing *Rude Pravo*, 25 January 1992).

[34] The relationship between the Czechs and the Slovaks is different from, for example, the conflict between the Serbs and Croats at least in one significant aspect. In the relatively recent past, during World War II, the Croatian fascists committed genocide on the Serbs, killing over half a million people. Although many Slovaks claim that the Czechs took advantage of them and benefitted from the Slovaks, nowhere in the history of the coexistence of these two "nations" can one find a chapter similar to the Serb-Croatian scenario.

[35] In 1918, the Slovaks felt unsatisfied with the unitary form of the First Republic. In 1938, they declared independence. Thirty years later, in 1968,

while the Czechs strived for more political freedoms the Slovaks pressed for more "national" sovereignty.

[36]See n. 49, and accompanying text. See also Sunstein, "Constitutionalism," 644.

[37]See n. 31, and accompanying text. This call for secession is self-destructive when one considers the bad economic conditions and forecasts for Slovakia, the relatively small population and territory, and a possibility of international isolation resulting from secession. Also, an important factor is the internal heterogeneity of Slovakia where the national minorities, notably Hungarians, may in turn also claim the right of self-determination, or even secession.

[38]See nn. 54–63, and accompanying text (discussing the 1990–1991 constitutional amendments).

[39]The Federal Assembly passed regulatory laws dealing with privatization, restitution, foreign exchange, banking, joint ventures, foreign investment, and the commercial and concession-based trades codes. The area that urgently needs but currently lacks regulation, especially during the ongoing privatization process, is securities regulation.

[40]See n. 24.

[41]1968 Federation amendment, Article 42. The majoritarian rule (a majority outvoting a minority) is prohibited; that is, deputies in the two parts of the Chambers of Nations have to vote separately, when voting on bills regulating taxes, price policy, customs, technological investment, labor, wages and social policy, press, media, economic administration, establishment of federal organs of state administration, foreign economic relations, any budgetary questions, and issues of citizenship. Interestingly, the prohibition of majoritarian rule does not apply to votes of no-confidence to the Government (the executive).

[42]1968 Federation amendment, Article 42.

[43]The United States Senate, for example, has two senators from each state regardless of its population. United States Constitution, Article I, Section 3.

[44]See nn. 53 and 117 and accompanying text (discussing the various Slovak nationalistic groups).

[44]1968 Federation amendment, Article 41.

[46]Currently, the Federal Assembly consists of sixteen parties. Czechoslovakia's political system traditionally consists of multiple political parties and coalition governments due to an election system based on proportional representation. Pre-1938 Czechoslovakia demonstrated the variety and domination of political parties over Czechoslovak public life. Edward Táborský, *Czechoslovak Democracy at Work* (London: Allen and Unwin, 1945), 94. See also Cutler and Schwartz, "Constitutional Reform," 513–14. As in the First Republic, the recently passed amendment to election law No. 47/1990 Zb. (on file with the *American University Journal of International Law and Policy*) is based on proportional representation. A natural result of the proportional electoral system is a proliferation of smaller parties. This is even truer in post-Communist Czechoslovakia where, as in Poland and Hungary, political life remains unstabilized and parties struggle to define their identity and their role and place in the political spectrum of the country.

[47]Canada, though consisting of ten provinces, resembles Czechoslovakia by the clear polarization and resulting controversies between the English-speaking population and the French-speaking population concentrated almost exclusively in the Québec province. India provides a similar situation, in which the division lies between the Hindu and Muslim populations.

[48]Blaustein and Flanz, *Constitutions: Belgium*. It is true, however, that despite the lack of any explicit constitutional provisions, Belgian parliamentary procedures are de facto based on a consensus and compromise among the various ethnic groups and communities.

[49]Currently, Slovak nationalists benefit from this mixed blessing, despite public opinion polls conducted in the CSFR during the last eighteen months showing that most people in both republics wish to continue living in a common state. "Nationwide Poll Shows Support for Federation Vote," *FBIS-EEU-91-222*, 18 November 1991, p. 13 (citing *Prague CSTK*, 15 November 1991). Indicative of the strong bargaining position of the Slovak opposition deputies in the Chamber of Nations is, among other things, their resistance to increasing the federation members to include Moravia and Silesia. These two parts of the Czech republic historically enjoyed a certain degree of self-governance thanks to a state structure similar to Germany's. Transferring the "dual" federation into one involving three, four, or more members would shift the balance of power to Slovakia's disadvantage. Despite recent proposals by a Moravian self-governance movement to offer Slovakia a special statute of autonomy in exchange for its support of the idea of a tripartite federation, the Slovak political representation remains opposed to this concept. "Moravian Deputy on Tripartite Federation Proposal," *FBIS-EEU-91-220*, 14 November 1991, p. 12 (citing *Národná Obroda*, 12 November 1991, p. 3).

[50]See Petr Brodský, "V Tatrách bez občanských práv" (In Tatras without human rights), *Respekt*, 11–17 November 1991, p. 8, quoting the Hungarian ambassador as saying "In the area of constitutional terminology, post-Communist Czechoslovakia represents a 'semantic black hole.'"

[51]See generally Grexa, "O jednote po jednote" (On unity after unity), *Kultúrny Život* 3 (1992): 1, criticizing the populistic call for unity of the entire Slovak nation. The semantic confusion, however, is not only a specific problem of Czechoslovakia. One commentator cites research that revealed no less than 255 different understandings of the term "federalism." See Gerloch, "Nad Variantami," 499, citing M. Frenkel, *Foederalismus und Bundesstaat, Bd. I: Foederalismus* (Bern and Frankfurt am Main, 1984), 113.

[52]A survey conducted by a Slovak Institute for Public Opinion Research in February 1992 illustrates this problem. In the survey, 48 percent of Slovak population expressed their wish to live in a federation "based upon the constitutions of two republics with equal rights." "Federation Most Favored State Form in Slovakia," *FBIS-EEU-92-044*, 5 March 1992, p. 12 (citing *Prague CSTK*, 27 February 1992). According to the same source, only 8 percent, however, accept the current model of federation, despite the strong safeguards that model provides for the Slovak Republic.

[53]There is only one party in Slovakia, the Slovak National Party, that openly expresses hopes for Slovakia's independence. Other parties—such as the Movement for Democratic Slovakia, a splinter from the movement Public Against Violence, and the Slovak Christian Democratic Movement, a

splinter of the Christian Democratic Movement, and some other smaller parties—hide behind "better sounding" and undefined terms like "confederation."

[54]Úst. zák č. 23/1991 Zb., uvádzajúci Listinu základných práv a slobôd (Czech. Const. Act No. 23/1991 Coll. of Laws, instituting the Charter of Fundamental Rights and Freedoms) [hereinafter Charter].

[55]See Sunstein, "Constitutionalism," 647 n. 82, noting that guaranteed rights mean little where there are no institutions through which individuals can claim their rights. In general, most of the Communist constitutions in Czechoslovakia and other former Communist countries provided for a full range of civil and political rights and liberties on paper. In practice, however, the government violated each of these rights. See Sunstein, "Constitutionalism," 647 n. 82, listing rights guaranteed by the former Soviet Constitution.

[56]Úst. zák. č. 556/1990 Zb., ktorým sa mení a dopl'ňa ústavný zákon č. 143/1968 Zb., o československej federácii (Czech. Const. Act No. 556/1990 Coll. of Laws, altering Czech. Const. Act No. 143/1968 Coll. of Laws, on the Czechoslovak Federation) [hereinafter 1990 constitutional act on power-sharing].

[57]Úst. zák. č. 91/1991 Zb., o ústavnom súde Českej a Slovenskej Federatívnej republiky (Czech. Const. Act No. 91/1991 Coll. of Laws, on the Constitutional Court of the Czech and Slovak Federal Republic).

[58]Úst. zák. č. 326/1991 Zb., ktorým sa mení a dopl'ňa Ústava Českej a Slovenskej Federatívnej Republiky v znení neskorších predpisov (Czech. Const. Act No. 326/1991 Coll. of Laws, altering the Constitution of the Czech and Slovak Federal Republic as amended).

[59]Úst. zák. č. 327/1991 Zb., o celoštátnom referende (Czech. Const. Act No. 327/1991 Coll. of Laws, on Referendum) [hereinafter Referendum Law].

[60]The Parliament's preoccupation with the intricacies of the federalism debate is the most obvious factor contributing to the lack of interest in important issues. There is, however, another related factor. Any problem that fails to connect directly with the main issue, federalism, still becomes a battleground for the Czech-Slovak dispute. In essence, the two rival nations compete on all fronts.

[61]See Úst. Zák. č. 23/1991 Zb., uvádzajúci Listinu základných práv a slobôd (Czech. Const. Act No. 23/1991 Coll. of Laws, instituting the Charter of Fundamental Rights and Freedoms) at Section 2, stating that "[i]nternational treaties on human rights and fundamental freedoms, ratified and promulgated by the Czech and Slovak Federal Republic, are universally binding on its territory and supersede its own laws." The issue of whether international treaties supersede only ordinary legislation or also constitutional acts, which require a super majority for adoption, remains unclear.

[62]The preamble of the 1960 Constitution, as amended in 1968 and 1991, states that "(1) The Czech and Slovak Federal Republic is a federal state of two equal, fraternal nations, the Czechs and the Slovaks," and that "(2) The Czech and Slovak Federative Republic is founded on the voluntary bond of the equal, national states of the Czech and the Slovak nations, based on the right of each of these nations to self-determination." Úst. zák. č. 100/1960 Zb., Czech. Const. of 1960, reprinted in Blaustein and Flanz, *Constitutions: Czechoslovakia*.

[63]Úst. zák. ČSFR č. 144/1968 Zb., o postavení národností v Československej socialistickej republike (Czech. Const. Act No. 144/1968 Coll. of Laws, concerning the status of ethnic groups in the Czechoslovak Socialist Republic).

[64]One danger that the wording of the former constitutional preambles poses is that pursuant to the Central European definition of a "nation," where "nation" means "people," there is not much room for national minorities. See n. 3, which explains the different definitions of the word "nation."

[65]This article uses the term "government" to refer to the prime minister and the council or cabinet of ministers. This use, which does not connote the entire governmental structure, is common in parliamentary systems.

[66] One of the most important changes in the amendment was a different structure of the federal parliament. The new parliament would consist of a Chamber of Representatives and a Senate located in Bratislava, the capital of Slovakia. Draft Úst. zák. ČSFR No. 1212/1992 altering Czech. Const. Act No. 143/1968 Coll. of Laws, as amended (on file with the *American University Journal of International Law and Policy*).

[67]"Federal Assembly Rejects Constitution Amendments," *FBIS-EEU-92-033*, 19 February 1992, p. 3 (citing *Prague CSTK*, 18 February 1992). Following a mandatory conciliation procedure, which is triggered any time a bill passes one chamber and not the other, the amendment failed to pass the Slovak part of the Chamber of Nations again on 3 March 1992. "Federal Assembly Fails to Amend Constitution," *FBIS-EEU-92-044*, 5 March 1992, p. 7 (citing Czechoslovak Radio, 3 March 1992). See also "Assembly Body Rejects Constitutional Amendment," *FBIS-EEU-92-041*, 2 March 1992, p. 15 (citing *Prague CSTK*, 27 February 1992).

[68]"Slovak Government Adopts Stand on 'Power-Sharing,'" *FBIS-EEU-91-226*, 22 November 1991, p. 8 (citing Czechoslovak Radio, 19 November 1991). This declaration became known as the "12:8 Declaration" because eight ministers, including the Slovak prime minister, refused to approve it. The Slovak prime minister stated that presenting the declaration at a government meeting was politically dangerous. Further, he asserted that the declaration is not legally binding for the political parties of the Slovak National Council. "Carnogursky Reacts to Declaration," *FBIS-EEU-91-226*, 22 November 1991, p. 9 (citing *Narodna Obroda*, 20 November 1991, pp. 1, 6).

[69]The declaration stated that, in addition to the existing powers, a common state should exercise legislative powers in the areas of labor, wages, and social policy. The declaration also recommended that a common state should exercise executive power in the areas of economic competition law, postal services, long-distance communication, the rail networks, and a single currency. "Carnogursky Reacts to Declaration," 1, 6.

[70]Ján Čarnogurský, the present Slovak prime minister and the chairman of the Christian Democratic Movement, introduced this concept in the spring of 1991. The negotiations recently terminated after the Presidium of the Slovak National Council failed to adopt an agreed text of the treaty. See nn. 77–87 and accompanying text, discussing the recently terminated negotiations on the state treaty.

[71] See nn. 4–21 and accompanying text, detailing Czech and Slovak attempts to shape the country's constitutional framework.

[72] The Slovak term *štátna zmluva* is hard to translate into English. *Zmluva* can be translated as treaty, contract, or agreement, hence the English "state treaty." The treaty was supposed to form a basis for a reformed federal institutional structure, including a new power-sharing arrangement between the federation and the republics.

[73] As of November 1991, "of the 88 provisions contained in the draft treaty, no accord could be reached [between the National Councils] on 22 of them." "Czech, Slovak Differences on Treaty Viewed," *FBIS-EEU-91-222*, 18 November 1991, p. 9 (citing *Lidove Noviny*, 14 November 1991, pp. 1, 3).

[74] Amy Barrett and James H. Ottaway, Jr., "In Czechoslovakia, the Political Pendulum Swings from Compromise to Confrontation," *Wall Street Journal Europe*, 27 January 1992, p. 7. This article argues that the privatization process may expand the already existing economic gap between the republics, because Slovakia is less developed, poorer, and subsidized by the federal budget.

[75] "Political Pendulum Swings," 7.

[76] "Havel, Carnogursky View Elections, State Treaty," *FBIS-EEU-92-014*, 22 January 1992, p. 11 (citing Bratislava Radio Network, 17 January 1992). In this same radio interview, the Slovak prime minister elaborated on the differing approaches to the state treaty: "We insist on the treaty being between the Slovak Republic and the Czech Republic. Although the republics would be represented by their respective [N]ational [C]ouncils, it would be a treaty between the republics. In this sense it would be a state treaty, because it would be a treaty between two states" (12).

[77] The chairman of the Slovak National Council, in an interview after a negotiating session in Milovy in February 1992, stated: "Indeed, Wednesday night we noted something incredible—that on the question of division of powers we actually are not very far apart." "Reaction to Czech-Slovak Draft Constitution Treaty; Miklosko: 'Acceptable Mechanism' Found," *FBIS-EEU-92-031*, 14 February 1992, p. 12 (citing *Naroda Obroda*, 10 February 1992).

[78] "Czech, Slovak National Councils Agree on Treaty," *FBIS-EEU-92-027*, 10 February 1992, p. 8 (citing Czechoslovak Radio, 8 February 1992); see also "Text of Draft Czech-Slovak Constitution Treaty," *FBIS-EEU-92-031*, 14 February 1992, p. 6 (citing *Hospodarske Noviny*, 11 February 1992), reprinting the entire text of the document.

[79] "Czech Deputies 'Welcome' Next Meeting," *FBIS-EEU-92-032*, 18 February 1992, p. 12 (citing Czechoslovak Radio, 13 February 1992), reprinting the entire text of the Czech National Council resolution of 13 February 1992.

[80] "Czech, Slovak National Councils Agree on Treaty," p. 8.

[81] "Slovak Council Fails to Pass Draft Treaty," *FBIS-EEU-92-030*, 13 February 1992, p. 5 (citing Prague Radio, 12 February 1992). Ten members of the Presidium voted to approve the treaty, and ten voted against it.

[82] "Klepac Spells Out Objections to Draft Treaty," *FBIS-EEU-92-038*, 26 February 1992, p. 10 (citing *Slovensky Dennik*, 15 February 1992).

[83] The chairman of the nationalist-oriented Slovak Christian Democratic Movement said: "The Czech side tenaciously tries to prevent Slovakia from

becoming more visible as a separate entity." "Klepac Spells Out Objections to Draft Treaty," 10.

[84]"Klepac Spells Out Objections to Draft Treaty," 10.

[85]"Czech, Slovak Leaders Suggest Talk Suspension," *FBIS-EEU-92-049*, 12 March 1992, p. 10 (citing *Prague CSTK*, 11 March 1992).

[86]The chairwoman of the Czech National Council called the treaty "a good document that could be a basis for transforming our state into an authentic federation." "Czech, Slovak Leaders Suggest Talk Suspension," 10.

[87]"Carnogursky: State Breakup 'Possible'," *FBIS-EEU-92-031*, 14 February 1992, p. 13 (citing Prague Radio, 13 February 1992).

[88]See "Slovak Republic's Draft of Sovereignty Declaration," *FBIS-EEU-91-049*, 13 March 1991, p. 17 (citing *Smena*, 2 March 1991), reprinting the full text of the declaration. The parties even organized rallies in support of the declaration. See "'Thousands' of Slovaks Demand State Sovereignty," *FBIS-EEU-91-048*, 12 March 1991, p. 10 (citing *Prague CSTK*, 12 March 1991).

[89]"Miklosko on Consequences of Treaty's Rejection," *FBIS-EEU-92-036*, 24 February 1992, p. 13 (citing *Narodna Obroda*, 18 February 1992), interviewing the chairman of the Slovak National Council on the effects of the rejection of the state treaty.

[90]The chairman of the Slovak National Council is of the opinion that "no party will dare to take such a risky step before the elections."

[91]See "Návrh Ústavy Slovenskej Republiky" (Draft of the Slovak Republic's Constitution), *Práca*, 8 January 1992, p. 4.

[92]"Návrh Ústavy Slovenskej Republiky," 4.

[93]See nn. 66–67 and accompanying text (detailing the reasons behind the Federal Assembly's failure to adopt three chapters of the new constitution).

[94]As one commentator put it: "[W]ith its hypocritical internationalism, the Communist regime covered up the existing conflicts, and made taboos of them. Problems were not being solved, they were covered up." Kováč, "Slováci a Česi," 1.

[95]"Havel Appeals for Support to Resolve Crisis," *FBIS-EEU-92-222*, 18 November 1991, p. 7 (citing the Prague Federal 1 Television Network, 17 November 1991), translating and reprinting the text of Havel's "Address to the Nation."

[96]"Havel Appeals for Support to Resolve Crisis," 7–8. See also nn. 102–17 and accompanying text (discussing the proposed bills).

[97]1968 Federation amendment, Article 61. The presidential powers pursuant to the amendment are limited. The president may appoint and recall the prime minister and other ministers, grant amnesty, dissolve the Federal Assembly if it cannot agree on a budget, conduct foreign affairs, serve as commander-in-chief of the army, and call for new elections.

[98]Concerned with the situation in the country, President Havel opened his 17 November speech with the following words: "Everything seems to indicate that, at present, our representative bodies are unable to reach a timely and reasonable agreement about future coexistence in our state. . . . [T]he talks have begun to go in circles and have gradually become the object

of opposition and even mockery by our citizens and the mass media." "Havel Appeals for Support to Resolve Crisis," 7.

[99]"Havel's New Year Speech Views Progress, Goals." *FBIS-EEU-92-001*, 2 January 1992, p. 14 (citing Czechoslovak Radio, 1 January 1992), explaining the reasons for his proposals. In this New Year's speech Havel stated: "[N]ot long ago, I submitted to the Federal Assembly several draft laws that could open the road to further negotiations, create a system of safeguards against a possible crisis, and at least make sure that there would be an election in June."

[100]"Havel Addresses Federal Assembly 3 Dec" [hereinafter "Havel's Proposals"], *FBIS-EEU-91-233*, 4 December 1991, p. 10 (citing Czechoslovak Radio, 3 December 1991), presenting his proposals in a speech to the Federal Assembly.

[101]In justifying the proposal, Havel noted that it corresponded to Czechoslovakia's unusual situation. The requirement of ratification originated with the Slovak representation and was opposed by the Czech and federal politicians. Ratification of the federal Constitution by the National Councils was accepted as a political trade-off in order to reach a consensus with the Slovak representatives on the constitutional framework. "Havel Addresses Federal Assembly 3 Dec," 10.

[102]"Legislators Reject Two Havel Draft Bills," *FBIS-EEU-92-014*, 22 January 1992, p. 11 (citing *Prague CSTK*, 21 January 1992).

[103]"Havel's Proposals," 13.

[104]"Havel's Proposals," 13.

[105]"Havel's Proposals," 13. According to the latest polls, 74 percent of the people in Czechoslovakia (78 percent in the Czech Republic, 66 percent in Slovakia) believe that the question of a future existence of a common state should be decided by a referendum. See "Nationwide Poll Shows Support for Federation Vote," 13. See also "Legislators Reject Two Havel Draft Bills," 11, noting requirements giving the president the right to call a referendum.

[106]Úst. zák. o referende č. 327/1991 Zb. (Constitutional Act No. 327/1991 Coll. of Laws, on Referendum).

[107]Even if a referendum was possible, however, it is not certain it would help the situation. The effectiveness of a referendum would depend on the question presented to the people, because most of the population of Czechoslovakia wants to preserve a common state. The issue that has resisted consensus so far is the form that this common state should have. As Příhoda noted, this issue "really cannot be solved by referendum. Such an attempt would shed light on the matter only if [a referendum] resulted in a decision to break up the common state." If the result of a referendum was a positive one, the protagonists of Slovak sovereignty might be silenced for a while, but the issue of the Czech-Slovak relationship would not be resolved. Příhoda, "Česke dilema," 1–2.

[108]"Legislators Reject Two Havel Draft Bills," 11. An interesting phenomenon occurred in Czechoslovakia. Typically, it is the ethnic minorities and administrative entities that exploit referenda in their efforts to gain independence, declare sovereignty, or achieve autonomy within larger units. Interestingly, in Czechoslovakia, the profederation parties in both the Czech and

Slovak republics pushed for a referendum, whereas the nationalistic parties in Slovakia fiercely opposed such a measure.

[109]"Havel's Proposals," 12.

[110]"Parliament Rejects Havel Presidential Powers Bill," *FBIS-EEU-92-019*, 29 January 1992, p. 7 (citing Czechoslovak Radio Prague, 28 January 1992).

[111]"Havel's Proposals,"13.

[112]The delegated representatives of the republics' National Councils would comprise the thirty members. The proposal would also give the Federal Council a suspensive veto over legislation. "Havel's Proposals,"13. It is doubtful whether such a structure would, if adopted, solve any potential deadlocks, because the proposal would still require the unicameral Federal Assembly to cast separate votes on many issues in the Czech and Slovak sections.

[113]"Havel Withdraws Proposal for Federal Assembly and Council: New Proposal Tabled," *BBC-EE-1287-B-1*, 25 January 1992, p. 1 (citing Czechoslovak Radio, 22 January 1992).

[114]"Havel's Proposals,"14; "Havel Briefs Journalists on Draft Election Law," *FBIS-EEU-91-247*, 24 December 1991, p. 6 (citing Czechoslovak Radio, 23 December 1991).

[115]"Prezident Kontra Parlament, Dva Návrhy Volebního Zákona" (President contra Parliament, two proposals of election law), *Respekt*, 16–22 December 1991, p. 4, discussing optional proposals.

[116]"Parliament Passes Amended Electoral Law," *FBIS-EEU-92-020*, 30 January 1992, p. 7 (citing *Prague CSTK*, 29 January 1992).

[117]See Marián Timoracký, "Otázka otázky" (Question of a question), *Respekt*, 25 November–1 December 1991, p. 4, discussing the referendum and political parties in Czechoslovakia. The most nationalistic parties in the Federal Assembly are the Slovak National Party, the Movement for Democratic Slovakia, the Party of the Democratic Left (formerly the Communist party), and the Slovak Christian Democratic Movement (a recent splinter of the Christian Democratic Movement). These parties vote together as the "Slovak bloc."

[118]The chairman of the Slovak National Council summarized the situation as follows: "We have agreed with the representatives of the Czech political scene and with the head of state that the situation should remain unchanged until the elections and that no risky experiments should be undertaken." "Miklosko on Consequences of Treaty's Rejection," 13.

[119]The Federal Assembly failed to adopt the three chapters of the constitution which would have changed the current setup. See nn. 66–67 and accompanying text. See also "Havel 'Afraid' of Presidential Election Problems," *FBIS-EEU-92-000*, 13 March 1992, p. 6 (citing *Mlada Fronta Dnes*, 10 March 1992).

[120]The 1968 Federation amendment, Article 62, states: "The election of the president . . . shall be held within the last fourteen days of the presidential term of office." It may be inferred that the incumbent president ceases to hold the office within fourteen days, regardless of whether a new president is elected.

[121]See "Havel 'Afraid' of Presidential Election Problems," 6. The article cites the first deputy of the Federal Assembly who, contrary to Havel, be-

lieves that "according to the currently valid constitution, the nonelection of a head of state would not have to provoke a constitutional crisis." Such an optimistic assessment of the law from one of its drafters is surprising under the circumstances. Despite his optimism, the first deputy proposed using a new method for electing the president. The method would consist of potentially three election runs. This first deputy's backup proposal is, of course, wholly unrealistic, for a simple reason; for its approval, the proposal would need to secure a three-fifths majority of the elected deputies in all three parts of the Federal Assembly.

[122]"Amendment to Presidential Election Law Passed," *FBIS-EEU-92-075*, 15 April 1992 (citing *Prague CSTK*, 15 April 1992). If the second round fails, the incumbent president remains in office, but only up to a maximum of three months. Consequently, Parliament may not be able to agree on a president.

[123]This possibility constitutes a worst-case scenario. Even if the country splits, however, it is doubtful a civil war like the one in Yugoslavia would ensue. The internal as well as international consequences of such a split are hard to imagine. An issue not yet sufficiently addressed is the question of succession, which merits a discussion separate from this chapter.

[124]If such a development was to follow, it could be terminated by the Czechs, who might decide that it was not worthwhile to remain in the union.

[125]One commentator suggested that the European Community, the Council of Europe, and the Conference on Security and Cooperation in Europe may, in fact, "exercise a salutary constraining influence" on the number of choices that the Eastern European countries have to face in their constitution-making processes. Elster, "Constitutionalism in Eastern Europe," 481.

Chapter 4

Constitutional Politics in Poland: A Report on the Constitutional Committee of the Polish Parliament

Andrzej Rapaczynski

This chapter is neither a comprehensive historical account of the work of the Constitutional Committee of the Polish Parliament nor a theoretical synthesis of recent constitutional developments in Poland. It is a mixture of theory, anecdote, and personal reminiscence. The work on the new Polish constitution has in some ways been overtaken by events that unfortunately have always lurked in the background of the drafters' work and influenced their decisions.

My personal perspective also accounts for my focus on constitutional questions of institutional structure. I have served as an adviser to the Subcommittee on Institutions of the Polish Parliament's Constitutional Committee, and both interest and experience lead me to provide information on the emerging institutional structure of the Polish state. Therefore, this chapter does not discuss the protection of individual rights in the next Polish constitution, except insofar as it relates to institutional considerations.

Background

THE COMMUNIST CONSTITUTION OF 1952

Poland still functions under the Constitution enacted in 1952,[1] even though the political and economic system codified in that

document, and even the symbolic name of the state it had introduced (People's Republic of Poland), have been changed. The
1952 Constitution was a product of the first postwar Polish Parliament, dominated by the Polish United Workers' Party (PUWP).
Although it was amended several times, it has been clear since
the moment of Solidarity's victory over the old system in 1989
that Poland must replace the 1952 Constitution—a primary symbol of the Communist regime—with a document reflecting the
country's democratic aspirations.

Like the People's Republic itself, the 1952 Constitution bears
the unmistakable stamp of the Soviet printing press and faithfully
reflects the vicissitudes of the history of the Socialist bloc. It
began with a copy of the so-called Stalinist Constitution, the 1936
Soviet model that formally established a fictitiously democratic
republic. A naive reader (and there were surprisingly many of
them around the world at the time)[2] would find little fault with
this document: it did not mandate a one-party system, for example, but in fact specifically provided for freedom of association
and most of the other political and individual rights typically
respected in Western democracies. But given the reality of political terror in the country,[3] the enactment in 1952 of a Polish-
language equivalent of the Soviet Constitution was simply a mark
of the Soviet conquest and the completion of the *Gleichschaltung*
(amalgamation) process after the war.

Surprisingly perhaps, but not really paradoxically, the constitutions of Eastern Europe became somewhat less liberal as the
Stalinist terror relaxed. The "leading role" of the Communist
parties was written into these documents,[4] as was the special role
of the Soviet Union in the countries' affairs.[5] The litany of un-
enforceable social and economic rights expanded with time,[6]
whereas American-style political rights were scaled down. The
introduction of many of these changes in the 1970s and 1980s
caused a number of protests in Poland. The constitutionalization
of Poland's ties to Moscow and to the Warsaw Pact was especially
troubling, because it seemed to undermine the very sovereignty
of the country.

In a somewhat perverse way, however, the reforms reflected a
movement toward the rule of law. The first postwar constitution
was a fiction in nearly every respect, and the authorities treated
it essentially as propaganda for foreign consumption. As time
went by, however, at least two reasons made the ruling elite move
toward a more realistic formulation of the basic law as well as of

other, more specific legal enactments. First, the Stalinist terror left an indelible imprint on the Communist leadership itself: the party apparatus had, after all, been among the most prominent victims of the great purges. Although the Communists clearly intended to continue relying on repression as a prime tool to maintain their power, they apparently concluded that legalizing the repression would protect members of the ruling elites against the most arbitrary and tyrannical abuses of power by the top leadership of the moment. Second, at least in Poland and Hungary, the leadership also tried to present a certain facade of legitimacy to the population at large. The regime made clear that it would tolerate no fundamental assaults on its core powers, but it permitted a certain amount of freedom at the margin. Therefore, the regimes returned in part to legality: at the very least a paper record was left of official action, and the increased publicity deterred most instances of the purely personal exercise of power by the lower echelons of the party and the state bureaucracy.

The implementation of such a system, however, required that legal norms become somewhat more realistic; they had to give the leadership the right to suppress opposition to the fundamental principles on which Communist authority was based, and with time these changes had to reach the constitutional level. The amendments concerning the "leading role" of the Communist party, for example, removed most legal ground from the potential claims of the opposition. Similarly, the codification of the dominant position of the Soviet Union and the unassailable status of the Warsaw Pact expressed a formal limitation on East European countries' sovereignty, and thus marked a relatively clear boundary (set by the Brezhnev Doctrine) for all possible internal reforms. At the same time, however, these changes signified that constitutions were beginning to mean something. In Poland the government even took some steps to introduce a watered-down version of judicial review.[7]

DOWNFALL OF THE COMMUNIST REGIME

The transition from communism to democracy in Poland took place before the fall of the other regimes in Eastern Europe, and it came about as a result of the so-called roundtable talks between the Communist leadership and the Solidarity-led opposition.[8] No one originally expected the roundtable agreement to lead to a complete transformation of the old regime. Following the introduction of martial law in December 1981 and the banning of the Solidarity union, the Polish authorities, led by General Wojciech Jaruzelski, largely blunted the ideological Communist edge of their power. The government made significant personnel changes at the top, increasing the influence of the military establishment at the party's expense. The regime also repeatedly attempted to improve Poland's economic situation and tried to legitimize the ruling elite by presenting it as the true defender of Polish national aspirations and as a buffer between Poland and the forces of Soviet imperialism.

Despite these efforts, the rump Communist regime went from one defeat to another. The economy continued to deteriorate, and the regime's attempts to gain a measure of social acceptance basically failed. Although its political power was firmly anchored in the military, the ruling elite faced a deepening social and economic crisis. Moreover, the changes in the Soviet Union under President Mikhail Gorbachev made clear that the authorities now had more room to maneuver and could no longer hide behind the threat of Soviet intervention. In the end, after some hesitation, the authorities decided to move in the direction of genuine power-sharing. At first, they tried to form a coalition with the Roman Catholic Church and other non-Solidarity opposition. But when it became clear that Solidarity was too powerful to be left out and that the underground leaders of the union were prepared to make reasonable compromises, the circle around General Jaruzelski resolved to include Solidarity as well.

In the winter of 1989, leaders of Solidarity and the Communist regime gathered at the roundtable to negotiate their respective roles under the new arrangement. Many Solidarity leaders believed that their only interest lay in the legal reestablishment of the union. In their view, the political compromise essentially benefitted the Communists and was a price to be paid for the legalization of the union. Others, however, took the Communists' political proposals seriously and worked hard for a bargain that would enable the union to participate meaningfully in the country's political institutions.

What had been anticipated as the stickiest part of the roundtable negotiations—the future status of the Solidarity labor union—was settled quickly and without difficulty. The real wrangling was about the future political structure of the country, and it continued for several weeks. The final political bargain assigned to the Communists and their allies (the Peasant Party and another traditional fig leaf for the Communists) 65 percent of the seats in the Sejm, the lower house of the Polish Parliament, with the remaining 35 percent to be filled through genuinely free elections. The compromise further provided for a restoration of the upper house, the Senate, which the Communists had abolished after the war.[9] With all one hundred members freely elected, the Senate was to have considerable legislative powers, the most important of which would be a veto on the initiatives of the Sejm, which the latter could override only with a two-thirds majority. A strong presidency would replace the ineffectual old Council of State. Although the president would not be the head of government, he or she would have a veto power similar to that of the United States president, and a large measure of control over the army.[10] The roundtable participants clearly designed that position for General Jaruzelski, who was to become a senior statesman and a guarantor of the compromise vis-à-vis the Soviet Union. Parliament quickly amended the 1952 Constitution to make the arrangement fully legal.

Both sides believed that the compromise guaranteed the Communists effective control over the political system, but also gave the opposition a possible veto over Communist initiatives. No one had imagined that the election, held on 4 June 1989, would bring such a crushing defeat to the Communists that its aftermath would transform the whole roundtable agreement beyond recognition. Solidarity's candidates won, often by huge majorities, all the seats in the Sejm for which they were eligible to compete, as well as 99 percent of the seats in the Senate. On the uncontested countrywide at-large election for the Sejm seats reserved for those loyal to the old regime, all but two of the Communist-approved candidates failed to receive the required majority of the votes,[11] with some of the most important Communist leaders failing to gain seats. The Communists thus could not fill even some of those uncontested seats that the compromise had assigned to them, and they needed the humiliating help of their Solidarity opponents to get their top candidates into the Sejm. The impasse was resolved only by modifying the election rules for the second round of voting; in that round, Solidarity leaders urged their followers to vote for the reform-minded Communists on the countrywide at-large list.

Following the election, the Communist-led coalition immediately began to crumble. To prevent their own extinction, the ex-allies of the Communists from the Peasant Party and Democratic

Alliance began to hint at their availability for a coalition excluding the Communists. The Communists themselves appealed for a broad-based government. And some influential members of Solidarity began to demand the leadership of the government as a price for their support of Jaruzelski's presidency.

Parliament eventually elected General Jaruzelski president by a humiliating majority of one vote; that the Solidarity leadership engineered the election in order to preserve the roundtable bargain only increased the embarrassment. Shortly afterward, Jaruzelski designated another Communist general, Czesław Kiszczak, as prime minister, but the latter failed to form a government. A Solidarity-led coalition was becoming inevitable. Finally, in August 1989, Jaruzelski asked Tadeusz Mazowiecki, a Catholic journalist and long-time adviser to Lech Wałęsa, to form a government.[12] Though Mazowiecki did invite a few Communists to join the new cabinet and gave them control over the army and the police, the Communist rule in Poland was in fact at an end.

Beginnings of the Current Constitutional Reform

The new Solidarity-led government soon proposed a series of constitutional amendments to provide the necessary legal basis for the functioning of democratic institutions. Adopted in December 1989, these amendments eliminated the constitutionally privileged role of the Polish United Workers' Party, introduced the principle of the equality of diverse forms of ownership (thus providing a constitutional foundation for private property and the emerging market economy), and established a number of housecleaning measures, enabling the new authorities to initiate the political reconstruction.

From the beginning, however, the amendments to the 1952 Constitution were intended to be temporary, and no effort was made to transform the old document into a permanent basic law of the newly free Poland. In particular, no attempt was made to change the hackneyed Communist phrases of the Bill of Rights in the old Constitution[13] to express the true aspirations of the new democratic order, even though some of the old provisions concerning the social and economic regime clearly contradicted the new emphasis on a market economy.[14] Everyone understood at the time, however, that the 1952 Constitution would soon be replaced by a new document establishing the legal foundation of democratic governance.

In accordance with these expectations, in early 1990 the Sejm appointed a special Constitutional Committee, charged with the task of preparing the new constitution. Chaired by one of the most important Solidarity leaders, Professor Bronisław Geremek, the committee was in turn divided into three subcommittees: the Subcommittee on Institutions, charged with designing a new governmental structure; the Subcommittee on Human Rights, charged with the preparation of a new bill of rights; and the Subcommittee on Social and Economic Provisions, charged with preparing the articles dealing with property, labor relations, and the new economic order. The committee also appointed a number of advisers (myself among them) for each subcommittee.

In the early stages of the Constitutional Committee's work, the committee met in plenary sessions to discuss matters such as the general tenets of the new constitutional order, the relation between Polish domestic law and the norms of international law, and the basic types of individual rights to be included in the constitution. Subcommittees met to discuss the more technical issues within their jurisdiction and further delegated the bulk of the drafting to individual experts or groups of experts.

As of this writing, the full Constitutional Committee has discussed, section by section, the proposals drafted in the subcommittees. The original plans called for the committee to make further revisions to the draft and then present the constitution to a joint session of both houses of Parliament (which passed a special law to this effect),[15] followed by a referendum.

Although these plans have never been officially revoked, the political situation in Poland has changed dramatically, and the fate of the draft is uncertain. From its inception, the Sejm's Constitutional Committee was a subject of considerable controversy. The roundtable Sejm was not a product of fully free elections. As a result, the Senate, with a sense of its greater representativeness, formed its own Constitutional Committee and began working on a separate draft, even though the 1952 Constitution placed the matter of constitutional changes in the Sejm.[16] The Senate committee has not played a large role, because no party leaders (including Solidarity's) approved of its formation; its drafts have not received serious attention. Consequently, the Sejm committee has managed to retain its predominant position. Yet repeated attempts to form a joint committee of both houses have also failed, and the lack of a clear commitment on the part of the Senate to the work of the Sejm's committee has cast a shadow on the Sejm's work.

The composition of the subcommittees also gave some grounds for concern. Solidarity deputies, who provided the impetus behind the project of a new constitution, dominated the Constitutional Committee as a whole. Strangely enough, most of these deputies had little interest in the overall institutional design that would emerge from the drafting. Many of them were veterans in the struggle for human rights, and they flocked to the subcommittee charged with preparing the new bill of rights. Others had strong ideological commitments to the free market and the dismantling of the command economy, and they chose to join the Social and Economic Provisions Subcommittee, although its work was of necessity limited to a few articles in the new constitution.

Unelected deputies tied to the old regime therefore came to dominate the Subcommittee on Institutions, charged with drafting the core of the new document: the sections dealing with the Parliament, the government,[17] the presidency, and the judiciary. Moreover, most experts attached to the Subcommittee on Institutions also had strong ties to the old regime, partly because the subcommittee members did and partly because most Polish experts in the area came from the once tightly controlled university law faculties. Even with the addition of two expatriate advisers clearly associated with the new regime, the Solidarity parliamentary leadership had good reason to be concerned about this crucial subcommittee.[18]

Other factors combined to weaken the Sejm committee even further. With its Communist deputies and their erstwhile allies occupying 65 percent of the seats, the Sejm had more legitimacy than one might expect, in part because the Communists quickly became demoralized. In addition to the crushing defeat in the parliamentary election, events in the region (above all, the disappearance of a realistic Soviet threat) made the Communists' role as the facilitator of the transition no longer credible. The Communists proceeded to dissolve their party, and individual Communist deputies scrambled to join the ranks of the democratic movement. The parties previously allied with the Communists (the Peasant Party, in particular) have similarly transformed themselves in order to fit into the new democratic order.

In some sense, then, the Sejm became much more representative than one would have expected.

Paradoxically, one could even venture the claim that the Sejm was more representative than if the elections had been entirely free. Compare the composition of the Sejm with that of the Senate, where the duel between Solidarity and the Communists allowed the union to sweep 99 percent of the seats. The Senate thus became a one-party institution, which included no genuine representation of the peasants or any of the social democratic or other leftist formations that exist in other European countries. The unelected members of the Sejm not only introduced some variety into its composition, but they also tried to behave in a responsible fashion: the dubious legitimacy of their position made them exercise great care in opposing the Solidarity-dominated government and its parliamentary leadership, at least so long as the latter was itself united and basking in the glow of popular approval.

As time went by, however, the legitimacy of the Sejm was gradually tarnished, not least of all because the Solidarity movement began to split between a group based in Gdańsk, centered around Wałęsa, and a group based in Warsaw, composed primarily of intellectuals who came to dominate the government. Clearly resenting the attempt of his erstwhile advisers to keep him at arm's length from the center of power, Wałęsa himself began a bruising campaign against what he presented as an alliance between the compromised ex-Communists and the "leftist" intellectuals in the government. Among other things, he attacked the idea that the roundtable Parliament could legitimately enact a new democratic constitution.

The Solidarity parliamentary leadership knew that the roundtable Sejm was not an ideal body to adopt the new constitution. At the same time, they felt that the Sejm—perhaps in part because many of its members knew that they held their seats by historical accident and should "redeem" themselves by good behavior—might actually be more cooperative than the next, democratically elected body, given the absence of a developed party system and the likely combination of inexperience and anarchic enthusiasm among the new deputies. (The unruly Senate was, again, quite instructive in this respect.) As a result, the Solidarity leadership in Parliament, firmly in the hands of the Warsaw group, decided quite early on a strategy for drafting and adoption of a new constitution. This strategy called for the roundtable legislature to prepare and vote on the new constitution. Then, in order to heighten the document's legitimacy, Parliament would submit it to a national referendum.[19] Furthermore, the leadership contemplated that the next parliament, then expected to be elected in the spring of 1991, could officially promulgate the new constitution, preferably on the symbolically important date of 3 May,[20] without, however, being given an opportunity to change a document already approved by the people themselves.

The parliamentary leadership also saw the new constitution in a more directly political perspective. The forces behind Wałęsa demanded that Jaruzelski resign or be removed from the presidency, to be replaced by someone more representative of the new order. The Gdańsk group felt that the new president must be Wałęsa, and the people around Wałęsa were probably prepared for his election by the roundtable Parliament. But the Warsaw group believed that it could field a candidate who would beat Wałęsa in a popular election,[21] and therefore pushed through Parliament a law providing for direct election of the president.[22] Having accomplished this, the Warsaw leaders quickly saw that the Gdańsk electrician would be much harder to beat than they had expected, and soon had to reckon with the likelihood of a powerful Wałęsa presidency. Wałęsa made no secret of his intention to be an active president. The Solidarity leadership in Warsaw, therefore, began to look to the new constitution as potentially a highly effective instrument for preventing Wałęsa's future dominance over Parliament and the government.[23] In response, the forces around Wałęsa became even more strongly opposed to the work of the Sejm committee and considered it ever more a symbol of an unholy alliance of old and new elites. The legitimacy of the Sejm committee's work, which could remain broadly acceptable only if viewed as expressing the ideas of a unified Solidarity leadership, lost support from a large segment of the public.

Other aspects of the Constitutional Committee also became politicized to a degree hardly compatible with proper consideration of the long-term interests of the country. The question of whether to include the basic principles of the electoral system in the text of the constitution, as well as which electoral system to adopt, came to be seen as largely a matter of party interest, rather than long-term considerations. A number of unelected deputies tied to the old regime viewed an extreme system of proportional representation as their best hope for preserving a niche for themselves in the new political order. Similarly, the questions of abortion and the separation between church and state became matters of intense controversy, in which immediate political gains or losses seemed to play as prominent a role as any deeper constitutional convictions.[24]

The December 1990 presidential election cast the greatest doubt on the work of the Constitutional Committee. Wałęsa won handily, whereas the Warsaw group's candidate, Prime Minister Mazowiecki, failed to qualify for the second round,[25] suffering an embarrassing defeat at the hands of a shady expatriate virtually unknown only a few weeks earlier. Both the new president and the people around him made it abundantly clear that they intended the focus of power to shift from the prime minister's office to the presidential palace. Sensing the diminution of the office, several people refused Wałęsa's offer of the post of prime minister, and the person who ultimately accepted it (Jan Krzysztof Bielecki) was a relatively obscure man without any political base of his own. At the same time, a kind of shadow government began to form around the new president. These developments undoubtedly have reduced the chances that the draft prepared by the Constitutional Committee will eventually become the new constitution. Wałęsa's associates had long argued that the roundtable Sejm did not have sufficient legitimacy to adopt a new constitution, and the draft (prepared under the leadership tied to Wałęsa's opponents) limited the power of the president to an extent presumably unacceptable to the new establishment.

Still, neither Wałęsa nor Parliament has officially repudiated the work of the Constitutional Committee. Indeed, in the first few weeks after Wałęsa took office, the Constitutional Committee continued its work, until a reasonably complete draft had been prepared, and then shifted its attention to the matter of the new election ordinance. Moreover, the draft constitution has not, at the time of this writing, become subject to the intense criticism one might have expected. Equally surprising, President Wałęsa, faced with a need to assure that his first months in office were not punctuated by a series of important elections and concomitant shifts in government policy and personnel, began to hint that the term of the roundtable Parliament might be extended (perhaps by as much as a year) beyond the spring of 1991.

Thus, once again, the roles have reversed. The Wałęsa camp, which had come to power with the help of its demand for a political "acceleration" that would eliminate the remnants of the

Communist regime from positions of authority, seemed to be planning an extension of the roundtable Parliament's term of office beyond anything that the allegedly lagging Warsaw group had in mind. After a few weeks, the Wałęsa camp changed course again and proposed 26 May as the date of the new elections, but in the absence of a consensus on the new election law, this date was unrealistic.[26]

This jockeying for position has left the Constitutional Committee in limbo. Its leadership remains largely in the hands of the Warsaw group, and there is a certain momentum in its commitment to the draft the experts and the subcommittees have prepared. But it has also become clear to most people that the new constitution will have to wait until the next parliament. As of this writing, it is impossible to predict what will happen. It is difficult to imagine, however, that the present draft will indeed become the new basic law without major changes, although it is also not clear how public opinion will react to changes introduced in response to narrow political considerations.[27] For this reason it may be unwise, except for a few special cases, to discuss in detail the particular provisions of the draft now under consideration. The process of preparing a new constitution and the general substantive concerns raised in the work of the Constitutional Committee may nonetheless have significance beyond this draft and beyond the Polish situation.

The Nature of a New Constitution

One of the most basic questions concerning a new Polish constitution was whether it would be primarily a legal norm rather than a political or symbolic document. This question, never explicitly discussed by the Constitutional Committee, colored a number of discussions concerning the individual rights provisions and the institutional model of the new political system. I examine three basic areas: judicial review, positive and negative rights, and amendment procedures. These three topics impart a flavor of how the drafters viewed the nature of a new Polish constitution.

JUDICIAL REVIEW

Most European countries, including Poland, have historically viewed their constitutions as primarily symbolic, uniting the people behind certain principles by which the state was morally and politically obliged to be guided, but which did not function as legal norms in the American sense.[28] In particular, though the courts would consider constitutional provisions when interpreting various aspects of the law, traditionally they were not supposed to enforce the Constitution by striking down conflicting normative pronouncements of the political organs of the state. Constitutions set the institutional framework of the state and defined the identity and the aspirations of the people in their sovereign capacity. European constitutions thus typically still contain many hortatory statements and confer rights that courts do not directly enforce.

Since World War II, many European countries have modified this tradition by adopting some form of judicial review, and this trend has led to an increased understanding of the constitution as the basic law of the land. In fact, the shift toward some form of judicial control over the political process had reached Eastern Europe even before the upheavals of 1989, and the Communist authorities in Poland experimented with limited judicial review.[29]

The new democratic leaders of Poland had additional reasons to look to the United States and those West European countries that had adopted the model of judicial enforcement of constitutional norms. In their struggles with the Communist regime, the opposition repeatedly pointed out the contrast between the constitutionally guaranteed freedoms of citizens and the niggardly embodiment of those freedoms in ordinary statutes and routine law enforcement, as well as the absence of a truly independent judiciary to curtail abuses of power by the government. As a result, everyone involved in the process of drafting the new constitution assumed that the new document would feature rather prominently some form of judicial review, including the possibility of a judicial invalidation of legislative enactments.

Poles both inside and outside the Constitutional Committee considered several models of judicial review.[30] One possibility was the American model, in which every judge (state and federal) has the power to declare all official actions, including legal enactments of the national legislature, void because of their unconstitutionality. This model is often viewed as peculiar to the common law tradition, and many people involved in the work of the Sejm committee considered it ill-suited to Polish conditions. Some believed that ordinary Polish judges did not have enough training to exercise such great power, nor could they receive adequate training within a reasonable amount of time. Others believed that the American system was unsuited to the civil law tradition, because the civil law judge, essentially a professional civil servant, lacks the prestige and experience of the common law judge, or because the civil law is too specialized (which, however, is not really true in Poland). I do not fully share some of these criticisms, but the committee never seriously considered following the American model in detail. Some members of the committee were inclined, however, to follow the American system of combining the power of judicial review with the other competencies of the existing Supreme Court, rather than creating a separate tribunal to deal exclusively with constitutional matters.

Another model was the German one. In Germany, a special Constitutional Court, endowed with the unique power to invalidate ordinary legislation incompatible with the provisions of the Constitution, has exclusive jurisdiction over constitutional cases.[31] Although most Polish specialists favored this model—for which some domestic precedents already exist—there was considerable anxiety that the German procedure of "individual complaint," by which any private person may test the constitutionality of legislation, would lead to a flood of frivolous litigation that could ultimately undermine the whole institution of judicial review. Those who voiced such fears preferred to limit constitutional review to cases in which certain specified actors (such as legislators or the president) bring their complaints before a constitutional tribunal, or in which lower court judges refer to the same tribunal those constitutional questions essential to the resolution of cases before them.

The Subcommittee on Institutions ultimately chose the German model and wrote a draft that allowed various official actors, as well as private individuals, to bring their complaints before a special constitutional tribunal.[32] The constitutional tribunal would be empowered to issue so-called abstract opinions (opinions issued, for instance, at the request of the president, which are nevertheless binding) but would not issue advisory opinions, nor could it be asked to confirm a law's constitutionality. At the same time, the draft proposes to follow the French system by separating judicial review of legislation from the review of the legality of executive and administrative action, vesting the latter power in a special administrative tribunal.

Negative and Positive Rights

Despite these differences concerning the form of judicial review, one might expect that the fact that some version of judicial review was taken for granted would settle the question of the symbolic or aspirational versus legal nature of the constitutional text. This was not the case, however, for the drafters faced strong political pressures to include in the constitutional text a number of provisions that are not readily judicially enforceable.

If a constitution is to be essentially a legal document, it must primarily include provisions that courts can enforce without upsetting the proper balance of power among the branches of government in a democracy. It is usual, of course, for a constitution as a legal document to include all kinds of political rights as well as a number of other so-called negative rights, which prevent the state from interfering with an individual's exercise of free speech or religion, or which limit the state's power in criminal proceedings. Often it is also believed, however, that a constitution must be sparing in its guarantee of so-called social and economic rights, such as the right to work or to decent housing, or the right to a clean environment. It might be difficult for a court to ensure that the government observes rights of this kind without taking on the role of a super-legislature, reallocating resources and reshuffling governmental priorities to a degree that healthy democratic systems ordinarily reserve for the legislature and executive. The provision of such entitlements usually requires the state to make substantial budgetary outlays, as well as a host of other decisions concerning the relative importance of various social concerns, such as full employment versus inflation, or spending on housing versus spending on education or defense.

Courts generally do not have the competence to make such decisions: neither their training nor the form of litigation provides them with the information and expertise required to structure governmental affairs at this level. Nor do courts have the legitimacy—that is, the democratic pedigree—to make their decisions palatable to the public, who must live with the consequences. Social rights are important; indeed, their achievement may be one of the most basic functions of a constitutional democracy. But the hard choices necessary to turn rights into realities are often thought to be better left to the political system rather than to a legally binding provision of the constitutional text.

Considerations of this kind became very important in the Polish context. First, Poland has a long tradition (antedating the Communist regime) of governmental paternalism, including large-scale government intervention in the economy. Furthermore, although Poland's new leaders rejected much of the Communist rhetoric along with the Communist regime, the Polish population's commitment to the free market may prove rather shallow. The Poles have had no experience with unemployment during the last forty years, and economic inequality, although present, was always both hidden and officially disparaged under the Communists. Finally, the present government's origins are in union activity; its enthusiasm for an unadulterated form of capitalism is tempered by a concern that the government's most powerful political constituency might not tolerate the resulting dislocations.

The drafters thus felt a significant pressure to retain some form of constitutional commitment to full employment, or at least to express an obligation of the state to extend special protection to labor. On the other hand, as the opponents of the right to work have pointed out, economic restructuring will inevitably produce relatively severe unemployment. A right to work, even if in principle enforceable as a matter of constitutional norms, could not be judicially (or otherwise) enforced in Poland until this restructuring is largely completed. Consequently, opponents have argued, including this right into the basic law would make the constitution a symbolic and aspirational document rather than a genuine legal norm.

The right-to-work question exemplifies a more general problem. Communist Poland had an extensive system of laws and constitutional provisions protecting the rudimentary welfare of the workers: free (if miserable) health care,[33] paid vacations,[34] maternity leaves,[35] and state retirement pensions, to cite a few examples. The drafters initially had to decide how much of this system should be constitutionalized in the future. To the extent that they chose to protect these social and economic rights through the constitution, the drafters then had to decide whether to guarantee a large number of specific rights or to use sweeping and majestic phrases that would later acquire meaning through judicial interpretation.

The Subcommittee on Social and Economic Provisions has found this problem particularly difficult and as of this writing has not produced its final proposals. The draft that is likely to emerge, however, will probably eschew the most explosive commitments, while stating a number of vague (and presumably not readily enforceable) aspirations. It is proposed, for example, not to guarantee a right to work, but to oblige the state "to protect labor." There are also proposals to constitutionalize a number of specific rights, such as minimum hours, that courts could enforce without crippling the economy.

The Amendment Procedure

A final issue that illustrates the nature of the constitution is the amendment procedure. Strangely enough, the drafters have neither prepared nor extensively discussed the text of any possible procedures for amending the document they are writing. Some voices have urged that the new draft follow the tradition of making constitutional amendments relatively easy; under the old Constitution, a two-thirds majority of the Sejm can amend the document.[36] Others have argued, however, that the new constitution should have more permanence. According to this view the drafters should strive to initiate a new tradition, influenced by the American model, in which the basic law would function as a focal point of the national and political identity of the Polish people.

Proponents of a relatively easy amendment procedure have pointed to the danger of entrenching a document that may hamper future development and ultimately weaken the new political order by removing much of its flexibility. Proponents of a more difficult procedure note the need for strong protection of individual rights and a lasting nonpartisan commitment to the basic institutional structure. They accordingly have proposed that the requirement of a two-thirds majority be strengthened by the added requirement of a national referendum whenever a sufficient number of parliamentary deputies so desire. Although the discussion has not been extensive, the intermittent intrusion of narrow political concerns into the drafting process has significantly weakened the position of those who argued for a deeper entrenchment of the norms being prepared under such circumstances; the ultimate document is likely to reflect shifting political considerations.

The Electoral System

A crucial aspect of the political order in the future Poland—indeed, the one that may more than any other determine the fate of democracy in Eastern Europe's largest country—is often not addressed in written constitutions: the nature of the electoral system used to fill the seats in the national legislature. Although the new Polish constitution will also probably leave this matter to ordinary legislation, the electoral system was part and parcel of the recent constitutional debates in Poland. The fact that Parliament conferred the task of drafting the electoral law on the Constitutional Committee underscores the significance of this issue.

The electoral problem may be approached in two related ways. The first is to view it in pragmatic or empirical terms: depending on the electoral system one chooses, one can readily predict that certain groups will acquire greater or lesser ability to shape the legislative process. To the extent that the executive depends on the outcome of legislative elections, these groups will also have greater or lesser ability to determine the outcomes of the political process as a whole. The second approach is to consider the issue in more lofty terms: by determining the way in which the nation chooses its representatives, the electoral system defines the very concept of democracy, the way in which the political institutions are related to the source of their own legitimacy.

East Europeans are much more likely to consider the issue in the latter terms. To be sure, their more narrow partisan interests sometimes track their ideological pronouncements, and a Western observer may take their rhetoric with a grain of salt. Thus, for example, the Communist epigones stand little chance of winning an outright majority in any electoral district and are also among the most ardent proponents of proportional representation, which may assure them of some seats despite their inability to get more than a few percent of the national vote. Nevertheless, the East Europeans' commitment to the discourse of principles goes beyond a calculation of party interest; in fact, it often contradicts such an interest, expressing a certain disdain for (and often ignorance of) an "engineering" approach, which examines practical consequences before delving into a discussion of abstract ideas. This tendency to maintain a relatively high level of abstraction sometimes results in a certain formalism: generalities such as the "sovereignty of the people" or "separation of powers" or a number of Latin rules and taxonomies often take precedence over hardheaded pragmatic considerations.

An example from the work of the Constitutional Committee illustrates this point. As explained earlier, the roundtable negotiations preceding the Communist departure from power resulted in a compromise to assure the opposition some meaningful form of participation while still preserving the core of Communist control. The main element in this compromise was the restoration of the Senate, in which the opposition could freely compete for seats with the Communists. But the opposition centered around Solidarity dealt such a decisive blow to the Communists and their allies in the first elections that Solidarity was able to form a broad-based government under its own leadership.

The restored Senate thus lacked most of its raison d'être from its inception. Its symbolic legitimacy did provide a certain balance to the still largely unelected Sejm, but at a significant price: it raised the specter of legislative paralysis. The roundtable negotiators had designed the Senate to function as a Solidarity veto instrument. The Senate not only could initiate its own legislation but also could propose amendments to the laws put forth by the Sejm. Unless the Sejm agreed to these amendments or rejected them by a two-thirds majority, the law could not go into effect. This arrangement turned out to be cumbersome. The legislators lost considerable time trying to synchronize the work of the two houses, and this effort, together with the lack of party discipline among the senators, significantly slowed the legislative process just when the government was trying to overhaul the foundations of the Polish state.

All the drafters of the new constitution therefore understood that the institution of the Senate could not remain unmodified. Yet they also knew they could not abolish it: the Senate would have to vote on the new constitution, and as a symbol of Solidarity's victory the Senate enjoyed considerable popularity among the Poles. The trick was to find some way to keep it and not to make it entirely insignificant, but also to prevent a legislative stalemate in the future.

The Subcommittee on Institutions proposed to solve this dilemma by providing for indirect election of senators and making the Senate into an organ representing the units of the newly created local government. In this way, the Senate's prestige would strengthen the democratic principle of local autonomy, while the diminished personal stature of the senators would make it easier for the party leaders to control them.

During discussion of this proposal at a plenary session of the Constitutional Committee, one of the advisers, Zbigniew Pelczynski of Oxford University, raised the following point. The purpose of local government reform, which Parliament had put into effect sometime before, was to create many small, autonomous districts, each of which could decide important local matters with extensive citizen initiative and participation. In planning these local districts, no one had thought about using them as a springboard for national representation; all that had been at issue was to calibrate local governments to their communities. The average rural district naturally was much smaller than the urban one, and the proportion of districts dominated by rural interests was much greater than the proportion of rural inhabitants in the country as a whole. If these local districts were now to become the basis for representation in the Senate, the adviser pointed out, the Senate would become the most potent rural lobby in existence, representing the interests of "provincial Poland" in a way that the drafters most likely had never intended.

No one on the committee had considered this consequence before Pelczynski pointed it out. Even more surprisingly, no one paid much attention to his point even after it was presented; committee members simply mustered no interest in such realpolitik.[37]

THE POLISH PREFERENCE FOR PROPORTIONAL REPRESENTATION

From the beginning, the Constitutional Committee considered the development of laws governing the election of the more important Sejm to be among its principal tasks. The old electoral ordinance, giving an artificial majority to the Communists and their allies, could not provide the basis of the next election. It was necessary to prepare a new ordinance before the end of Parliament's term, regardless of the progress of work on the constitution.

The drafters faced a basic choice between some version of proportional representation and what the Poles call a "majoritarian" system, which requires the winning candidate to obtain at some point in the process a plurality or majority of the votes cast. Most of those who expressed an opinion felt that only a system of proportional representation was truly democratic, although some supported the majoritarian system (especially its French version, which requires an absolute majority and provides for a two-round election when necessary to accomplish this goal). A number of reasons were given for this preference for proportional representation, ranging from appeals to tradition to a rather confused belief that proportional representation better protects the interests of the minorities.[38] But the most basic source of the preference, which some groups expressed despite a potential party interest to the contrary, was a certain vision of democracy or, more precisely, of the idea of representation.

Proponents of proportional representation essentially argued that it better expresses the will of the electorate. This argument assumes, in turn, that we should understand representation quite literally, as a faithful reflection (re-presentation) of the constellation of political forces in society. Social groups sharing a common interest or agreeing on a vision of the public interest should be able to organize in political parties of their own, and these parties should then be given a chance to represent themselves in Parliament. The legislature would then constitute a microcosm of society; each significant social group would have its own voice.

Going one level deeper in the analysis of the Polish preference for proportional representation, one can discern in it a certain view of the relation between the government and the governed. According to this view, which is common in continental Europe, the people are the true "sovereign," endowed with a will of their own from which all legitimate political authority stems. A legitimate government must thus be grounded in a legislature that is really *of* the people in the strong sense of the *identity* of the rulers and the ruled. This identity guarantees against governmental repression and ensures that citizens are truly free (that is, following their own will) in obeying the laws of their country.[39] Only when the parliament contains all the essential ideological ingredients that make up the nation as a whole is the soul of the people present in its pronouncements. Legislation emanating from such a parliament wears the mantle of democratic legitimacy.

Many arguments can be made against this account of democratic legitimacy. The objection raised most often in Poland was essentially pragmatic: proportional representation will lead to an excessive fragmentation of political life, with the concomitant danger of weak, revolving-door governments, ultimately leading to anarchy. Such a danger is particularly great in a country in crisis, with an acute need for a strong and decisive government. This argument did not sway the proponents of proportional representation. It seems that the Poles, having achieved freedom after so many years of struggle, could not take seriously the idea that the choice of one electoral structure over another could threaten the long-term health of democracy. Advocates of a proportional system believed that greater diversity could only strengthen Parliament's legitimacy, whereas limiting it might give rise to the unhealthy and much-feared phenomenon of extraparliamentary opposition.

Those who acknowledged some strength in the antifragmentation argument simply responded by proposing a limitation on the size of electoral districts[40] or the institution of a threshold (such as 5 percent of the vote) that a party would have to achieve before gaining representation. But interestingly enough, the more theoretical arguments against the concept of democracy underlying proportional representation were neither commonly made nor well received. It was rarely pointed out, for example, that the idea of the "identity" of the popular will with the products of a representative legislature is riddled with theoretical difficulties, stemming from the fact that no aggregation of individual (or group) preferences into a single social choice is in principle free from paradoxes.[41] It was also rarely noted that the assumption of the possible identity of the people with its representatives flies in the face of the oft-repeated allegiance to the ideas of liberalism. Most liberals see the government as a powerful special interest of its own, always potentially inimical to the interests of the governed. Consequently, liberals regard the democratic system of representation (and the electoral process itself) not as a positive emanation from the sovereign, but as a purely negative device, allowing the voters to cashier a government that they perceive is not doing its job.

Every system of representation involves some form of aggregation of private preferences into a collective choice, but most participants in the drafting process have not clearly observed this point. In this respect the different electoral systems differ only with respect to the point at which the various groups must strike a compromise to produce an effective majority. In the system of proportional representation, this bargain is struck after the elections, when the parties must agree to form a government or pass new legislation. In the majoritarian system, by contrast, the key compromises are made before the election, when various social interests must coalesce around a party program that can gain a majority of the popular vote. In the majoritarian system, therefore, diverse social interests tend to form two political blocs, each tending toward the center of the political spectrum,[42] and the election itself tends to become a plebiscite on the fate of the bloc in power.

The system of proportional representation, on the other hand, provides no premium for shaping broad coalition programs. On the contrary, the most rational policy is to form narrowly based parties and enter into coalitions only after elections.[43] But then the voters can hold no single party to account for the government's policies: each party can still claim to represent the interests of its constituency, and if the government's program does not correspond to the preferences of a party's voters, the party can always attempt to shift the blame to other parties with which it formed a postelection coalition. Consequently, the most important political decisions, namely those that aggregate individual (or group) choices into social policies, are never directly subjected to popular approval. The strong theory of representation underlying proportional representation, affirming the identity of governors and the governed, thus clashes with the strong theory of governmental responsibility, which allows for direct electoral control of the team in power.[44]

THE RELATIONSHIP BETWEEN ELECTORAL LAW AND THE DEVELOPMENT OF POLITICAL PARTIES

Participants in the drafting of the electoral law had to consider the fact that Poland's transition to democracy did not lead to the quick formation of effective political parties. The need to preserve unity in order to oppose the Communists, and later the overwhelming victory of the Solidarity bloc, gave the politicians centered around the union a near monopoly of political power. The only effective political organization took the form of the so-called Citizens' Committees, a loose alliance of anti-Communists hastily formed under the auspices of Solidarity for the purpose of winning the 1989 election. All attempts to transform the Citizens' Committees into a political party eventually foundered as a result of the personal ambitions of the various contenders for power in Warsaw, and the committees remained essentially a dominant, nonparty political machine.

A number of small parties also appeared on the scene, some of which were reincarnations of the political movements from the Communist regime, above all the Social Democratic Party, which is a new organization of former Communist activists. Other parties anachronistically harkened back to pre–World War II divisions. Efforts to form new parties, one supporting Wałęsa and the Gdańsk group,[45] the other centered around Prime Minister Mazowiecki and the Warsaw intellectuals,[46] have failed so far, with the polls showing a low level of recognition or support for both movements.

In this situation, both the proportional and the majoritarian systems carry a number of dangers. On the one hand, proportional representation cannot work without a party system; its adoption could simply mean that the existing parties—including the anachronistic and sterile prewar groups that would ordinarily disappear with their geriatric leadership—are frozen into the permanent political landscape of Poland. The majoritarian system, on the other hand, can function with a weak party system by focusing representation around strong political personalities or regional interests. This system might create a situation like that in Mexico, with the political structure dominated by the political machine of the Citizens' Committees. Alternatively, the majoritarian system might create a caricature of the U.S. Congress devoid of even the weak American party system. Without the offsetting strength of the presidential office, this could result in legislative paralysis and endemic rent-seeking localism.

Even if a stable party system were developed, it would be subject to yet another worry. A two-party system has many virtues in the abstract. It presupposes, however, that the various social interests are able to coalesce into two basic, lasting political groupings, with all the compromises and ideological ambiguities that this process involves. On this score, however, there were good reasons to wonder whether the social structure and the political tradition of Poland could comfortably accommodate a two-party system. Presumably, like every European country, Poland will one day have a party representing the interests of the workers and other social democratic constituencies and another party representing the interest of the large and small owners of capital. Yet many people had great difficulty imagining the Polish political landscape without a powerful peasant party or the complicating factors of nationalism and Catholicism. Although most Western countries have managed to integrate these interests into basically two-bloc politics, an artificial attempt to accelerate this development in Poland could misfire. For this reason, many opponents of proportional representation advocated the more complex French system, in which the absolute majority requirement in a two-stage electoral process allows for a multiparty system while creating strong incentives to form two-bloc electoral alliances.

The Absence of Electoral Law from the Draft Constitution

Work on the new electoral law remains incomplete as of this writing. But even a cursory look at further developments shows continuing instability. At one time, the parliamentary leadership was ready to propose a moderately proportional system of representation.[47] Then a majoritarian system was seriously considered, and a mixed ordinance was actually proposed and extensively debated. A number of competing proposals were presented from the floor, most of them strongly proportional, but the presidential election intervened, and the work on the parliamentary election law was postponed, to be resumed at the beginning of 1991. This work is still in progress, with the Constitutional Committee and the presidential palace putting forth two competing proposals.[48]

Precisely because the discussion of the new electoral law has been rather chaotic, with the moods shifting often in quite opposite directions and opportunistic considerations playing an increasingly important role, some voices demanded that the constitution itself spell out the most basic electoral principles. This would preclude a constantly changing set of rules—in which parties temporarily in control seek to preserve their power by tampering with the electoral laws—and might provide a permanent stimulus to the formation of a broadly supported party system. After some initial momentum, the move to include the basic choice of an electoral system in the constitution lost most of its support. Among the common arguments against it was the unconvincing (and factually inaccurate) claim that few countries have such constitutional provisions.[49] The more convincing argument was that the roundtable Parliament, containing the Communist epigones committed to proportional representation, would oppose any constitutional provisions mandating a majoritarian system. And since most people who took the idea seriously favored some form of the majoritarian system, attempts to include such a provision were discontinued.

The Parliament, the Government, and the President

East Europeans have not only a long-standing commitment to democratic institutions but also an intuitive understanding of democratic procedures that is often surprising in people who lived under dictatorship for fifty years. My favorite example comes from personal experience of many years ago, when I participated in an illegal meeting during the student demonstrations at the University of Warsaw in 1968. I remember vividly my astonishment that the meeting of several thousand people was run—with practically no supervision on the part of the leaders of the revolt, most of whom had been arrested before the demonstrations began—as if most of the participants had thoroughly studied *Robert's Rules of Order*, though in fact not one of them had probably ever heard of the famous rule book. I recall thinking that democracy, or at least its procedural aspects, must simply run in the blood of twentieth-century Europeans.

Yet the Poles and other East Europeans sometimes take certain democratic clichés too literally. The East European intelligentsia's common attitude toward the role of the national legislature in the political life of the country exemplifies this tendency.

THE POLISH PREFERENCE FOR A POWERFUL LEGISLATURE

I have described already the prevailing Polish ideas concerning the concept of political representation and the resulting view of the relationship between the people and their elected representatives. When applied to the Parliament, Polish views usually yield the following reasoning: all legitimate political power flows from the people. The depository and embodiment of the people's own sovereignty is the national legislature, chosen in universal, equal, direct, secret, and proportional elections. Therefore, the Parliament, as the most direct representative of the people, reflecting the principal voices of the nation, should be the supreme organ of government and determine the policy of the nation.

Added to this belief is the extremely widespread view that free and unfettered debate is the essence of all democratic institutions. Although this conviction is of course particularly strong with respect to the Parliament, it often extends to other collective bodies, such as labor unions or political parties. One can easily understand this attitude among people who for years endured staged discussions with a predetermined outcome, and who fought hard for the freedom to air their true convictions.[50] But the result is that the Poles are highly suspicious of all forms of authority and do not fully appreciate the role that leadership plays in cutting through a multitude of opinions and making necessary decisions. Just as Poles see representation as not really a delegation but a microcosmic reconstitution of the polity at large, they conceive of responsibility in decision making as a submission to direct and specific authorization (in the literal sense in which the principal becomes the author of the agent's actions), rather than as the presence of external controls over an essentially autonomous agent. This means in practice that the Poles often oppose even the most reasonable limitations that the leadership may want to impose on the freedom of debate (and of parliamentary debate in particular), considering such limitations essentially undemocratic.

Altogether the Poles' attachments to the principle of legislative supremacy and to free debate potentially interfere with the sensible allocation of powers among the branches of government. In structuring the institutional framework of their new democracy, many Poles, along with other East Europeans, are ready to endow their national legislature with all conceivable powers and to view the government as needing constant parliamentary authorization. Typically, this yields a significant constituency for such arrangements as: a largely unlimited power of the parliamentary deputies to initiate legislation (with no priority given to governmental proposals); the deputies' ability to propose amendments to governmental legislation at nearly all stages of the legislative process; the Parliament's power to vote no-confidence for the government or any particular minister at any time; and the requirement of parliamentary approval for both appointments and dismissals of government officials.[51] At the same time, little attention is paid to streamlining parliamentary procedure (it is usually left for the Parliament's internal rules), and drafters are prone to ignore the party system that is likely to prevail when they consider the structure of the Parliament.

What many East Europeans seem to be missing is some pragmatic and up-to-date political science—the knowledge of how democratic institutions in the West operate on a day-to-day basis and the practical consequences of particular institutional arrangements.[52] It should be easy to see that a bicameral body composed of 560 members, organized in six or seven political parties, all lacking genuine control over their members, may not be the most appropriate organ to formulate a coherent national policy and supervise its execution—especially in a country facing monumental social, economic, and political problems related to the transition to a market economy, which requires a leadership capable of making effective decisions. Among those East Europeans who recognize this dilemma, many seem to think that all democratic governments must operate in this inefficient fashion. What they generally do not realize is that parliaments in the West do not have the all-encompassing powers East Europeans want to bestow on their own and do not, as a rule, participate actively in the formulation of national policy.

Even in those countries in which the rhetoric of parliamentary supremacy still dominates the discourse of national politics, the principle of party discipline, combined with a variety of procedural rules, places the job of formulating the national policy squarely with the executive; Britain is perhaps the clearest example. Parliamentary deliberation is thus more reactive than originative. It functions as a highly visible forum for discussion and criticism of governmental policies by the opposition, rather than as a creative mechanism for shaping directives for the government to follow. In practice, proposals put forth by the executive are not genuinely tested in the process of debate. On the contrary, their passage is normally assured in advance by party discipline in the governmental majority. The long-term effect of the open monitoring of the majority's actions, rather than the legislature's ability to contribute to policy formation, determines the parliament's proper role in the democratic process.

THE POTENTIALLY CONTRADICTORY PREFERENCE FOR A STRONG PRESIDENCY

Since most Poles do not view the parliament in the customary role of reactor, those who observe the often disorganized proceedings of their legislature and the government's occasional inability to control the legislative agenda tend to view these phenomena as a necessary corollary of the parliamentary system, and sometimes fear that anarchy may lie ahead for the still fragile Polish state. They look for a remedy in the creation of a strong office of the president. Unlike the government, which emanates from the Parliament and is not directly invested with its power by the people, a popularly elected president may constitute a proper counterweight to the Parliament, because he or she can claim an equally strong link to the source of all legitimate authority.

There is thus a peculiar tension among the Poles, perhaps more than among other East Europeans. A rather anarchic view of democracy, emphasizing the supremacy of undisciplined parliamentary power, coexists with a readiness to support a highly personal embodiment of popular will in the office of a potentially authoritarian president. Discussions surrounding the recent presidential election made this duality evident. Lech Wałęsa gained considerable support for his promise to be a roving people's representative, demanding the power to solve by decree the problems that supposedly clogged the channels of political and economic change. Although Wałęsa presented himself as a problem solver, his opponents depicted him as lacking the slightest understanding or respect for the democratic institutions of his own country.[53] Much of this debate went beyond the exaggerations characteristic of an election campaign. The people in the Wałęsa camp sincerely believed that their defeat would bring about governmental paralysis, whereas many sophisticated members of the opposition believed with equal sincerity that a Wałęsa victory might lead to dictatorship.

THE DRAFT CONSTITUTION: RECONCILING THE CONFLICTING PREFERENCES

In light of this intellectual climate, the Subcommittee on Institutions produced a remarkable proposal, rejecting both a strong presidential office and unfettered parliamentary authority. Instead, the subcommittee proposed to institute a strong government, capable of imposing discipline on the parliamentary proceedings, with a president functioning as an impartial arbiter, empowered to break impasses at moments of political crisis.

The proposals drafted by the Subcommittee on Institutions emerged from a long and cumbersome process. The subcommittee met frequently during 1990 to discuss the text of various provisions provided by individual experts. Because the sections prepared in this piecemeal way lacked sufficient unity, and because the subcommittee did not vote to accept or reject any of the drafts presented to it, a number of members were frustrated by the apparently unfocused proceedings. Nevertheless, after a considerable amount of time was spent in this process, those members and experts who took part came to know each other quite well, and bonds of respect and understanding began to develop despite the participants' greatly varying backgrounds and convictions. Then, in the fall of 1990, a smaller group of self-selected advisers and a few deputies gathered near Warsaw for several marathon sessions, during which they agreed upon drafts of the most important sections on the Parliament, the government, and the presidency. The full Constitutional Committee later approved this draft with very few changes.

The subcommittee started its final deliberations with the outlines of a broad agreement: the office of the president would not be purely ceremonial, but the president would be neither the chief executive nor a dominant figure in the policy-making arena. Parliament would control the government and provide a public forum for discussing policy matters, but would not become an executive committee of several hundred members. The agenda for the nation and the ability to shape policy would be firmly in the hands of the government.

The main problem facing the subcommittee in the last stages of its work was to translate these principles into the language of concrete constitutional provisions. Above all, the subcommittee had to determine how to confer on the government the powers that would enable it to exercise undisputed leadership in the policy-making area, without undermining its democratic responsibility to the Parliament. The task appeared particularly difficult in light of two circumstances: the country did not have an established party system to assure a smooth functioning of the Parliament, and (for reasons discussed in the preceding section entitled "The Electoral System") the drafters knew that they could not resolve this problem by imposing a majoritarian electoral system that would foster the formation of strong governmental majorities in the legislature.

The drafters therefore chose a number of lesser measures, each of which would strengthen somewhat the hand of the government, with the hope that together they would provide sufficient leverage for the emergence of a strong governmental leadership. In particular, the drafters attempted to create a series of mechanisms to differentiate strongly between the positions of the supporters and the opponents of the government, as well as produce significant incentives for the deputies, even in the absence of strong party discipline, to toe the line on matters considered important by the government.

The first device used was to make the government relatively independent of small shifts in parliamentary opinion and capable of riding through moments of dissatisfaction. This goal was achieved, initially, in two ways: first, by making the office of the prime minister dominant in the government and, second, by making it difficult to remove the government from power without a broad consensus. The drafters intended, in other words, to shift the burden of parliamentary inertia (which may become substantial in a body with many weakly organized parties) from the government to the opposition, thus making the same forces that potentially contribute to chaos work in favor of the constituted authority.

The predominance of the prime minister was assured in several ways. To begin with, the president—not the legislature—was to designate the prime minister. When an already constituted majority existed in Parliament, the president would have little choice but to designate its leader, because the Parliament could twice reject the president's candidates and then designate a prime minister of its own choice. When Parliament did not have a clear candidate of its own, however, the support of the head of state would considerably strengthen the new prime minister. Not only would the nomination confer a degree of nonpartisan prestige, but the president and the prime minister, acting together, would enjoy extensive powers. The most important of these would be the president's ability to dissolve Parliament upon the failure of a vote of confidence that the prime minister could request in connection with significant legislative proposals of the government.[54]

The prime minister would be further strengthened by his or her dominant position among the ministers. The presidential designee would be empowered to choose members of the new government, who would be submitted for Parliament's approval as a unit. Any minister could then be dismissed by the prime minister acting alone,[55] whereas Parliament would have no power to remove any of the ministers, without bringing down the government as a whole. The draft also clearly gives the prime minister a leading role in the government and makes him or her the official superior of every member of the state administration.

To entrench the position of the government, the draft makes it removable by Parliament only through the procedure of the so-called constructive no-confidence, a device borrowed from the

Federal Republic of Germany.[56] According to this procedure (to be distinguished from the "confidence vote" discussed earlier, which only the government could initiate), Parliament can remove the government from office only by designating a new prime minister and voting him or her in by a majority of all votes, following a seven-day cooling period.[57]

The draft also invests the government with a number of other tools intended to strengthen its stability and freedom to maneuver. It facilitates its legislative agenda by giving priority to governmental legislative initiatives and prohibiting amendments to its legislative proposals from the floor (amendments brought in committees are allowed). Furthermore, it allows the president to dissolve Parliament if the budget is not passed within three months from its submission by the government. If Parliament is not dissolved, the government may spend according to its proposed budget; if the budget is not passed within six months, dissolution is automatic. Finally, any proposed amendment to the budget, as well as any other legislation proposed from the floor that involves increased expenditures, must indicate the revenue sources for these expenditures.

Having assured the government a large degree of independence, the draft proceeds to vest Parliament with a series of tools to exercise its supervisory functions. It requires the government to provide, within three days, oral explanations on the floor concerning any questions from the deputies, and to provide within twenty-one days a written answer to any parliamentary request for information. A special parliamentary body is charged with watching over the administration's accounts and investigating financial abuses. Parliamentary commissions are given wide powers of inquiry, with a right to call all government officials before them.

The system proposed by the draft of the Subcommittee on Institutions makes it clear that the policy of the nation is determined by the government. Consequently, although the proposal allows the president, if he or she believes a law passed by Parliament to be unconstitutional, to submit it to the Constitutional Tribunal prior to final approval, the draft does not give the president the power of legislative initiative, and requires a countersignature of the prime minister in connection with most exercises of the president's authority.

Although the draft thus generally tends to empower the president as a guardian of the constitutional order, rather than a political figure, there are some aspects of the presidential power in which the subcommittee departed from its vision. The most important of these was the conferral on the president of the veto power, subject to being overridden by a two-thirds vote of the Sejm. A result of instructions from the Constitutional Committee, this concession does create a potential for an increase in the president's power that might undermine the institutional structure the drafters attempted to establish, especially if the ratifiers choose (as proposed in one of the two variants of the draft) to make the president popularly elected. Generally speaking, the chapter dealing with the president was the most difficult for the subcommittee; the pressure of events leading to the presidential election of 1990 could be felt throughout the final stages of the subcommittee's deliberations.

Conclusion

The work on the new constitution of the Polish Republic is not yet complete, and it is not clear to what extent the present draft will be retained by the current Parliament, which will have the ultimate responsibility for enacting the new basic law. But the experience of drafting brings to the fore the most fundamental problem facing the constitution makers of Eastern Europe—the fact that the new constitutions must be prepared at a time of profound and rapid changes in the political and economic structure of the country. These changes revealed, among other things, that the broad consensus among the members of the erstwhile opposition to the Communist dictatorship tended to disintegrate rather quickly, once the enemy had been defeated. This consensus was not shallow, insofar as it expressed a shared commitment to the most fundamental values of personal liberty and political democracy. But precisely because the consensus was extremely broad and opposition to the Communists did not require the elaboration of a more concrete conception of democracy and its institutions, those opposed to the Communists never developed a unified vision of the institutional arrangements that must now replace the old dictatorship. Consequently, Poland, like the other countries of Eastern Europe, is drifting into a new political structure. The lack of clear models and the absence of experience in designing practical solutions to the basic problems of the polity make the efforts to establish the new constitutional order both exhilarating and fraught with danger. Perhaps the most interesting question in this regard is to what extent the people involved in this process will be able to control it, and to what extent the events of the moment will obscure a vision of the more distant future.

Notes

Professor Rapaczynski's analysis focuses on the drafting process as it was unfolding during 1990. In August 1992 the Sejm approved a "Little Constitution." This Constitution represents a compromise between presidential and parliamentary forms of government. It reflects not so much political theory as compromises turning upon current Polish politics.—ED.

[1]The most recent version of this Constitution generally available in English translation is in Gisbert H. Flanz, "Poland," in Albert P. Blaustein and Gisbert H. Flanz, eds., *Constitutions of the Countries of the World* (Dobbs Ferry, NY: Oceana, 1990) [hereinafter Recent Constitution]. This translation incorporates most amendments made before December 1989. Unless otherwise specified, all citations to the existing Polish Constitution refer to this version.

[2]See David Caute, *The Fellow Travellers: Intellectual Friends of Communism* (New Haven, Conn.: Yale University Press, 1988).

[3]For an account of Poland and other countries during that period, see generally Zbigniew Brzezinski, *The Soviet Bloc: Unity and Conflict* (Cambridge, Mass.: Harvard University Press, 1967). For a discussion of the terror of these regimes, see especially pp. 85–104, and sources cited therein.

[4]See, for example, Recent Constitution, p. 5, Article 3, Section 1. Parliament has since amended this section to end the privileged status of the Communist party and to guarantee the free formation of political parties. (Recent Constitution, p. v).

[5] See, for example, Recent Constitution, p. 7, Article 6, Section 7, Clause 2: "In its policy the Polish People's Republic . . . shall consolidate friendship and cooperation with the Union of Soviet Socialist Republics and other socialist States."

[6]See, for example, Recent Constitution, p. 27, Article 69, Section 1 (right to "rest and leisure"); p. 28, Article 71 (right to a clean environment); and p. 28, Article 72, Section 1 (right to education).

[7]Recent Constitution, p. 18, Article 33a; see also Note, "Constitutional Heritage and Renewal: The Case of Poland," *Virginia Law Review* 77 (1991):49.

[8]A more detailed history of the roundtable talks and the elections of 1989 is found in Timothy Garton Ash, *The Magic Lantern* (New York: Random House, 1990), 25–46. See also Wiktor Osiatynski, *The Round Table Negotiations in Poland* (Working Paper, Center for the Study of Constitutionalism in Eastern Europe, University of Chicago Law School, 1991) and sources cited therein; Zbigniew Pelczynski and Sergiusz Kowalski, "Poland," *Electoral Studies* 9 (December 1990): 346.

[9]Ironically, it was the Communists who initiated the idea of the Senate's reconstitution.

[10]Recent Constitution, p. 14, Article 32, Section 2.

[11]One of these two candidates apparently passed only because his name appeared last on the electoral list. Voters had to cross out the names of any candidates whom they did not wish to elect. It seems that many voters, intending to cross out all the names on the ballot, drew x-shaped lines that did not reach the very bottom of the page.

[12]Ironically, Mazowiecki had been one of the Solidarity leaders who did not believe in the significance of the political compromise during the round-table negotiations He was active in the negotiations for reinstatement of the union but, following the election (in which he refused to run), he wrote an article decrying as irresponsible the call for a Solidarity-led government. Once in the government, however, Mazowiecki quickly moved to consolidate his power and independence, and his kingmaker, Wałęsa, soon regretted his nomination.

[13]Recent Constitution, p. 26, Clause 8.

[14]Thus Article 68 still refers to "the Socialist economic systems" and central planning, whereas the new Article 6 guarantees "freedom of economic activity without regard to the form of ownership."

[15]See n. 18.

[16]Recent Constitution, p. 35, Article 106.This has been changed in the meantime. See n. 18.

[17]I use "government" here, and elsewhere in this chapter, in the sense in which the term is commonly used in parliamentary systems: to refer to the prime minister, the cabinet ministers (typically also members of Parliament), and the departments they head, and not to the entire governmental structure.

[18]This concern turned out to have been quite unnecessary. Experts and a few self-selected deputies undertook the bulk of the subcommittee's work, and the Polish experts' Communist loyalties turned out to be superficial. Following the demise of the Communists as an organized force, these experts had no ideological ax to grind and worked quite harmoniously to produce the best possible draft under the circumstances.

[19]Parliament formalized this strategy in a statute passed in the fall of 1990, specifying that the two houses of Parliament sitting together as a "National Assembly" must approve the new constitution by a two-thirds majority and then submit it to a referendum. Although technically the referendum would be nonbinding, the new constitution would clearly derive much of its legitimacy from the direct popular approval.

[20]The first Polish Constitution was adopted on 3 May 1791. According to some reckonings, the May 3 Constitution (as it came to be known) was the first European constitution, and it is a symbol of the Polish Enlightenment. As of this writing, it is clear that the new parliament will not be elected by the time of the bicentennial (with the election scheduled to take place in October 1991), but the roundtable Parliament might still choose the date of 3 May 1991 as the official publication date of the results of the work of this Constitutional Committee.

[21]A number of politicians associated with the Warsaw group were, at the time, riding high in the polls, while Wałęsa, with his habit of speaking before thinking, appeared less and less popular. Shortly after the decision to go to a direct election, however, the winds began to shift, and Wałęsa started to gain ground against the "Warsaw" candidate, Prime Minister Mazowiecki.

[22]Wałęsa's backers could hardly oppose the call for a popular election, after their attacks on the legitimacy of the roundtable Sejm. The role reversal was nearly complete: the Warsaw group in principle preferred an indirect election.

[23]This is not to say that the Warsaw leadership acted in a purely opportunistic fashion; its opposition to a strong presidency was also grounded in principle.

[24] The matter of church-state relations illustrates the predominance of immediate political concerns. In August 1990, two weeks before the beginning of the school year and without any prior consultations with Parliament, the government issued a regulation introducing religion in public schools, despite the fact that public opinion polls had indicated that most parents opposed the move. Apparently, however, the government had been under intense pressure from the Church and decided to settle the matter before the upcoming presidential elections. The government's calculations may have been correct, in that the public mood shifted rather quickly in favor of change once the decision had been made, and the matter was removed from the election campaign. But very little attention seems to have been paid to its long-term consequences on the separation of church and state.

[25]To be elected, a candidate had to obtain an absolute majority of the vote. If no candidate received the required majority in the first round the two candidates with the greatest numbers of votes were entitled to take part in a run-off election. Wałęsa polled twice as many votes as the next candidate (Stanisław Tymiński) in the first round, but failed to win outright. In the second round, he won close to 80 percent of the vote.

[26]The election was eventually held in October 1991.

[27]The most obvious example of such response would be a strong shift toward a more presidential regime that could be viewed as tailored to satisfy Wałęsa's appetite for more power.

[28]See generally Francisco Rubio Llorente, "Constitutional Jurisdiction in Law-making," in Alesandro Pizzorusso, ed., *Law in the Making: A Comparative Survey* (Hamburg: Springer, 1988), 156.

[29]See "Constitutional Heritage and Renewal," 49.

[30]For a general discussion of judicial review in a comparative context, see Mauro Cappelletti, *The Judicial Process in Comparative Perspective* (Oxford: Clarendon, 1989).

[31]For the Basic Law, see Gisbert H. Flanz, "The Federal Republic of Germany," in Blaustein and Flanz, *Constitutions of the Countries of the World*, vol. 6, 75, 93.

[32]This text has not yet been translated.

[33]Recent Constitution, p. 28, Article 70, Section 2.

[34]Recent Constitution, p. 27, Article 69, Section 2.

[35]Recent Constitution, p. 29, Article 78, Section 2, Clause 2. The same article provides more general and sweeping guarantees of equality for women.

[36]Recent Constitution, p. 35, Article 106.

[37] The matter was ultimately considered by the experts who produced the final draft. The principle of tying the election of senators to the local units of self-government was preserved (with the vote being given to all local councilmen), but representation was made proportional to the population of each district. In addition, the Senate was given the right to amend legislation (without any additional approval by the Sejm), but the Sejm was given the power to reject the Senate's amendments by a majority vote.

[38]There is no a priori reason to believe that proportional representation better protects the interests of minorities. As I argue later in this chapter, the relevant difference simply concerns the point at which minorities can bargain for concessions with the other groups comprising a potential majority.

[39]The philosophical underpinning of this conception of popular democracy, which came to the fore during the French Revolution, had been provided by Jean-Jacques Rousseau and was further developed by Immanuel Kant.

[40]Under most systems of proportional representation, the smaller the district, the greater the departures from the principle of proportionality.

[41]The canonical text here is Kenneth Arrow, *Social Choice and Individual Values*, 2d ed. (New Haven, Conn.: Yale University Press, 1963). Arrow's work has generated a whole literature. For a review of later developments, see Russell Hardin, *Collective Action* (Baltimore, Md.: Johns Hopkins University Press, 1982).

[42]Assuming that the political spectrum can be represented by a straight line (a controversial assumption) and that the people on both extremes vote (an assumption that is not always justified), each bloc can take for granted the extremes on its side of the spectrum (the right-of-center bloc the extreme right, the left-of-center the extreme left). As a result, both blocs tend to compete for the votes in the center.

[43]Any coalition program will contain points with which any particular interest group will disagree. In a system of proportional representation (especially in its extreme versions), however, there is no premium on achieving any particular percentage of the vote in order to gain representation. Consequently, any time a party adopts a broadly based program and holds on to it for a sufficiently long time, another party is likely to be formed that reflects more closely the views of some section of the first party's constituency and scoops some of its votes.

[44]The foregoing argument applies to the rather pure and idealized versions of the two electoral systems. In practice, the systems are often not "pure" and other constraints, such as minimum thresholds or the size of districts in proportional representation, modify the consequences of the electoral rules themselves. But these pure cases help us analyze the tendencies that a given electoral system will exhibit. It is the relative scarcity of such an analysis in the Polish context that I found disturbing.

[45]The Center Alliance.

[46]The Civic Movement–Democratic Action, known by its Polish acronym ROAD.

[47]This system of representation used the d'Hondt method and rather small districts. For a full explanation of the d'Hondt system, see Enid Lakeman, *How Democracies Vote: A Study of Electoral Systems*, 4th ed. (London: Faber and Faber, 1974).

[48] The presidential proposal contains a larger number of single-member districts and a countrywide system of proportional representation for the rest of the seats. The Constitutional Committee's proposal has a smaller number of single-member districts, but limits somewhat more the chances of the smallest parties by having a number of small multimember districts. A minority of the committee proposed to privilege the larger parties still further by the use of a 5 percent threshold and a d'Hondt system of seat assignment.

[49]Among the countries whose constitutions contain such provisions are: Australia, Chapter I, Part II, Section 9 (Senate elections); Belgium, Article 48; Canada, Article 40; Greece, Article 54, Section 3 (partial); India, Article 80, Section 4 (Upper House); Ireland, Articles 16.2.5, 18.5; Italy, Article 56; Mexico, Article 52; The Netherlands, Chapter 3, Articles 53–55; Portugal, Article 155; Sweden, The Instruments of Government, Chapter 3, Articles 6–9; and Switzerland, Articles 73, 80. These texts are available in various volumes of Blaustein and Flanz, *Constitutions of the Countries of the World*.

[50]The Polish distaste for authority, however, clearly dates back further than the rejection of the Communist oppression. The history of Poland is replete with anarchic institutions, such as the famous *liberum veto* (the requirement of parliamentary unanimity).

[51]In the fall of 1990, when Prime Minister Mazowiecki decided to introduce some cabinet changes, Parliament refused to confirm his dismissal of an otherwise nondescript minister of telecommunications. The prime minister then told the minister to go on an extended vacation, and one of the most important government departments, charged at that time with some of the most difficult decisions concerning the future development of the country, remained without its head for several months.

[52]I am painting here with a broad brush, obviously. Many people in Eastern Europe are very learned in political and constitutional theory; I met a number of such men and women during my work in Poland. What I am describing here, however, is a widespread view among many important people, including several members of the Constitutional Committee and other influential opinion makers, whose support for any constitutional solutions chosen by the drafters would be essential for the final adoption of the committee's work.

[53]The Polish daily press contained numerous articles discussing this debate.

[54]Parliament could avoid dissolution in such cases only by voting the confidence requested, or transforming the vote of confidence into a constructive no-confidence vote, as explained in the next section of this chapter. The failure of a vote of confidence would not by itself lead to the government's resignation, even if the Parliament were not dissolved.

[55]When dismissing a minister, the prime minister would be obliged to inform the Sejm and explain his or her decision. Any new minister would have to be confirmed by the Sejm.

[56]Basic Law of Germany, Article 67, reprinted in Flanz, "The Federal Republic of Germany," in Blaustein and Flanz, *Constitutions of the Countries of the World*.

[57]A motion by sixty deputies is required to put a no-confidence matter on the agenda.

Chapter 5

Self-Governance or Central Control? Rewriting Constitutions in Central and Eastern Europe

Joanna Regulska

I am not an advocate for frequent changes in laws and constitutions. But laws and institutions must go hand in hand with the progress of the human mind.

—*Thomas Jefferson*

The fundamental political and organizational transformation occurring in the countries of Central and Eastern Europe focuses on the restructuring of central control and the establishment of new political institutions. This process of building new institutions—initiated about three years ago in Poland, Hungary, and the Czech and Slovak republics, and slowly beginning now in Bulgaria, Romania, Albania, and the newly independent states of the former Soviet Union—faces major challenges and barriers.

The obstacles are the result of a forty-five-year legacy of totalitarian, centralized, and command authority. Vladimir Lenin's notion of "democratic centralism" prevailed and for many decades retained a hierarchical structure of government, institutions, and society.[1] Although the Communist regimes formally adopted new constitutions, they generally ignored the principles of those constitutions: the rule of law became the rule of party, and the separation of powers ceased to exist. As a result, members of these societies have been denied basic democratic freedoms, especially the freedom of self-determination.

Even when constitutions provided for basic rights, those rights could only be exercised within the context of the overriding principles of the leading role of the Communist party and of socialism. In the Soviet Union, Article 125 of the "Stalin" Constitution of 1936 stated this notion very plainly: "In conformity with the interests of the working people, and in order to strengthen the socialist system, the citizens of U.S.S.R. are guaranteed by law: freedom of speech, freedom of the press, freedom of the assembly."[2] Thus the rights that could be exercised within the Communist framework were seen also as the citizens' obligations to build socialism.

Under this system constitutions served as tools for maintaining order, not as means for protecting individual freedoms. By designating the Communist party as "the vanguard of the working people in their struggle to build a Communist society and [as a] leading core of all organizations" (Article 126), the Soviet Constitution established an overall goal to which civil liberties needed to conform. Yet, at the same time, provisions establishing judicial enforcement of constitutional rights were nowhere to be found.

The constitutions of Central and Eastern Europe that were modeled after the Soviet blueprint automatically inherited this arbitrary, authoritarian use of power and control needed for the legitimization of their Communist regimes. They rejected the distinction between private and public spheres; they created prohibitions and permissions not only for the government but also for individuals; and they imposed duties on private persons, rather than preserving the rights of those persons. And most important for the current topic, the separation of powers, an essential feature of democratic constitutions, was replaced by the concentration of powers and the subordination of lower levels to higher ones.

Theoretically, the current rewriting of past Socialist constitutions represents an attempt to introduce democratic principles, to empower people by providing them with freedoms and rights, and to signify the transition to a new political system. These constitutions are presented as symbols of progress and as guarantees that the new changes will be institutionalized. For local self-government the new constitutions are supposed to secure autonomy. A review of two already approved constitutions (Bulgarian and Romanian) and another half dozen drafts, however, has led me to question some of these assumptions.[3]

Do the constitutions of newly emerging democracies indeed represent a complete transition from totalitarian regimes to democratic systems? Do they represent a step forward away from Sovietlike constitutions, or are they grounded in their predecessors' philosophy? Do they support the emergence of a civil society and provide for the protection of civil and political rights, including economic liberties? Do they not only acknowledge but also reinforce the existence of autonomous local self-government, the essential means of political participation for the public?

This chapter will address these questions and examine one aspect of the current political and economic transformation developing in post-Communist societies, namely the emergence of local autonomy as exemplified by the establishment of local self-government. Specifically, I will attempt to determine the extent to which the current process of rewriting the constitutions of Central and Eastern Europe fosters democratic decentralization. In all Central and Eastern European states, constitutional remaking represents a determination to regain self-governance. This chapter presents my search for evidence that the rights of local self-governance are adequately protected by these new constitutions. The fundamental question, then, is to what extent new constitutions will adhere to the principle of separation of powers and allow for the autonomy of territorial units.

The chapter is composed of three parts. The first section reviews the criteria that can be used to define autonomy of local self-government and discusses the current status of local government reform in the region. The second part reviews tendencies in constitutional development in Central and Eastern Europe, and the third part analyzes this process in regard to protection of the rights of local self-governance. The research for this chapter was conducted during 1991 and consisted of interviews and consultations with parliamentary leaders and local government officials in Central and Eastern Europe.[4]

Local Self-Government: Theory and Practice

Before selected constitutions of Central and Eastern Europe are reviewed, it is important to consider the usual understanding of the nature and importance of local self-government. This background is all the more important because the theoretical understanding of the state has come into direct and sometimes costly conflict with the realities of rapid political and economic changes in the region. These changes have created barriers that obstruct the effective development and implementation of reform at the local level.

First, as Brian Smith[5] and others have argued, decentralized government implies "self-governing through political institutions" at the local level, where these units "will not be administered by the agents of a superior government but will be governed by institutions that are founded on the politics of the area." Second, it implies that these institutions will be run by representatives democratically elected by citizens inhabiting the area. In the context of this framework, decentralization is seen as a question of central-local relations, a "formal relationship of power and influence . . . expressed through . . . legislative, judicial and administrative channels."[6]

It is important to make a distinction between decentralization and local autonomy. Decentralization is an indispensable but not a sufficient condition for local autonomy. As Smith argues, the "level of autonomy devolved to subnational governments will reflect the political interests represented at the centre."[7]

These criteria are often elaborated in terms of the intellectual perspective from which local self-government is viewed. Here I will mention only the two theories most relevant to the discussion about the concept of local self-government in Central and Eastern Europe. Liberals employ two arguments in support of local government. One group, those who see local government as important to national democracy, stress three functions: political education, training in leadership, and political stability.[8] The other camp, those who support local government's contribution at the local level, emphasize equality, liberty, and responsiveness to people's needs.

In contrast, Marxist scholars have argued that the local state must be analyzed in terms of its role in the reproduction of capitalist relations. Perhaps most important, local government has a long tradition of providing the conditions necessary for the reproduction of labor. At the same time, local government is involved in the process of allocation of resources to profitable production and unprofitable consumption. The distinction between the national state and the local state, whereby the former is more preoccupied with the social investment expenditure and the latter with social consumption, has led to the creation of "dual-state" theory.[9] This perceived duality becomes less distinct, however, if one considers that the local state contributes to the productive sphere "on behalf of capital as its political agent in the provision of roads, water supplies, energy, communications, physical planning, and urban development."[10]

In analyzing these interpretations, one cannot ignore the fact that a country's decision to instate a more centralized or decentralized government is not simply a technical effort; indeed, it is fundamentally a political undertaking. The process will depend on political struggles among parties, elected officials, and bureaucrats, to mention only a few of the interest groups that may lose or gain as a result of the restructuring of the central-local relations. It will also result in the fulfillment of political objectives and determination of the state's ideological shape by some factions, to the exclusion of others. The struggle over the writing of the Polish constitution is a case in point. Between 1989 and 1991 more than eleven drafts of the Polish constitution were prepared.[11] Not only both chambers of the Parliament (the Sejm and the Senate) but also several political parties (for example, the Confederation for an Independent Poland and the Peasant Party), as well as individuals, were involved in creating draft constitutions. Such a diversity of proposals suggests that the outcome is important for many. Interestingly, ten of the proposed versions contain separate chapters devoted to local self-government.

Although students of the nature of the state may differ in their perspectives, they agree on the importance of local government and its role in the contemporary state. It is not surprising that the Central and Eastern European states, as a part of their political transformation, claim to support the autonomy of local government, as exemplified through holding local elections, creating local institutions, and fostering political pluralism. What is debatable is the degree of power and influence that the central governments are ready to devolve to the local level.

In all the countries of Central and Eastern Europe, local government reform was launched as a deliberate move from the centrally controlled system in which hierarchical dependencies and the unity of power were at the core of the administrative structure. In the period of 1989–90, most countries of the region put in power new, independent central governments. The speed with which new political leaders attempted to move toward the establishment of principles of self-governance was remarkable. In 1990, we witnessed the approval of local self-government legislation in Poland, Hungary, and the Czech and Slovak republics. The year 1991 brought changes in Bulgaria. In 1992, Romania joined the trend. Albania and the newly independent states of the former Soviet Union are at various stages of drafting their legislation.

Although the speed with which these changes were achieved was extraordinary, the price paid has been high. In over one hundred interviews conducted in the summer and fall of 1991 with parliamentary leaders, local government officials, lawmakers, and citizens, I discerned a general feeling of distress and dissatisfaction with the outcomes of the decentralization efforts undertaken by governments and politicians. The mayor of the Hungarian city of Nagynyarad suggested that "centralization is even stronger than before the reform was launched, because most of the financial resources are still coming from the state," and that although new responsibilities of local governments have been approved by the Parliament and the government, no new monies have been delegated." He saw this as a constitutional issue, claiming that the "constitution should guarantee financial resources for the new tasks required by the legislation. In that way autonomy of local government will be secured."[12]

The lack of appropriate legislation and the ambiguity of the legislation being created have been also frequently mentioned. Hungary lacked a "property law," which was supposed to clarify communal property ownership, and a "capital law," which aimed to clear the relationship between twenty-four districts of Budapest and the city's general assembly.[13] Lajos Szabó, chief of the Division for Autonomous Bodies, in the Ministry of the Interior, presented a similar list: "The missing law concerns the clarification of local government property. A law that specifies the assets that belong to the treasury is needed before local governments can tell what belongs to them. A land law, and laws concerning concessions and privatization, are also needed."[14]

Bulgarians, on the other hand, were faced with writing legislation pertinent to local government structure, division of responsibilities between the central and local levels, and questions related to fiscal arrangements.[15] Bulgarian district officials in Plovdiv voiced similar concerns to those indicated by the Hungarians: "There is far too much of central government intervention in controlling and coordinating county and local activities."[16] Scholars pointed to conceptual weaknesses of the effort: the "law is too liberal and often ideal a picture, but in this form cannot be used by local authorities."[17]

Although each country is undertaking the challenge of reforming its central-local relations on its own terms and with the speed allowed by its specific circumstances, the similarity of the messages that have been sent is striking: the legacy of communism and new challenges brought by the current changes make the establishment of autonomous local self-government more difficult than expected. The major barriers, as seen by Central and East European analysts of local government, can be summarized into five problem areas: conceptual weaknesses of local government reform; increasing tendency toward centralization; politicization of the local level; alienation of society and of local self-governing bodies; and inertia of the old administrative system.

This list is by no means exhaustive; rather, it reflects a spectrum of the difficulties that the region faced in the second year of transition. The intensity with which these problems emerged in the individual countries varied. A brief examination of two of the barriers—the lack of a clearly defined framework of local government reform, and the tensions between centralist and decentralist tendencies—is of special interest to this inquiry, as they are directly relevant to the question of how local government is addressed in new constitutions. Two examples, Poland and Romania, will be used to illustrate these dilemmas. Poland, which began a legislative debate on local government reform in the summer of 1989, represents a case of unprecedented progress during a brief period, but which also became quickly entangled in serious conflicts and disputes over the desired level of local self-governance. Romania, a member of the "southern tier," did not even begin discussions about the future shape of local government until the summer of 1991. Nevertheless, the similarity of experience left recognizable marks on both nations.

POLAND

In Poland, in May 1990, local government officials were promised power, autonomy, and full self-governance. The Local Self-Government Act of March 1990 and subsequent changes in the constitution were guarantors of the self-governing rights of local authorities.[18] Although the enacted legislation pertinent to local government reform presented an overall model of a new local government structure and focused on selected technical aspects, the shortage of time for conceptual debate before the legislation could be approved has resulted in a persistent misunderstanding by Parliament and consecutive governments of the conceptual framework of the reform. Issues that were not adequately discussed before enactment of the legislation included the division of powers and responsibilities between the central and local levels, the role of intermediary levels (regional and subregional) in the overall system of self-governance, and service organization and delivery under decentralized governance and market economy. Similarly, debates regarding fiscal arrangements, such as revenue sources and their collection and redistribution, were conducted in many cases after the principal legislation had been approved. The issue of fiscal autonomy as a prerequisite for local autonomy was put aside.[19] Subsequently, this lack of discussion between practitioners and politicians has been translated into a lack of political support for restructuring central-local relations and for continuing political and administrative decentralization.

The first signs that the new central administration was not ready to pass all appropriate responsibilities on to local government were already visible in the spring of 1990, during the parliamentary debates on the final shape of the Division of Duties and Responsibilities (DDR) Act. Individual sectoral ministries, with the exception of the Ministry of Finance, failed to engage fully in discussions of their future role in a decentralized state.[20] This reluctance could be interpreted, on the one hand, as a failure to understand that their contribution in the form of new, revised legislation is essential for the implementation of local government reform. On the other hand, it might be a sign of the recognition that any change would in the long run result in a loss of power and central control.[21] Parliament was rather quiet in this debate, because it had more to lose than to gain by advancing decentralization. Matters were not settled by the passage of legislation, and the problems intensified in the summer of 1990, when the interpretation of recently enacted laws began to take place.

The DDR Act provided local government with numerous new responsibilities in the area of land management, public transportation, housing, infrastructure, preschool and primary education, and provision of water and sewage.[22] Several ambiguities regarding the distribution of functions among different levels of government were left intact.[23] Further complicating matters, *rejony* (district authorities) were established. They were immediately perceived by many as the antithesis of self-governance and a dangerous source of potential failure for the entire reform.[24]

At the same time, there were those who supported a new, extended tier of central administration. The representatives of the Public Administration Office in the Council of Ministers argued that such an extension is necessary for a central administration to have control over newly established local self-government.[25] At the meeting of the National Assembly of Local Authorities in July 1990 in Poznan, Jerzy Kozłowski, at that time secretary of state for public administration in Prime Minister Mazowiecki's cabinet, argued for the necessity of the existence of an "administrative police" and of a large number of other duties to be placed under the jurisdiction of district authorities. This was the beginning of a quick return to "sectoral Poland." Subsequently, regional offices of the ministries of Building and Construction, National Education, and Health were opened.[26] Indeed, the central administration persistently attempted to extend its control by establishing new institutions at the local level under the banner of special administration.

Senator Jerzy Stępień, commissioner general for local elections, argued in his statement during the hearings of the Senate Constitutional Commission (November 1990) for the need to give more attention to local self-government in the new constitution and to use that occasion to resolve problems and conflicts whose existence was already evident after the first six months of self-governance. His list repeated several complaints already mentioned: the ill-formed DDR Act, which contributed to conflicts between central and local levels; the establishment of district offices, which in effect assumed many local self-government responsibilities; and the lack of legislation designing new fiscal relations between central and local levels.[27] In addition, he argued that the creation of a second level of self-governing authorities is imperative for the future of the entire reform. He stressed that this latter issue especially must be discussed before a new constitution is adopted; the constitutional provisions pertinent to local government "should not be written in such a way as to foreclose the possibility of creating in the future self-governing authorities at the higher level."[28]

Thus, after the initial proclamation of decentralization, it became apparent that *deconcentration* rather than *decentralization* was in fact occurring. The former term signifies only a change in the structure of the system, whereas the latter refers to a devolution of power and decision making to the local level. A power struggle emerged between the central level accustomed to full control, strongly supported by existing legislation and an extensive bureaucracy, and the newly elected local government officials, equipped only with fragile and incomplete legislation.

The signs that deconcentration is taking place have been numerous. First of all, they include the creation by the central level of new institutions at the regional and local levels. This increased tendency by individual ministries and branches of central government to establish their own branch offices at the lower level, as opposed to allowing for self-government representation to emerge from the bottom up, has been seen by local government officials as a direct threat to decentralized government.[29] In addition, numerous special tasks are routinely delegated to local government without consultation with regional levels of the public administration. Local government officials have become targets of direct dealings with the central administration.[30] Not only have they felt cheated as a certain degree of authority was taken away from them, but, more important, those who became their supervisors often represented members of the old *nomenklatura* (party appointees) transferred from the abandoned *voivodship* (provincial) administration. This was a real psychological blow; those who had been democratically elected found themselves governed once again by representatives of the old Communist regime.

Second, although the initial legislation provided for extended powers of local self-governance, specific laws subsequently passed narrowed those powers drastically, or established structures in such a way that the fulfillment of tasks by local government took place under the supervision of the central state. Third, increased fiscal control of resources by the central level, and the delegation of new responsibilities to local government without the allocation of appropriate financial resources to fulfill them, severely limited the ability of local government officials to exercise powers devolved to them earlier. Finally, a hectic and uncoordinated legislative process, carried out by several generations of politicians with short tenure, resulted in new legislation often in direct conflict with previously enacted laws.

Over the last two years, the problems in Poland have accelerated dramatically. The conflict between central administration and local self-governing bodies became an open one, with the public administration arguing that decentralization had proceeded too far—even further than in such West European countries as France.[31] The proponents of self-government persistently voiced their own concerns, arguing that not enough had been done. Grzegorz Grzelak, deputy chairman of the National Assembly of Local Authorities and former secretary for self-government affairs in the Presidential Chancellery, claimed that

> reform has unfortunately introduced only one, the basic *gmina*, level of local government and defined very narrowly the scope of its activities. In contrast, it defined broadly the duties that local government may be instructed to perform by the national government. In this connection, the system for monitoring and funding these duties was so conceived as to result, in practice, in the government's becoming a sort of watchdog over the local governments receiving these duties.[32]

Others argued that the undesirable establishment of a bipolar system—local self-government and central administration—fosters centralization of the state activities, and that this is taking place despite declarations by all post-1989 governments of their commitment to the establishment of autonomous local self-government.[33]

At the moment the losers are on both sides. The conflict has hampered the implementation of local government reform. It has alienated local government officials and the public at large, and resulted in many resignations, recalls, and referenda. In short, it has contributed to an already unstable political and economic climate. Both sides are in agreement that the ambiguities in law and the lack of a constitution establishing the form of the future Polish state also are to be blamed. Everyone is calling for a second stage of the reform, but, as expected, as many different models are available as there are proponents and opponents.[34]

ROMANIA

In 1991 conditions in Romania were drastically different from those in Poland. The legacy of Nicolae Ceausescu meant the destruction of society, political institutions, the legal system, and the economy.[35] A Romanian discussion about local government reform could not begin until the immediate crisis was over. As Romanian scholars have pointed out, the establishment of local self-government would require not only overcoming the problems that the entire country faces, but, in addition, creating new local institutions and laws that would address the needs of the local population; gaining the central government's support for reform; overcoming the existing local bureaucracy; and, most important, establishing sources of financial support.[36]

The weakness of Romania's government and Parliament, along with the suppressed legal system or the actual lack of one, created a climate of "no authority."[37] The pervasive feeling was that there was no government that could govern and no Parliament that could enact popularly desired laws, since Parliament, which passes laws, did not have the support of the population. Other Central and East European countries had also confronted many of these factors. The case of Romania was different, however, due to the absence of a well-established political opposition, the severity of its problems, and the rural character of the country. In this light, accomplishing decentralization will be problematic; many analysts have argued that the extent and success of local government reform will depend heavily on the response of the rural communities.[38]

The extreme isolation of villages—their lack of access to education, their exclusion from cultural, political, and economic information, and the resultant difficulties in forming local networks—has represented a barrier to change, especially given the limited financial resources. Rural households are poor and primitive; they could not present their full political force unless major resources were directed toward increasing the standard of living in the countryside. Progressive Romanian groups have argued that "in the present situation, sending a hundred political activists into the countryside will achieve less than giving one tractor to the farmers," and that the "only viable economy is the peasant economy."[39] Trăilă Cernescu, a sociologist from the Center for Urban and Regional Sociology, pointed out that at least three conditions need to be met for Romanian local government reform to succeed: political transformation on the rural level; adoption of legislation on land reform and reprivatization; and infusion of capital investments into housing, infrastructure, and education.[40]

A step in the right direction has been made. The Ion Iliescu regime did enact in 1990 a new land law, which gave land to local authorities and set the procedure for its redistribution to previous and potential owners. Even as this decision was being awaited, its limits became clear. Its inadequacy is a result of the demand for financial resources and equipment, and, most important, for guidelines on how to depart from the existing feudal system. Educational opportunities remain limited to members of state cooperatives, excluding new landowners. Furthermore, the legislation has appeared to be too narrow, since it did not include any of the other aspects of agricultural or financial reform, and thus did not set the framework for a more decentralized system. Because almost all of the executive power remained at the central level, peasants were not strong enough to oppose the law.[41] The lack of procedures for local government using the new land law to determine past land ownership, to guarantee the participation of the local population in the decision-making process, and to appraise land facilitated chaos, tensions, and frequent episodes of violence in rural communities.[42]

The response of the central government was limited at best; superficial changes were implemented, but with a clear agenda of maintaining control at the central level and providing legitimacy for the National Salvation Front to position itself correctly for the upcoming local elections.[43] For example, the Governmental Council for Reform, Public Relations, and Information fostered the creation of the Department of Social and Political Structures (DSPS), which carried the status of "a special department for political analysis and planning . . . within the government."[44] The DSPS has been charged with the development of strategies and mechanisms for the implementation of government reform. In its report on past and projected activities, local self-governance failed to find a place among issues to be addressed. What remains is the old ideology of central control and dominance; the report discusses the need for developing mechanisms focused on "sectoral strategic programs: implementation and control programs (the government)" and "the administration (subordinate structures: departments and counties)."[45] Clearly the style of governance from the top down has prevailed.

The issues raised here present serious challenges to local government reform across the region. In light of these challenges, one needs to ask whether the new constitutions are able—or even attempt—to guarantee "democratic decentralization" or local self-government.

The New Constitutions of Central and Eastern Europe

Because these constitutions are works in progress and the process of negotiation continues, it is difficult to present an extensive comparison and to predict their future. Thus the following section is a sketchy description of the tendencies that have emerged in the writing of constitutional documents. Although this section addresses general issues, the next one focuses specifically on the provisions made for local government in these constitutions.

The international community views the new constitutions of the post-Communist societies as a necessary step, one that will acknowledge the emergence of the Central and East European countries as independent nations. Those documents are seen as elements of a new political stability, providing legitimacy through new credentials and thereby enhancing the national capabilities for self-governance. The international community regards constitutions both as mechanisms for imposing restraints on government and as tools for legitimizing the power of those governments. But in the case of Central and Eastern European societies, these constitutions have a more specific meaning: they are often seen as safeguards against the past, and thus as a means for protecting the rights that were abused by the Communist regimes, such as the right to hold meetings, to associate, to demonstrate, and to strike.

In most Western democracies, constitutions have been codified in a single written document (the exception is Great Britain), which presents directives for governing bodies and standards against which their performance can be measured. But because the limitations of governmental activities typically have been formulated only when the danger of losing rights could be foreseen, rights that have not been in question were not subject to explicit protection. This is the case in Central and East European countries, where most of the new governments still fail to distinguish between private and public actors, and thus, in general, standards apply in equal measure to the governmental and private spheres.

Frequently, Western constitutions have not been limited to describing existing functions and circumstances. They have also incorporated the intentions of the nation to achieve new social, political, or economic goals. These so-called prospective provisions have varied, reflecting specific national circumstances, as in the case of the West German Constitution, which refers to missing territory.[46]

In the case of the Central and Eastern European constitutions, these prospective provisions are expressed in a long list of "aspirational rights," which in most cases translate into numerous measures to protect social welfare. For example, the Albanian, Czech, and Polish drafts and the Bulgarian Constitution include the right to work. The right to a healthy environment is written into the Bulgarian Constitution and the drafts of the constitutions of the Czech and Slovak republics, Hungary, and Romania. Several other rights, including education, social security, and recreation, are also protected.

In this context should be mentioned the increasing ethnic strife and nationalist politics in the region. Although most of the constitutions have room for provisions relevant to the protection of minority language and religious rights, several documents have included severe limits on these rights. The Bulgarian and Romanian Constitutions are the most explicit in this respect. The Romanian Constitution declares Romanian as the country's official language, allowing the mayor of Cluj in Transylvania to interpret the document as grounds to eliminate the teaching of Hungarian from schools in his city.[47] The Bulgarian Constitution not only restricts language instruction in schools to Bulgarian but also does not permit ethnically based institutions and organizations to exist. These issues have rarely been mentioned in the context of local self-governance and its rights, even though in reality the consequences, or absence, of any of these provisions will be felt at the local level. In the long run, they will affect relations within local communities and between them and their self-governing authorities.

Such provisions are unique to the Central and Eastern European constitutions. They indicate how strongly Socialist ideology, although theoretically dismissed, in practice continues to influence the process of constitution making. At the same time, these provisions indicate the role that social structures and institutions, as well as values and traditions, exercise in this process.

The issue here is, however, more than the simple acknowledgment of the fact that tradition dies hard. The inclusion of these provisions has presented another dilemma: many of the rights mentioned earlier will never be fulfilled. The fulfillment of others may take years, because currently most of the economies in the region are too weak and too poor to guarantee decent living conditions on a collective level. The constitutions contain rights and guarantees that from the outset cannot be met. What power can such documents have?

From the perspective of newly reestablished local self-government, which has been given the responsibility to deliver most of the goods and services prescribed by those provisions, another question should be raised. How will the populations evaluate the performance of its institutions, and to what extent will they trust a system that cannot do what it is supposed to? Barbara Zawadzka, in her article "The Local Self-Government: Difficulties and Dangers," points out the "danger of alienating the organs of self-government from their own community." Furthermore, she notes, "Neither residents nor their elected council representatives are in a position to improve upon status quo regarding the satisfaction of urgent needs in the areas of housing, construction, the equipping of the material base of education, the health service (not to mention culture), and the expansion and repair of municipal engineering equipment and the like. The impossible situation emanates primarily from the lack of funds."[48] Clearly, one of the functions that local government is supposed to perform—responsiveness to citizens' needs—must await better economic times. The price that will be paid for this delay is yet to be determined.

The foregoing review by no means presents an exhaustive list of the functions and purposes that should be served by constitutions. But it does point out the complexity of the issues that need to be addressed and with which the post-Communist regimes are struggling. The circumstances surrounding the current drafting process are both similar to and drastically different from the experiences of Western democracies in the eighteenth and nineteenth centuries. One might argue that the purpose of presenting a constitution in the United States or France was to obtain sovereignty or to transfer authority and power by establishing a contract between the people and their government. Are the post-Communist societies not discussing the same notion? Is the drafting of the current constitutions not precisely the attempt to write an internal contract between society and authority?

Indeed, this view has been implicit in Poland's attempts to hold nationwide constitutional referenda. In the draft legislation "On the Preparation and Adoption of the Constitution of the Polish Republic," which was prepared for President Lech Wałęsa and introduced to the Parliament in March 1992, Wiktor Osiatyński (former adviser to the constitutional Committee of the Senate) argued that the "constitution should become an occasion for at least a minimal bridging of the increasing gap between the political elites and the society."[49] He argued further that holding a nationwide referendum would provide the best opportunity for educating society about democratic principles. Since the adoption of the constitution would require the approval of the document by two-thirds of the local authorities, the constitution would be tested directly by people. By first promoting a dialogue about the importance and the purpose of the constitution in a democratic state, Osiatyński hopes to bridge the gulf between those who rule and those who are ruled.[50] As a true believer in local democracy, he sees the constitution as a new contract between Polish society and its political leaders.

His proposal has been seen, however, as a direct threat to the power and legitimacy of the Parliament. During the first reading of the proposal, several deputies argued against it. Their arguments claimed that such legislation would "do more harm than good." They "worried" that few people would go to vote, and that those who did would be unable to understand what they were voting for.[51] Finally, the fact that the president would have the power to call a referendum to vote on specific aspects of the constitution, but the Parliament would be denied such powers, was interpreted as yet another attempt by the president to capture more power. In the end the proposal was defeated and sent back to the Legislative Committee for further revisions. On 24 March 1992 an agreement was reached that the new constitution will in the future be adopted by the Parliament and then ratified by the entire nation. It was not until 1 August 1992 that the so-called Little Constitution was approved. It combines a presidential form of government with the parliamentary system. Local self-government found its rightful place among the five chapters of the document.[52]

The current process in Central and Eastern Europe is distinctly different from the writing of Western constitutions because there exists no precedent for shifting from Communist totalitarianism to democracy. Apart from seeking inspiration in its own past constitutions, Poland has looked toward the German and French models of state. Albania has increasingly turned toward the Italian experience and its model of central-local relations.

The process of writing is made additionally troublesome by the fact that among those participating in the preparation of the new constitutions are representatives of the old regimes seeking to retain power. Faced with a dramatic loss of control, these proponents of communism have adopted a wide range of tactics, ranging from a willingness to compromise and engage in coalition building to a far more aggressive opposition to constitutional development. In this light, the fact that currently only Bulgaria and Romania have adopted new constitutions is not surprising. The success of those two countries can be attributed in part to the decision by members of the old Communist guard—who knew that their days were numbered but at the same time wished to preserve whatever legitimacy possible—to choose to present themselves as the founding fathers of progress.

The proliferation of political parties represents another new feature of constitutional development. Whereas in the eighteenth and nineteenth centuries political parties remained outside the constitutional process, today they are playing a significant role in drafting constitutions. And as the parties are themselves in an early stage of development and much of their activity is focused on fighting for legitimacy, their agendas tend to represent particular rather than collective interests; their goal is often to bring liberty and justice to one group but not to others.

On the basis of the discussion in this section, several general conclusions can be reached. First, the contents of the new constitutional documents clearly reflect both the unusual circumstances in which they were created and their countries' legacies. The necessity of addressing past abuses and the perceived need to guard against their resurfacing are visible in every constitution already adopted, as well as in the drafts awaiting approval. Second, the constitutions are indirectly intended to be used as mechanisms for dealing with specific problems. This is often their unstated purpose, but frequently it is an angle used by a variety of political parties in their struggle to gain power. Third, the process of drafting the constitutions in Central and Eastern Europe differs from the circumstances and practices established by Western democracies. The existence of Western models invites comparisons and assistance from foreign advisers. Although on the one hand this input is desirable, especially in current conditions, on the other hand it presents a problem because these new documents are becoming less a product of the societies that will be subject to them. The new constitutions thus threaten to impose foreign practices that will conflict with prevailing values and attitudes. Finally, the political instability and power struggles between numerous parties delay the process and often force temporary solutions.

In this context, the attempt to redefine the meaning, purpose, and content of the new constitutions with respect to the establishment of autonomous local self-government produces mixed results, at best.

Constitutions and Local Self-Government

The first section of this chapter identified several features that could be used to evaluate states' commitment to decentralized government. Two broad areas of concern were discussed: the existence of self-governing institutions rooted in the area under their jurisdiction, and the existence of democratically elected representatives. This is not to say that the mere existence of self-governing institutions is sufficient for achieving decentralization. Rather, it should be seen as an essential element for establishing conditions for the evolution of central-local relations. In effect, depending on the interrelationship between political ideology and the legislative, judicial, and administrative spheres, central-local relations will take different shapes and will lead to the development of different types of decentralized systems.

Existing constitutions have addressed these issues in various ways. Western constitutions lay out the rights and obligations of different levels of government. By distributing responsibilities and powers, and thus establishing a framework for intergovernmental relations, constitutions reinforce the centralized or decentralized form of government. Such an arrangement has been especially crucial in the case of the federal form of government, for instance in Germany.[53] But these constitutions most often refer explicitly to the central and regional levels and only implicitly to the local level. The German and French Constitutions are typical of this arrangement.

Only in Japan have local self-government provisions been written into the core principles of its unitary state Constitution, and India is the only federal state whose constitution contains such a statement.[54] Nevertheless, local government has gained a permanent place in most constitutions; it has become part of the unwritten constitution, reinforced by checks and balances placed within the body of the written document, such as in the United States.[55]

The new constitutions, as well as the drafts of those not yet approved, differ drastically in this regard. All of them contain separate chapters devoted to local government. Yet they vary significantly in the language used to describe constitutional provisions. From that perspective they can be categorized into two groups: (1) those that make a clear reference to local self-government: Hungary (Chapter 9: local autonomous governing bodies); Poland (Chapter 11: local government); Bulgaria (Chapter 7: local self-government and local administration); Ukraine

(Chapter 7: city and regional self-governance); Estonia (Chapter 14: local government); and Lithuania (Chapter 8: local governments); (2) those that avoid direct reference to local government but emphasize only administrative issues, or make no reference to either of the two: Romania (Chapter 5: local public administration); Czech Republic (Chapter 7: territorial self-administration and state administration); Slovak Republic (Chapter 8: national committees); and Albania (Chapter 4: organization and administration of local government). Although this is only a simple classification, it reflects an important distinction in the understanding of the role and importance that local government should have in the overall structure of new democratic states.

Analysts who engage in the comparative study of constitutions often examine the order in which individual matters are addressed as a measure of their importance. From this point of view, the attitude toward local government seems to be consistent throughout Central and Eastern Europe: chapters on local government are placed at the end of the constitutions. Still, there are some interesting differences in this regard. For example, the Hungarian Constitution (the oldest "new" constitution, passed in 1989) is the most explicit about autonomy and self-governance at the local level. In fact, it places this chapter before the one addressing fundamental rights and duties of citizens (Chapter 12), but nonetheless almost at the end of the document. On the other hand, in the Romanian Constitution (one of the two adopted by the new government, although not by the democratically elected Parliament) the chapter on local government is included in Title III on Public Authorities (out of a total of nine titles). It is located before the articles and chapters on the economy, property rights, and the financial system. One might conclude from this that Romania is more committed to local autonomy and self-governance; in fact, however, the reverse is true, which points out the obvious limitation of this form of analysis.

If constitutions vary in the way in which they explicitly discuss local government, they also differ in the extent to which they discuss it. There is a tendency in countries that were more oppressed and controlled in the past (for example, Albania and Ukraine) to include more detail in their new constitutions or in their drafts, whereas countries that in the past had slightly more flexibility and freedom show less concern with details. This discrepancy is not entirely unexpected, for two reasons. First, as discussed earlier, a general desire to guard and protect is currently prevalent. Rights and responsibilities that in the past were not guaranteed are now often included, even when this appears to lead to an overregulation of local government and to the inclusion of matters that should be discussed in specific laws, as in the case of details regarding the specification of the duties and responsibilities of local government.

Second, this excess detail results from attempts by some groups to use the new constitutions to their advantage. Constitutions, due to their supreme legal status, are difficult to change, and therefore including certain elements will make these features more permanent. For example, in the case of Albania, the local government provisions intended to be included in the constitution were on the one hand extensive and on the other hand incomplete. If a proposed draft had been adopted, it would have introduced an incomplete but highly centralized system of administration. Week-long working sessions, which I conducted with members of Albania's Parliamentary Local Government Subcommittee of the Constitutional Drafting Commission in December 1991, pointed out that the inclusion of the large number of details could also be interpreted in the context of the political struggle.[56] Because constitutions are difficult to change (in the case of Albania a two-thirds vote in the Parliament and an electoral majority in the referendum are required), by including many details the writers could secure the protection of certain elements of the new system. A similar tendency for intense concern with details is also apparent in the draft constitution of Ukraine.

The existence of indigenous institutions at the local level is relatively easy to measure. The greater difficulty is assessing the extent to which they are indeed self-governing.[57] At this point, it is difficult to generalize: only two new constitutions have been adopted (Bulgaria and Romania), several others are at various stages of drafting, and Hungary is not even considering the rewriting of its constitution. Nonetheless, it is possible to lay out a framework for comparing central-local relations based on the following elements:

(1) The establishment of local councils or executive boards (Romania, Estonia, Czech Republic, Slovak Republic, Ukraine, Lithuania, Bulgaria)

(2) Permission to create municipal associations and other alliances (Hungary, Estonia, Czech Republic, Ukraine, Bulgaria)

(3) Indication of the separation of powers between the executive and legislative branches (Poland, Hungary, Ukraine, Lithuania, Bulgaria)

(4) Devolution of legislative power to the local level (Poland, Hungary, Ukraine)

(5) Goals of local government are to satisfy either popular needs (Poland, Hungary, Slovak Republic, Lithuania) or other needs (Romania—public services in country interests)

(6) Right of local governments to judicial appeal (Poland, Hungary, Lithuania, Bulgaria)

(7) Legal status for the local government (Poland)

(8) Right of local governments to set taxes (Poland, Romania, Hungary, Slovak Republic, Ukraine, Lithuania)

(9) Right of local governments to receive central government grants and subsidies (Poland, Hungary, Slovak Republic, Lithuania, Bulgaria)

(10) Right of local governments to establish independent budgets (Estonia, Czech Republic, Slovak Republic, Ukraine, Lithuania, Bulgaria)

(11) Guarantees of property and ownership rights (Poland, Hungary, Czech Republic, Slovak Republic, Lithuania, Bulgaria) or right to govern and maintain (Ukraine)

(12) Right to proclaim ordinances (Poland, Estonia, Czech Republic, Slovak Republic)

(13) Clear reference to independent governance at local level (Hungary, Czech Republic, Poland, Estonia, Ukraine)

(14) Reference to economic independence (Czech Republic)

(15) Clear requirements for public consultation prior to decision making (Slovak Republic, Lithuania)

(16) Right to suspend local government by the central administration (Estonia, Romania, Ukraine)

(17) Strong interference of state administration in local government affairs (Romania, Albania, Ukraine, Lithuania).

What conclusions can be drawn from this list? First, visible tendencies toward centralization and difficulties in conceptualization of local government reform are not easy to detect in the constitutions. Constitutions are meant to guarantee fundamentals, with subsequent laws addressing details, and this is the case here.[58] One may conclude, however, that by providing several of the listed guarantees, the new constitutions are establishing the general principles of local autonomy. In only a couple of cases (Albania and Ukraine) is the structure of central-local relations left incomplete.

Second, although most of the constitutions protect the crucial rights of local government (such as budgets and property), the central state can still curtail the extent to which the local government is able to exercise them. For example, although local government can establish local taxes in general, it may be told specifically by the center what the sources of these revenues should be. In areas where the assigned sources do not provide for a high level of income, the right to collect funds will have minimal de facto effect on the local budget.[59]

Third, the most often referenced statements are those related to the independence of governance (point 13) at the local level, yet a more careful examination of other statements indicates that this commitment is not necessarily unquestionable. Indeed, in a few cases the constitutions provide the central administration with the right to suspend local government; thus, though in principle these countries are committed to local autonomy, the central state retains control over it (for example, Ukraine and Estonia).

Fourth, because the actual framework of decentralized government will be shaped by practice and will stem from political negotiations and subsequent legal initiatives and changes, numerous provisions (for example, those related to central state intervention in local affairs) could bring further control or could be eliminated altogether in due process.[60]

In summary, the new constitutions in general protect local autonomy, but at the same time there remains a clear indication of tendencies to retain central control. Indeed, it seems that only the structure has changed, though the power distribution remains the same, at least in the Romanian Constitution and in the Ukrainian and Albanian drafts.

In regard to the second issue, determining local autonomy, a clear commitment to local democratic elections can be found in the new constitutions. In general, provisions are made for direct election of local councillors, and in few cases mayors are also mentioned. Not all constitutions make explicit reference to the duration of the term of office. Those Central and East European countries that did specify set limits of four years. In the newly independent post-Soviet states, the term is shorter: in Ukraine and Lithuania two years and in Estonia three years. Such limitations, of course, imply a guarantee that subsequent elections will be called. Constitutions vary in regard to limitations imposed on the potential candidates, although in general all citizens of the specific locality who are eighteen and older can vote.

This review clearly indicates that citizens' participation in governmental activities is guaranteed by all constitutions. Several constitutions also specify the need for public consultation and provide for local referenda.[61] It is interesting to note, however, that although the government has provided those liberties, the people have not necessarily exercised them when the opportunity arose. In many Central and Eastern European countries, voter turnout in local elections has been surprisingly low. In the Czech and Slovak republics, just over 30 percent of eligible voters participated in the fall 1990 election of their representatives to the local government. Similarly low participation in elections on the local level has been observed in Hungary, where in many districts elections needed to be repeated for lack of the necessary minimum of votes (40.18 percent in first round and 28.94 percent in the second round). In Romania, although over 64.9 percent of eligible voters came to the polls in February 1992, the public was dissatisfied with the results. The Romanian Opinion Poll Institute, in a postelection survey conducted for the national news agency ROMPRES in 1992, stated, "The vote in the local polls in Romania was strongly affected by a general climate of frustration and concern over the emergence of overwhelming, almost paralysing social issues . . . a lower standard of living, insecure employment, diminished legality, spiralling corruption, hesitations in the rural reform and a prevalent feeling that the situation will only get worse."[62]

Although the issue of low voter turnout is not the subject of this inquiry, it is nonetheless symptomatic of the difficulties in establishing participatory democracy in post-Communist societies, and it will undoubtedly surface again during the next round of local elections.[63] The analysts of turnouts in the region were consistent in pointing out that ultimately it is the overall political and economic climate that will affect voting patterns.

Many difficulties lie ahead for the development and maintenance of local democracy in post-Communist states, but no one doubts that each nation in its own way is striving to reach that goal. The constitutional dilemmas presented here are shaping the future structure of Central and East European states. At the same time, a political struggle among hundreds of new parties delays this process of transformation. This is inevitable when building a new order—on the one hand there is the push for individual freedoms, on the other hand there is the reluctance to provide full devolution of power to autonomous local institutions. The signs are, however, that those countries that make explicit reference to local self-government in their constitutions are indeed committed to the establishment of self-governing institutions and to the increase in the discretionary decision-making powers of their local governments.

Notes

The following drafts and final constitutions were consulted during the preparation of this chapter:

(1) Albania, Constitution of, November 1991. Draft prepared by Constitutional Drafting Commission. Unofficial translation. Tirana, Albania.

(2) The Republic of Bulgaria, Constitution of, July 1991. Final text adopted by Grand National Assembly on 12 July 1991. Sofia Press Agency. Sofia, Bulgaria.

(3) The Czech Republic, Constitution of, July 1990. First working draft. Working translation. Prague, Czech Republic.

(4) The Republic of Estonia, Constitution of, April 1992. Draft prepared by Constitutional Assembly. Unofficial translation. Tallin, Estonia.

(5) The Republic of Hungary, Constitution of, 1990. Published in *Hungarian Rules of Law in Force*, vol. 1, no. 26. Budapest, Hungary.

(6) The Republic of Lithuania, Constitution of, February 1992. Draft prepared by the Committee for the Preparation of the Draft of the Constitution. Vilnius, Lithuania.

(7) The Republic of Poland, Constitution of, October 1991. Draft prepared by the Constitutional Committee of Sejm. Warsaw, Poland.

(8) Romania, Constitution of, 1991. Final text adopted by the Constitutional Assembly on 21 November 1991. Agentia Nationala de Presa, ROMPRES. Bucharest, Romania.

(9) The Slovak Republic, Constitution of, 1990. First working draft prepared by the Slovak National Council for Drafting the Constitution of the Slovak Republic.

(10) Ukraine, Constitution of, January 1992. Draft prepared by the Working Group of the Constitutional Commission of the Parliament of Ukraine. Kiev, Ukraine.

[1]W. Hardy Wickwar, *The Political Theory of Local Government* (Columbia: University of South Carolina Press, 1970), 82–83.

[2]William G. Andrews, *Constitutions and Constitutionalism*, 3d ed. (Princeton, N.J.: D. Van Nostrand Company, 1963), 176.

[3]Eight constitutional drafts (Albania, Czech Republic, Estonia, Hungary, Lithuania, Poland, Slovak Republic, Ukraine) and two constitutions (Romania and Bulgaria) have been reviewed.

[4]In the summer and fall of 1991 I visited Poland, Hungary, Bulgaria, the Czech and Slovak republics, Romania, and Albania and conducted lengthy interviews regarding local government reforms with local government officials, parliamentary and government leaders, politicians, lawyers, and citizens.

[5]Brian C. Smith, *Decentralization: The Territorial Dimension of the State* (London: Allen & Unwin, 1985), 18.

[6]Smith, *Decentralization*, 91.

[7]Smith, *Decentralization*, 59.

[8]Charles M. Wilson, *Essays on Local Government* (Oxford: Blackwell, 1948), 13; Smith, *Decentralization*, 18–20.

[9]James R. O'Connor, *The Fiscal Crisis of the State* (New York: St. Martin's Press, 1973), 124–144; Claus Offe, "The Theory of the Capitalist State and the Problem of the Policy Formation," in Leon Lindberg, Robert Alford, Colin Crouch, and Claus Offe, eds., *Stress and Contradiction in Modern Capitalism* (Lexington, Mass.: Lexington Books, 1975), 125–144.

[10]Smith, *Decentralization*, 40. For criticism of "dual state" thesis see Peter Saunders, "Reflections on the Dual Politics Thesis: The Argument, Its Origins and Its Critics," in Michael Goldsmith and Søren Villadsen, eds., *Urban Political Theory and the Management of the Fiscal Stress* (Hants, England: Gower Publishing Company, 1986).

[11]Marian Kallas, *Projekty Konstytucyjne 1989–1991* (Constitutional drafts 1989–1991) (Warsaw: Wydawnictwo Sejmowe, 1992).

[12]Personal interviews with Mayor Hargitai Fanos conducted in June 1991, in the City Office of Nagynyarad.

[13]These comments are based on personal interviews conducted in May 1991 in Budapest with Pál Belluszky, council member of District 1, Budapest; Gábor Demszky, mayor of Budapest; and with Ilona P. Kovács, political scientist at the Hungarian Academy of Sciences, Pécs.

[14]Lajos Szabó, "Autonomous Local Governments Are Waiting for Laws," *Joint Publication Research Service—Eastern Europe Report* [hereinafter *JPRS-EER*]-91-044, 5 April 1991 (citing *Uj Dunantuli Naplo*, 5 January 1991, 3).

[15]Comments based on personal interviews with the members of the Bulgarian Parliamentary Local Government Commission: Boris T. Kolev, Stefan V. Gaitandjiev, and Snezhana Bothusharova, conducted in Sofia, June 1991.

[16]These comments are based on personal interviews conducted in June 1991 with Mayor Mihail Mihov of the District Council of Plovdiv.

[17]Interview with Ilona Kovács.

[18]For extensive discussion see Jerzy Regulski, "Polish Local Government in Transition," *Environment and Planning* 7 (1989): 423–44; Joanna Regulska, "Democratic Elections and Political Restructuring in Poland," in John O'Loughlin and Herman Van der Wusten, eds., *New Political Geography of Eastern Europe* (London: Belhaven Press, 1993): 217–234; Jan Kubik, "Local

Government: The Basic Laws and Most Common Problems," *Report on Eastern Europe*, 31 May 1991: 19–22.

[19]See Michael E. Bell and Joanna Regulska, "Centralization Versus Decentralization: The Case of Financing Autonomous Local Governments in Poland," in Pierre Pestieau, ed., *Public Finance in a World of Transition*, Proceeding of the 47th Congress of the International Institute of Public Finance/Institut International de Finances Publiques, St. Petersburg, 1991; 1993.

[20]This statement is based on comments made by Ambassador Jerzy Regulski, former Plenipotentiary for Local Self-Government Reform in the cabinet of Prime Minister Tadeusz Mazowiecki. See also Regulski, "The Beginning of the Road: Local Self-Government," *Rzeczpospolita*, no. 138 (16–17 June 1990): 2.

[21]Jerzy Stępień, personal communication, 1990.

[22]"Ustawa z dn. 17 maja 1990r. o podziale zadan i kompetencji okreslonych w ustawach szczególnych pomiędzy organy gminy a organy administracji rządowej oraz o zmianie niektórych ustaw" (The legal division of areas of competence and functions between the bodies of local government and those of government administration, 17 May 1990), *Dziennik Ustaw Rzeczpospolitej Polskiej*, no. 34, 26 May 1990.

[23]Jan Kubik, "Local Government: The Basic Laws and Most Common Problems," Włodzimierz Kocon, "Conflicts in Local Government," paper presented at the conference "The Development of Local Democracy and Applied Conflict Resolution in Poland: A Dialogue," Warsaw, 23–25 May 1991.

[24]For extensive discussion see Jerzy Regulski, "Czy nie mogł Pan złożyć dymisji?" (Couldn't you resign?) *Wspólnota*, 9 February 1991; Regulski, "Rejony były błędem: Oddanie władzy trzeba było wymuszać" (Districts were mistake: Forceful confiscation of power), *Gazeta Wyborcza*, 22 February 1991: 11; Michał Kulesza, "Związek? Powiat? Wyższy Szczebel?" (Association? District? Higher Administrative Level?) Roundtable discussion. *Wspolnota* 37 (27 November 1990): 13–15.

[25]This comment is based on remarks made by Jerzy Kozłowski in Poznań at the Meeting of the National Assembly of Local Authorities, July 1990.

[26]Grzegorz Grzelak, "A Strong and Modern State," *Lad*, no. 5 (3 February 1991): 4.

[27]Jerzy Stępień, "Samorząd terytorialny w nowej konstytucji" (Local self-government in the new constitution), paper presented to the constitution drafters at the Senate hearing on 21 November 1990.

[28]Stępień, "Samorząd terytorialny."

[29]See Grzelak, "A Strong and Modern State," Jerzy Stępień, "Kilka ostrożnych kroków" (A few cautious steps), mimeograph, Warsaw, 3 February 1991; Josef Antal, "Diminishing Party Policy Considerations," *Foreign Broadcast Information Service* [hereinafter *FBIS*] EEU-91-204, 22 October 1991 (citing *Magyar Hirlap*, 16 October 1991), 23.

[30]Stępień, "Kilka ostrożnych kroków."

[31]Barbara Helka, "Koniec rejonowej administracji rządowej?" (The end of Subregional public administration?), *Rzeczpospolita*, no. 101 (30 April–1 May 1991).

[32]Grzelak, "A Strong and Modern State."

[33]Lech Mażewski, "Regionalizm: trzy ostrożne kroki" (Regionalization: three cautious steps), *Rzeczpospolita*, 7 July 1992, no. 158 (3196): 3.

[34]Lech Mażewski, "Regionalizm"; Jerzy Stępień et al., *"Wstępne Zatożenia Przebudowy Administracji Publicznej"* (Introductory assumptions for reconstruction of public administration), Committee for Reorganization of Public Administration, Warsaw, March 1992; Wisła Surażska, "Miedzy centrum a prowincją: Polska nie może czekać w administracyjnej próżni na polityczną stabilizację centrum" (Between central and provincial Poland: Poland cannot be in an administrative vacuum waiting for political stability of the central institutions), *Rzeczpospolita*, 16 July 1992, no. 166 (3204): 3.

[35]Michael Shafir, "Romania," *RFE/RL Research Report*, no. 27 (3 July 1992): 34–40.

[36]These comments are based on personal interviews conducted with sociologists Georgeta M. Gheorghe and Trăilă Cernescu from the Center for Urban and Regional Sociology, Bucharest, August 1991.

[37]Personal interview with Trăilă Cernescu.

[38]Personal interviews with Trăilă Cernescu, and with Petre M. Băcanu, editor of *Romania Libera*, Bucharest, August 1991.

[39]Personal interviews with Petre M. Băcanu.

[40]Personal interview with Trăilă Cernescu.

[41]Personal interview with Petre M. Băcanu.

[42]Personal interview with Georgeta M. Gheorghe.

[43]Dimitri Coru-Chirca, "Will the American Come?" *FBIS-EEU-92-047*, 10 March 1992, p. 28 (citing *Romania Libera*, 3 March 1992, 1).

[44]"Annual Report of the Council for Reform, Public Relations, and Information," mimeograph, August 1991, Government of Romania.

[45]"Annual Report of the Council for Reform," 19.

[46]Andrews, *Constitutions and Constitutionalism*, 25.

[47]Shafir, "Romania," 37.

[48]Barbara Zawadzka, "The Local Self-Government: Difficulties and Dangers," *JPRS-EER-91-068*, 20 May 1991, 4 (citing *Rzeczpospolita*, 12 April 1991, no. 86 [3029]: 3).

[49]Interview with Wiktor Osiatyński, "Not gift but social contract" in *Gazeta Wyborcza*, 19 March 1992, no. 67 (839): 3.

[50]Personal communication, Wiktor Osiatyński, 1992.

[51]*Gazeta Wyborcza*, 20 March 1992, no. 68 (840): 1.

[52]For discussion see "Mała konstytucja: ile komu władzy" (The small constitution: to whom how much power), *Rzeczpospolita*, 7 August 1992, no. 485 (3228), p. viii; and Lech Winiarski, "Twórczy kompromis" (Creative compromise), *Wspolnota*, 15 August 1992, no. 33 (127), 3.

[53]Andrews, *Constitutions and Constitutionalism*, 91, 119.

[54]Wickwar, *Political Theory of Local Government*, 87.

[55]Wickwar, *Political Theory of Local Government*, 44.

[56]I participated in a mission of the American Bar Association's Central and East European Law Initiative to Tirana, Albania, 2–9 December 1991. The delegation was hosted by the Parliamentary Local Government Subcommittee of the Constitutional Drafting Commission. The three-member team worked on the local government provisions proposed for inclusion in the new constitution.

[57]Eight drafts and two constitutions were reviewed for the presence or absence of these features. Although the presence of some statements can serve as a good indicator of the existence of a specific element, the absence of such statements does not rule out the possibility of its existence. Caution should be used when interpreting this list, since the subsequent drafts in some cases might already have altered the situation described here.

[58]The relevant elements are included in points 1–7.

[59]See points 10, 11, 12, 14, and 19.

[60]The pertinent rights are included in points 16 and 17.

[61]See especially the constitutions of Hungary, Lithuania, Poland, and the Slovak Republic.

[62]"Institute Examines Turnout, Trends," *FBIS-EEU-92-047*, 10 March 1992 (citing *Bucharest ROMPRES*, 10 March 1992): 28.

[63]For more discussion, see Regulska, "Democratic Elections and Political Restructuring in Poland," 228–232.

Chapter 6

The New East European Constitutional Courts

Herman Schwartz

Before World War II, few European states had constitutional courts, and virtually none exercised any significant judicial review over legislation.[1] After 1945 that changed. West Germany, Italy, Austria, Cyprus, Turkey, Yugoslavia, Greece, Spain, Portugal, and even France, one of the last bastions of parliamentary sovereignty, created tribunals with power to annul legislative enactments inconsistent with constitutional requirements.[2] Many of these courts, most notably the German Constitutional Court, have become powerful institutions. It was hardly surprising that the newly liberated nations in East and Central Europe and the former Soviet Union have decided to establish such courts.[3]

Because these countries have only recently shaken off Communist domination—and even that is not clear in Romania—some of these new courts, such as those in Czechoslovakia and Romania, have barely begun to function. Of the regularly functioning East European constitutional courts, some have operated with surprising independence, often insisting on protection of human rights and the rule of law. In this respect, these courts are following the lead of many of their West European predecessors.[4]

This chapter will describe some aspects of the different tribunals in Russia, Hungary, Poland, Czechoslovakia, Bulgaria, and Romania and will compare them with each other and with the U.S. Supreme Court. The first part will explore some basic differences between the American and continental systems of judicial review and describe the functions of the new East European constitutional courts. The second part will analyze a few decisions of the Russian Constitutional Court and then summarize some recent activities of a few other new constitutional courts.

Constitutional Courts and Judicial Review

DIFFUSE VERSUS CONCENTRATED: THE AMERICAN AND EUROPEAN MODELS

Most of the disparities between the Eastern European constitutional courts and the U.S. Supreme Court are rooted in differences in the fundamental premises underlying the respective institutions. The U.S. Supreme Court is not a court for constitutional issues in the strict sense, but rather the final appellate tribunal in the American judicial system.[5] Although it is the highest court in the system, the Supreme Court is still just a part of the federal judiciary, adjudicating controversies referred to it from the lower federal and state courts. While engaged in the business of resolving these disputes, the U.S. Supreme Court may decide constitutional questions, interpret federal law, assert the supremacy of federal law over state law, and resolve jurisdictional conflicts between state and federal governments, or within the federal government itself. Like any other federal court, the Supreme Court performs all these functions only as incident to settling live controversies between contending parties in a suit brought into the system for resolution. The U.S. Constitution does not explicitly grant the Supreme Court power to review and possibly annul legislative acts, and some judges and scholars still challenge the exercise of such power, at least in certain cases.[6] With respect to this dispute-resolving function, the U.S. Supreme Court resembles the traditional highest courts in conventional European judicial systems, although the latter are not empowered to strike down legislative enactments in the course of their adjudicatory activities. If the Supreme Court can resolve the case without deciding any fundamental issues, constitutional or otherwise, it is obliged to do so. Usually, the narrower the basis for the decision, the better.

One consequence of the incidental nature of such constitutional decision making has been that, since all courts are supposed to resolve these cases completely, definitively, and without the need for further judicial action by a higher court, all United States courts can resolve the constitutional issues. Comparativists call this approach the "diffuse system" of judicial review.

The continental European system of constitutional judicial review differs theoretically. As opposed to the American diffuse system, the European approach is to concentrate the power to review the constitutionality of legislation in one special tribunal that is not a part of the ordinary judiciary and does not adjudicate conventional litigation,[7] a function left for ordinary courts. Thus the constitutional provisions for the constitutional courts do not usually appear in the judiciary section of European constitutions but in a separate section, after the articles on the structure of the national government.[8]

Unlike its counterpart in the United States, the European constitutional court's primary function is not to adjudicate controversies between individuals or between them and their government, but to provide interpretations of its nation's constitution, regardless of how the interpretational issue arises. As one Italian expert explained, the European constitutional court "is neither part of the judicial order, nor part of the judicial organization in its widest sense: . . . the Constitutional Court remains outside the traditional categories of state power. It is an independent power whose function consists in [e]nsuring that the Constitution is respected in all areas."[9]

The constitutional court thus stands apart from the rest of the governmental apparatus, including the judiciary, and is responsible only to the nation's constitution and the values it incorporates. It is concerned not with resolving concrete live disputes between people or with their government, but with "defense of the constitution."

Accordingly, German, French, and other continental constitutional tribunals have neither hesitated nor apologized when issuing wide-ranging decisions on basic constitutional issues, often drawing on unwritten or historical principles and values.[10] A French decision on freedom of association and an abortion decision in Germany are good examples: the French court drew on the preamble to the 1789 Declaration on the Rights of Man for its ruling;[11] the German court interpreted the "right to life" in Article 2 (2) 1 to limit abortion rights, relying in part on its notions of "the dignity of man" and sociopolitical considerations, as well as its reaction to the Nazi policy of destroying "life unworthy to live."[12]

The new East European constitutional courts appear willing to take a similarly broad approach to constitutional analysis. With the exception of the Russian court, virtually no political-question limits restrain the jurisprudence of many of these courts. Indeed, contrary to U.S. practice, the justiciability provisions in many of these countries seem designed not to impede but rather to encourage judicial resolution of volatile political disputes. And East European political figures have not hesitated to go to their constitutional courts in highly charged political situations.

The broad decision-making powers and authority to resolve political issues that are vested in the constitutional courts extend far beyond the range of the typical civil law judge, whose approach to the judicial function is usually narrow and mechanical. As Louis Favoreu notes:

> Continental European [civil law] judges are "career judges" and in a sense bureaucrats. Before an all-powerful parliament they do not dare insist on their conception of the law. This is especially true in view of the fact that, unlike American judges who mostly pass on the constitutionality of state laws, European judges would have to verify—above all and even sometimes exclusively—the constitutionality of national laws, emanating from the representatives of the whole of the nation. That is why Continental European judges have never dared to start down the path to judicial review.[13]

Indeed, in cases of statutory ambiguity, the French originally insisted that judges refer the matter back to the legislature, to resolve the ambiguity, though this idea was abandoned quickly.[14] This attitude was obviously a far cry from how European constitutional court judges view themselves today.[15] In this respect, judges on the constitutional courts in Europe are much closer to their American counterparts than to their colleagues in the regular continental judiciary.[16]

Why have all these countries adopted such institutions? After all, the European tradition involves parliamentary supremacy. The answer lies partly in these nations' quest to protect civil and political liberties. For apart from the East Europeans' desire to follow Western models in order to be thought fit to join the Western community of nations, East Europeans have realized that while one must rely primarily on popular sovereignty in a democracy, the legislature and the executive may well abuse their powers, and an independent judiciary is necessary to protect the rights of the people.[17] Judge Learned Hand once noted that when liberty dies in the hearts of a nation, "no constitution, no court, no law can save it."[18] This is quite true, but a court can interpose obstacles to tyranny, and it can embarrass the tyrant. Moreover, as the American Founding Fathers realized, even a free society is prone to "ill humors" that can oppress its minorities and others.[19] Free and independent courts can provide some protection against this as well.

THE NEW EAST EUROPEAN CONSTITUTIONAL COURTS

What kinds of institutions are these East European constitutional courts? Perhaps the best way to answer this is to describe what they are supposed to do—the subject-matter jurisdiction of the constitutional courts of Bulgaria, Czechoslovakia, Hungary, Russia, Poland, and Romania, their interpretive and adjudicative roles, as well as the other functions, some of which seem quite different (though perhaps only superficially) from those required of the U.S. Supreme Court. Justiciability matters such as standing and mootness will be examined. Then the discussion will turn to the individual courts' authority to enforce their decisions and the selection and tenure of the constitutional court judges.

Subject-Matter Jurisdiction

The constitutional jurisdiction of the U.S. Supreme Court, as set out in Article III, Section 2 of the U.S. Constitution, does not differ much from the jurisdiction of an ordinary American court. In practice, the Supreme Court has come to limit its jurisdiction almost entirely to cases involving important questions of federal statutory and constitutional law and review of federal agency action. Indeed, except for state and federal criminal cases, the bulk of the U.S. Supreme Court's civil work in recent years has been the interpretation of federal statutes.

Unlike the U.S. Supreme Court, the new East European courts concentrate their judicial activity on constitutional questions. They do not often deal with such matters as statutory interpretation, which are handled by the traditional court system, except when necessary to resolve jurisdictional conflicts and the occasional referral from ordinary courts.[20]

All six countries under discussion—Bulgaria, Czechoslovakia, Hungary, Russia, Poland, and Romania—explicitly grant their constitutional courts the authority to determine the constitutionality of federal[21] laws and, in some cases, other legislative acts. Each of these nations, except perhaps Romania, authorizes review of presidential and ministerial decrees and orders. Only three—Czechoslovakia, Romania, and Russia—explicitly authorize their courts to review the constitutionality of state or local law.[22] Poland, Hungary, and Russia give their courts the authority to review the constitutionality of treaties, either proposed or adopted. Czechoslovakia, Hungary, and Bulgaria appear to consider treaties superior to domestic law,[23] whereas Romania, Russia, and Poland do not explicitly authorize their courts to compare domestic law with international treaties or international law. One rather odd piece of jurisdiction appears in both the Romanian and Hungarian Constitutions: the authority to rule on the constitutionality of parliamentary procedures.[24]

Jurisdictional disputes also fall within the East European constitutional courts' explicit subject-matter jurisdiction. Federal-state disputes are mentioned in the Czechoslovak, Bulgarian, Russian, and Hungarian provisions. Intragovernmental disputes between and among the president, Parliament, and cabinet are also included in the Bulgarian and Russian laws, whereas Czechoslovakia and Hungary empower their courts to resolve interagency disputes.[25]

Federal-state disputes raise particularly delicate questions that will likely test these courts' authority. Such disputes are especially sensitive in ethnically diverse nations like Russia, where the Republic of Tatarstan's decision to hold its referendum despite a Russian Constitutional Court declaration that doing so was unconstitutional raised questions about the Constitutional Court's ability to enforce its decisions,[26] and in Czechoslovakia, where federal-state questions reflect deep divisions in the country between Czechs and Slovaks.

The Czechoslovak Constitutional Court Act does not contain a clause making Czech or Slovak law—either constitutional or statutory—subordinate to Czechoslovak federal *legislation*, but only to the Czechoslovak federal Constitution.[27] Even the Czechoslovak court's authority to subordinate Czech or Slovak constitutional acts (though not ordinary legislation) to the

Czechoslovak federal Constitution will become effective only if and when a new federal constitution is adopted.[28] This may not occur for a long time, if ever, given the current impasse between the Czechs and Slovaks over a new constitution. The impact of the federal Constitutional Court's ruling that a Czech or Slovak constitutional act violates the federal Constitution is also uncertain. When the court finds an ordinary law unconstitutional, the appropriate legislature has six months to change it, and if it fails to do so, the law becomes "null and void." But this ruling does "not apply to Constitutional Acts" of the republics.[29] The Czechoslovak Constitutional Court Act is silent, however, as to what is then the constitutional status of a republic's constitutional law that the court has found inconsistent with the federal Constitution.[30] The court's jurisdiction over such disputes may thus be quite limited, even if its rulings are obeyed in full, which itself remains to be seen.

The Constitutions of Czechoslovakia, Russia, and Hungary specifically grant their courts human rights jurisdiction. Under these provisions, private parties may bring complaints directly to those constitutional courts, subject to certain procedural requirements. No such right exists in the other three countries, where it seems that human rights issues may be raised only in the regular court systems. Some of the problems this procedure creates will be discussed below.

Romania, Bulgaria, and Czechoslovakia also give their constitutional courts authority beyond the adjudicative function. Constitutional courts in these countries may outlaw political parties and political associations for "unconstitutionality," as in the case of Romania and Bulgaria, or unconstitutional or illegal "activities," as in Czechoslovakia.[31]

In several countries, the constitutional courts supervise elections. Romania, for example, gives its court the responsibility of "watch[ing] over the observance of the procedure for the election of the president of Romania and to confirm the returns thereof . . . [the] organization and holding of a referendum and to confirm its returns . . . [and] check[ing] on . . . the exercise of legislative initiative by citizens."[32] The Bulgarian court is required to monitor parliamentary as well as presidential elections. Turning over the delicate function of supervising elections to the constitutional courts seems to reflect a confidence that these institutions are above the fray and can be entrusted with supervising political activities.[33] Finally, since the bulk of the European constitutional courts' work is original jurisdiction, they may take evidence and make factual findings, unlike the overwhelmingly appellate U.S. Supreme Court.

Justiciability

U.S. justiciability requirements enable the federal courts to avoid deciding many questions of major constitutional significance, a goal frequently invoked in American constitutional jurisprudence.[34] The U.S. Supreme Court has limited its own authority by requiring that constitutional issues affecting legislation may only be challenged through adversary proceedings. Issues may not be raised before their resolution becomes necessary or in broader terms than are required by the specific facts of the issue before the court. Challengers must demonstrate that they were injured by the statute's operation or have availed themselves of its benefits. Furthermore, if the record before the court presents some nonconstitutional ground on which the case may be disposed of, the court must rely on the nonconstitutional rationale. As Justice Wiley Rutledge wrote in 1947:

> The policy's ultimate foundations, some if not all of which also sustain the jurisdictional limitation . . . are found in the delicacy of that function, particularly in view of possible consequences for others stemming also from constitutional roots; the comparative finality of those consequences; the consideration due to the judgment of other repositories of constitutional power concerning the scope of their authority; the necessity, if government is to function constitutionally, for each to keep within its power, including the courts; the inherent limitations of the judicial process, arising especially from its largely negative character and limited resources of enforcement; withal in the paramount importance of constitutional adjudication in our system.[35]

These notions are alien to the Europeans, who have created the constitutional court for the express purpose of deciding constitutional issues, not evading them. Unlike the U.S. model, standing is not based solely on the adversary process; abstract judicial review is welcomed, rather than avoided; questions may be considered both before the question arises as well as after it has been rendered moot; and finally, political questions lie well within the European court's judicial authority.

Who May Sue   The United States law of standing, which has gone through several phases, is premised on the nineteenth-century notion of a conventional lawsuit—two adversaries, one of whom has allegedly been injured by the other and is seeking redress through the courts. The East European approach is quite different. First, for most kinds of cases, these constitutions or constitutional acts generally allow one or more categories of public official—and only such officials—to bring a given issue to the constitutional court at a certain time with no additional requirements. This is consistent with the original purpose of these courts: to ensure compliance with the constitutionally mandated government structure and to provide legislators with impartial and expert advice about the constitutionality of proposed or enacted legislation.[36] Private persons are allowed to sue only occasionally. Human rights violations are one occasion that has been added, and even there the specific requirements that plaintiffs must meet to achieve standing are often somewhat unclear, possibly for the kinds of considerations the U.S. Supreme Court has fashioned.[37]

The Bulgarian provisions seem most restrictive: standing is given only to the president, a fifth of the national legislature, the government, the chief prosecutor, both the Supreme Administrative Court and the highest regular court, and in some cases, municipal councils; no direct private access seems available.[38]

Other countries are much more open. The Hungarian court's approach is the most generous. In Hungary, anyone can challenge "legal rules and other legal means of state guidance" as well as human rights violations. There are no standing restrictions for any legal rule that has become effective, thereby allowing challenges to all existing as well as newly enacted legislation.[39] But where a *preliminary* examination of bills, parliamentary acts enacted but not yet implemented, standing orders of Parliament, or international treaties are concerned, standing is given only to the president, Parliament,[40] a standing parliamentary committee, groups of deputies greater than fifty, and apparently the collective government, not just a single minister. Conflicts of jurisdiction also can be raised only by the parties involved. Parliament, however, can extend standing to those not already included in the various categories.

In Czechoslovakia challenges to laws or decrees as violative of federal constitutional, international, or statutory law may be filed by any of numerous federal, Czech, or Slovak officials, or one-fifth of the members of the federal or republic legislatures. Conflicts of jurisdiction may be brought to the Czechoslovak court by one of the agencies involved. When a political party is banned, the representative of that party, of course, may bring the action, and where human rights are concerned, a private complaint is enough "under conditions set by an Act of the Federal Assembly." Since the Constitutional Act says nothing more, the federal law—presumably by an ordinary law and not a constitutional act—will set the requirements private persons must meet in order to have their cases heard.[41]

Like the others, Polish law allows high government officials to initiate Constitutional Tribunal review, as well as "committees of fifty deputies" and the ombudsman; the latter is a particularly fertile source of Constitutional Tribunal cases.[42] In addition, certain private organizations such as trade unions and trade associations are allowed to file Constitutional Court actions in matters affecting them. The latter petitioners must go through an initial screening by a single judge, but may be rejected if their petition "fails to meet the requirements set by provisions of this law or when it is obviously unfounded or misaddressed."[43] These objections would seem applicable to all petitions, however, not just those brought by such groups as unions and trade associations, and it is difficult to see what additional requirements the screening process is supposed to impose.

The Romanian Constitution sets out only a few standing rules. The only judicial review allowed is for legislation prior to promulgation or about parliamentary procedure, in which case standing is limited to high government officials, a parliamentary "group" and fifty or more deputies, or twenty-five or more senators.[44] Specific legislation may set out the rules for invoking the court's jurisdiction in other matters.

The Russian Constitutional Act, which includes hundreds of detailed paragraphs and subparagraphs, sets up a complex system in which a wide variety of public officials can petition the court to hold "international treaties or enforceable enactments" unconstitutional,[45] and individual citizens can challenge "law-applying practices" in accordance with customary law and practice.[46] Whereas review is mandatory in the former case, private complaints can be refused if "inadvisable."[47] This latter provision, of course, allows the Russian court to develop standing and other justiciability requirements. At the request of a few high Russian officials of one of the Russian republics, or on its own initiative, the Russian court may also issue "findings," which are binding on other courts in their decision making.

In another departure from conventional U.S. practice, several of these courts—the Russian, Romanian, and Hungarian—can in some cases initiate actions on their own, without a complaining party.[48] Indeed, the Russian court even has the right to initiate legislation[49] and is encouraged to do so. Such broad-ranging judicial authority seems like a serious encroachment on principles of the separation of powers. Who, for example, would pass upon a law originally proposed by the Constitutional Court if it were challenged as violative of either the constitution or a treaty?

Finally, unlike the U.S. Supreme Court, these courts may rarely decline jurisdiction. The Russian provision allowing a refusal to hear private complaints as "inadvisable" seems to be the exception, rather than the rule. This has created serious overload difficulties for the Hungarian court because of its enormously broad standing provision.[50]

Ripeness and Mootness   Unlike U.S. courts, none of the East European constitutional courts under consideration seems to require a particular live dispute between adversaries, for all allow the appropriate bodies to challenge and test laws simply by filing the requisite papers by the appropriate bodies. The Romanian and Hungarian Constitutions allow review even of unimplemented laws. Thus all permit, and indeed provide, that the normal review procedure will be *abstract*: a legislative act, treaty, or executive decree is to be analyzed on its face, and not as it applies in a particular disputed instance. Only the Russian provisions for complaints by individual citizens about practices of law application seem to contemplate an existing controversy.

Also, there is no indication that mootness will end the courts' obligation to pass on the challenged legislation or treaty. Indeed, the Russian Constitutional Court Act expressly requires that court to continue a proceeding that has begun despite a repeal or expiration of the act in question.[51]

This combination of public-official standing and the abstract nature of the review underscores the special nature of the European constitutional courts, another difference from U.S. courts, which avoid ruling on abstract or moot issues.

The European system can continually plunge constitutional courts into political controversies by giving standing to relatively small groups of legislators who have lost a legislative battle. In

France, the 1974 expansion of standing to sixty deputies of the French National Assembly transformed the Conseil Constitutionnel from a protector of the executive against the legislature to a legislative weapon against executive action.[52] This is quite common in the European systems.[53] Perhaps for this reason very few of these new courts are precluded from deciding "political questions." Only the Russian court is under such a ban,[54] and the meaning of that phrase in the Russian Constitutional Court Act is unclear. This sharply contrasts with the case in the United States, where congressional standing is narrowly confined to prevent losing political factions from turning to the courts to win judicially what they lost legislatively.[55]

Cases also come before the constitutional courts through referral from the regular courts. It is inaccurate to say that the ordinary East European judges are barred from deciding constitutional questions. They can, but they are permitted to rule only one way: they may not ordinarily strike down statutes. If the ordinary courts find a statute to be unconstitutional, they must refer the case to the constitutional court, a practice similar to that found in German law. Thus, in Bulgaria and Hungary, the regular courts must refer a case to the constitutional court if they find a "discrepancy" between a law or a treaty and the constitution.[56] The ordinary courts must suspend proceedings and await the constitutional court's ruling. This, of course, reflects the continental style of "concentrated" judicial review, as opposed to the diffuse American style in which every court is theoretically authorized to strike down an unconstitutional statute.

Such a referral requirement has several disadvantages. Apart from the delay involved in the referral, the procedure is one-sided. Because referral is mandatory only if the regular or administrative court finds a "discrepancy" or "considers unconstitutional a legal rule," only a *successful* challenge to that law is referred to the constitutional court. To frame this stipulation in the context of litigation, only the government—the usual defender of such a law—has an automatic right of appeal to the constitutional court. If the regular court does not find a "discrepancy," and the challenger does not have a right to appeal, the matter will end there.

This is not a great problem in Germany and Hungary, where private parties have a right to go to the constitutional court, but this right does not exist in Bulgaria, Poland, or Romania, and only in a modified form in Russia and Czechoslovakia.[57] Moreover, given the normal timidity of traditional continental court judges toward striking down legislation, few will be inclined to find the "discrepancy," which, in Germany at least, they must justify in writing.

Thus, when a nation creates a special constitutional tribunal because it either lacks confidence in the capacity of the ordinary court system to decide constitutional questions or considers it inappropriate for such courts to review the acts of the legislature—the primary reasons for the "concentrated" approach to judicial review—a referral should be required whenever a regular court considers that a constitutional challenge simply presents a *serious question*, as the Polish Constitutional Court Act provides in certain situations.[58] Otherwise, judicial review by constitutional courts of constitutional issues arising out of ordinary litigation will operate largely to the benefit of the defenders of the law and not the challengers. The latter will get to the constitutional court only if they have already won, and not if their challenge failed. Such one-sidedness does not belong in a system of justice.

Selection and Tenure

The political nature of these courts is reflected also in the way constitutional court judges are appointed, which is through explicitly political methods. In each country, the constitutional court judges are selected in whole or in part by the parliaments, sometimes by simple majority rule.[59] In Czechoslovakia, the president chooses from among lists submitted by the federal, Czech, and Slovak legislatures. In Romania and Bulgaria, the nations' respective presidents also select some members, and in Bulgaria the chief judges of the administrative and ordinary courts select a third.

Only the Russian court judges have life tenure, though only until retirement at age sixty-five.[60] The other countries, possibly concerned about concentrating too much power in such a group, usually limit their judges to one term of seven to nine years. The only exceptions are Hungary, which allows one renewal of a nine-year term, and Czechoslovakia, where the Constitutional Court Act[61] is silent as to renewability, thereby implicitly allowing it.

Despite the lack of life tenure and the inevitably political nature of the selection process—which, incidentally, is equally political for the courts of other countries including France, Germany, and the United States—those East European courts that have decided cases have shown little deference to the governments and legislatures that appointed them. In this respect, these judges are following the pattern laid down by the French and German constitutional court judges, who have also been quite independent, despite the political selection process in those countries.[62] In part this may be because the almost universal limitation to one judicial term means that there is little to gain from deferring to the politicians; this may also be because many of the lawyers chosen as judges have been distinguished lawyers—especially the chief judges, who may be relatively apolitical—though some have not had good reputations. And finally, it may follow because few are professional politicians with continuing political ambitions.

The uncertain effect of some European constitutional rulings may also be different from the emphatic finality insisted upon by the U.S. Supreme Court for its rulings and those of its fellow federal courts, though that is not certain.[63] Although the decisions of most of these continental constitutional courts also are said to be final, in Romania prepromulgation decisions on the constitutionality of legislative enactments and parliamentary rules may be overridden by a two-thirds vote of *either* legislative chamber. Since a two-thirds vote of *both* chambers is necessary for a constitutional change in Romania, the override possibility represents a true intrusion on the finality of constitutional decisions, except that it applies only to prepromulgation enactments and parliamentary procedures, not to enacted laws. In Poland, a Constitutional Tribunal decision annulling a law may also be overridden by a two-thirds vote of the Sejm, the primary legislative chamber, in the presence of at least half of its deputies.[64] But since these are the same requirements as those for a constitutional amendment,[65] the override is tantamount to such an amendment, which can always override a constitutional nullification. So far, only one minor tribunal decision has been overturned by the Sejm.

The East European Constitutional Courts in Action

As of this writing, only five of these new constitutional courts have become operational—those in Czechoslovakia, Bulgaria, Poland, Hungary, and Russia.[66] Of these five, the Hungarian and

Russian courts are perhaps the most powerful. The following discussion will focus on the Russian court, with a summary of some recent actions of the Bulgarian, Polish, and Czechoslovak courts.[67]

THE RUSSIAN CONSTITUTIONAL COURT

Established in October 1991, the Russian Constitutional Court's first few months in office provide many lessons about the scope and limits of a constitutional court's power.[68] In a nation without a history of either judicial review or even an independent judiciary, the court first struck down a decree by a popular president and then a proposed referendum by an autonomous republic. Between the two, it responded to private citizens' complaints on a pension matter and decided another jurisdictional dispute between the president and the Parliament, this time in favor of the president. On its docket are many more delicate questions, including the legality of President Boris Yeltsin's ban on the Communist party.

Prior to the arrival of Mikhail Gorbachev, Soviet Communist law did not acknowledge the need for an independent judiciary and certainly not for an independent tribunal exercising judicial review over the acts of officialdom.[69] All authority—including judicial authority—came from and was supervised by the leadership of the Communist party.

A tentative move toward judicial review was made in January 1990 with the creation of the USSR Committee on Constitutional Supervision, a part of Gorbachev's reforms. The committee exercised some independent authority, striking down several of Gorbachev's decrees, yet some considered it a failure.[70] With the demise of the Soviet Union, the committee disbanded on 23 December 1991.

As part of the constitutional reform for the Russian Soviet Federal Socialist Republic (RSFSR)—not the USSR, which never made it to that stage—a constitutional court was proposed in the November 1990 draft constitution, with very broad powers of judicial review. Without waiting for a new constitution,[71] on 12 July 1991 the RSFSR adopted an elaborate eighty-nine–article statute containing hundreds of detailed provisions establishing a fifteen-member Constitutional Court with automatic tenure until retirement at age sixty-five and vast powers only slightly diminished from those listed in the November draft constitution.[72] At the end of October, thirteen of the fifteen judges, including Chairman Valery Zorkin,[73] were appointed from among twenty-three candidates proposed by President Yeltsin.[74] Many feared that the court would be as ineffectual as the USSR Committee on Constitutional Supervision was thought to have been.

Within days of the judges' appointment, a group of thirty-six legislators, mostly former Communist party officials, filed a petition with the court presenting it with its first political hot potato: a constitutional challenge to Yeltsin's postcoup decrees outlawing the Communist party, confiscating its property, and banning its activity. Before the court reached that question, however, another challenge to Yeltsin's authority was thrust onto the newly created court: a parliamentary challenge to a presidential decree merging what was left of the Russian KGB with the Ministry of Interior (MVD), which controls the police. This case became the vehicle for the court's baptism by fire.

The KGB (ISS)-MVD Merger Decree

Shortly after the August 1991 attempted coup, the KGB was partially dismantled, renamed the Interrepublic Security Service (ISS), and some of its more notorious units were reportedly abolished. The change left few differences between the remains of the ISS and the MVD and a good deal of overlap, according to government officials who supported the decree on the merger. The merger was executed allegedly to save money and increase crime-fighting efficiency, a major concern in a country facing a steep rise in crime. Accordingly, exercising decree powers given him by the Supreme Soviet on 1 November 1991 in connection with economic reform, Yeltsin ordered the merger on 19 December 1991, effective immediately, and appointed Victor Barannikov, a friend from his hometown of Sverdlovsk, to run the consolidated agency.[75]

The public reacted with shock and fear. The last such merger, in 1936, was immediately followed by Stalin's murderous purges, and the Yeltsin merger aroused memories and fears of a recurrence. There were also signs that the many remaining KGB members were entrenching themselves in key positions in both federal and local governments. President Yeltsin's commitment to constitutional democracy was also questioned by some human rights activists and former dissidents. These fears were compounded by a simultaneous press law proposal that would have severely inhibited journalists. An *Izvestia* headline on the merger decree and press proposal read "A Chill Runs Down One's Spine."[76]

Such concerns[77] prompted a petition by fifty-one deputies to the Constitutional Court challenging the merger decree, and on 26 December 1992 the Supreme Soviet passed a resolution directing President Yeltsin to annul the decree. The next day, the Constitutional Court met quickly and issued an order temporarily suspending the merger decree until a definitive ruling, with a hearing set for 14 January 1992. At the same time, Chairman Zorkin began to make a series of public statements on the court's role and other matters that to an American observer seem startlingly outspoken for a judge. For example, the day the court issued its suspension order, Zorkin

> expressed his deep concern over instances in which legislative and executive authorities have clearly ignored constitutional principles and norms. He said that in its activity the Presidium of the Russian Federation Supreme Soviet frequently goes beyond its constitutional powers, usurping the powers of legislative and executive authorities. The Russian President's decree on organizing a Russian Ministry of Security and Internal Affairs is contrary to the principles of organizing a state based on the rule of law.[78]

Shortly after the suspension order, the press reported that one judge had received anonymous threats against him and his family, the wife and daughter of another judge were accosted in the hallway of their home, and a third judge managed to escape injury after two "explosive devices" were hurled at him. I am told that, since the court's ruling, Chairman Zorkin has received two death threats. A confidential source told a newspaper that this harassment was a reaction to the Constitutional Court's suspension order.[79] It was also alleged that some members of the MVD and ISS began to destroy files.[80]

In the meantime, the government had accelerated the merger after the petition was filed and began planning the forcible suppression of any disruptions that might result from the lifting of price constraints. These plans were kept secret, which angered the court; others described them as a restoration of "the repressive functions of security organs inside the country."[81] In addition, the court was told that Barannikov, who headed the merged agency, had said to his staff on 27 December 1992, the day after the court's first order, "The people are fed up with *perestroika.*

The President's only support is the Armed Forces and the security and internal affairs agencies. . . . I will investigate the lobby that is opposing the merger and the enforcement of the President's decree."[82]

At first President Yeltsin tried to postpone the hearing indefinitely, perhaps in order to continue with the merger despite the suspension order, but his request was brusquely denied. The challengers argued that the decree was a threat to democracy and to individual rights; Sergei Shakhrai, state counselor for legal policy, disputed this and stated that it was within the Russian president's powers.[83]

After eight hours of argument and two hours' deliberation, a unanimous court declared the merger unconstitutional because the decree violated principles of the separation of powers under the 1977 Russian Constitution, which has remained in effect pending the adoption of a new constitution.[84] A full opinion was issued approximately two weeks later, confirming that decision. Specifically, the court held that the 1977 Constitution granted only the Supreme Soviet, and not the executive, the power to create ministries, which the Supreme Soviet has exercised through laws and resolutions since 1990. Whatever powers the president was given by the Supreme Soviet's action of November 1991 remained subject to the Supreme Soviet's approval, creating "a special mechanism . . . for preliminary monitoring" over executive decrees. Such monitoring, the court found, "is an element of the system of checks and balances, inherent in the principle of separation of powers."[85]

The court also stressed that the Supreme Soviet has the constitutional authority to participate in the development of basic defense and state security measures, and that other branches of government could not remove such issues from the Supreme Soviet's authority. Furthermore, the court noted that a week after Yeltsin announced the merger, the Supreme Soviet had passed a resolution directing him "to annul his decree."[86]

Concluding that the decree violated the spirit and letter of numerous other resolutions of the Supreme Soviet, the court found that the decree "in practice deprived the RSFSR Supreme Soviet of the opportunity to participate in the formation of basic measures in . . . defense and . . . national security," in violation of the Constitution. This, the court found, affected the most fundamental citizens' rights, "such as the right of inviolability of the person, of privacy, of the home, and of the secrecy of . . . communications."[87]

The immediate aftermath was confusing. Although Shakhrai was supposed to have harbored doubts about the merits of his case,[88] he deplored the decision as not "juridical" but based on "political and ideological motives" derived from the ambiguities of the current Constitution.[89] At first Shakhrai warned, "This does not mean the decree ceases to be in effect," but then added, "The government should obey the Constitutional Court."[90] This raised doubts as to whether the government would comply with the court's decision. Zorkin and a court spokeswoman threatened Shakhrai with impeachment if he repeated his comments either about the "political" nature of the ruling or about the effect of the decree.[91]

President Yeltsin's first reaction also was ambiguous. Zorkin reported that it took him an hour to persuade Yeltsin that he had to obey the court's ruling.[92] A few days later Yeltsin issued an order separating the two agencies. But because he put Barannikov, who had been head of the MVD, in charge of the security agency (ISS) and Barannikov's former deputy in charge of the MVD, one newspaper suggested that Yeltsin had "outwitted both the Russian Parliament and Constitutional Court."[93]

The court's first foray into judicial review—albeit only of an executive decree, not legislative action—clearly shows a determination to insist on the rule of law. This determination is reflected not only in the decision but also in the many extrajudicial statements by its chairman.[94] The decision involved a good deal of courage, for it challenged a popular president, though the decree itself was unpopular and was opposed by a variety of constituencies. And although there was nervousness about whether it would be obeyed—a nervousness that continues because of the possible de facto union, given that the heads of the now formally separated agencies are Barannikov and his former deputy—President Yeltsin's willingness to accept the decree, at least formally, is a hopeful sign.

As to the merits of the decision, experts on Soviet law have informed me that it is clearly sound.[95] The opinion is cast in a dry, technical, almost legalistic style, but that approach may be appropriate during the court's early years, particularly because the opinion does point to the possible harm the decree might inflict on individual rights.

On the other hand, State Counselor Shakhrai's lament about the difficulties of working with an old constitution is well-founded and echoed in Hungary and elsewhere. The new constitutional courts are trying to apply new laws, concepts, and constitutional provisions to old laws and amended constitutions based on very different concepts. The problem is compounded by the fact that since so few of these countries have adopted wholly new constitutions, but have simply amended their existing charters, the courts are often trying to reconcile old and new provisions in the same constitution.

Finally, it is fortunate that the court's most visible judge, Chairman Zorkin, was known not as an opponent of a strong executive, but as quite the opposite, someone whose objectivity was questioned because of his support for a strong president and his prior government service. As he said to me with a faint smile, "No one can accuse me of harboring any hostility to the president."[96]

The Tatarstan Referendum

The court was not so lucky when it was forced, again unexpectedly and by events, to consider the constitutionality of the March 1992 Tatarstan referendum.

It was expected that Russia would face monumental problems after the breakup of the Soviet Union: creating a market economy that can provide adequately for its people, building a democracy, and establishing relations with Ukraine and the other members of the former Soviet Union. What few expected was that Russia itself, a collection of many different republics, ethnic units, and religions, would face the same centrifugal forces as those that had destroyed the Soviet Union.[97] What Yeltsin did to Gorbachev and the Soviet Union is now being done to Yeltsin by several of the constituent republics of the Russian Federation.[98]

The problems with Tatarstan[99] began to take constitutional form on 30 August 1990, when its government issued a Declaration of State Sovereignty just three months after Russia declared its sovereignty. Tatarstan's declaration, which was to be the basis for a new Tatarstan constitution and laws, omitted any reference to Tatarstan remaining part of Russia. The Russian authorities, preoccupied with their own problems vis-à-vis the country at large, did nothing. Thereafter, in April 1991, Tatarstan revised the preamble to its constitution and the titles of certain constitutional articles so that they no longer included Tatarstan in the Russian Federation or accepted the supremacy of Russian law over the laws of Tatarstan.[100] Russian authorities continued to ignore the issue.

Then, on 29 November 1991 and 21 February 1992, Tatarstan nationalist pressure produced a series of laws that scheduled a referendum on 21 March 1992 on the following question: "Do you agree that the Tatarstan Republic is a sovereign state and a party to international law, basing its relations with the Russian Federation and other republics and states on treaties between equal partners? Yes or no?"[101] At the same time, in late January or early February 1992, Tatarstan stopped transmitting tax collections to Moscow. This time the Russian authorities reacted, and strongly.

The real meaning of the question posed in the referendum remains obscure. Assertions that it meant secession were repeatedly denied by Tatarstan leaders, who declared that they simply wanted to be treated as a "sovereign state," a "subject of international law" that would "build relations with Russia on the basis of a treaty . . . to be on an equal footing."[102] They did not intend that Tatarstan have either a separate currency, its own defense forces, or separate embassies abroad.[103] Tatarstan representatives admitted, however, that the question was deliberately ambiguous so that people would vote "yes" without realizing that they were voting for secession.[104]

Opposition party leaders in Tatarstan and others suggested that the referendum and possible secession were a way of keeping in power Tatarstan's current rulers, who are old-line Communists; Tatarstan President Mintimer Shaimiyev supported the August coup, and reform in Tatarstan has moved very slowly. "Secession here does not mean democracy," warned one Western diplomat.[105]

Fearing the referendum proposal as both a vehicle of Tatarstan secession and an example to other restive groups in the Russian Federation, on 5 March 1992 a group of Russian deputies led by Constitutional Commission Secretary General Oleg Rumyantsev petitioned the Russian Constitutional Court to review the constitutionality of the referendum. The deputies argued that the referendum might lead to a change in the Russian Federation's territory, a move that the Constitution forbids republics to attempt unilaterally.[106]

The court promptly scheduled a hearing for 13 March. Representatives of the Tatarstan Republic refused to attend, later claiming they did not have enough time to prepare.[107] The only parties in court were representatives of the Russian Federation deputies and the Supreme Soviet itself.[108] After several hours of argument and testimony, all of it inevitably one-sided, the court found that both the 1990 Declaration of Sovereignty and the referendum question violated the Russian Constitution in several respects:

(1) The denial of the supremacy of federal laws over the laws of members of the federation is contrary to the constitutional status of the republics in a federated state and precludes the establishment of a law-governed state.

"[(2)] The decree is . . . a legislative instrument, predetermining the direction and content of the legislative process.

"[(3) W]ithout denying the national group's right to self-determination exercised by means of a legal expression of the electorate's will, we must proceed from the fact that international law limits it to the observance of the requirements of the principle of territorial integrity and the observance of human rights.

"(4) According to the Constitution of the RSFSR, the Tatarstan Republic is part of the RSFSR (Article 71); the territory of the Tatarstan Republic is part of the territory of the RSFSR and may not be changed without its consent (Article 70); the Constitution of the Tatarstan Republic must correspond to the RSFSR Constitution (Article 78); the RSFSR Constitution must be observed by state and public organizations and officials (Article 4); a change in the national-state structure of the RSFSR requires a constitutional amendment, which is within the exclusive jurisdiction of the RSFSR, represented by its supreme bodies of government (Clause 1 of Article 72, Clause 3 of Article 104, and Clause 12 of Article 109).

"The RSFSR Constitution does not specify the right of the republics making up the RSFSR to withdraw from the federation. This right is not specified in the Constitution of the Tatarstan Republic. The unilateral declaration of this right by the Tatarstan Republic would be an affirmation of the legality of a complete or partial violation of the territorial unity of the sovereign federated state and the national unity of the national groups inhabiting it. Any actions intended to violate this unity will damage the constitutional order of the RSFSR and will be incompatible with international rules on human rights and the rights of national groups."

(5) The ambiguity of the question deprives citizens of the right "to express their will freely [and] to participate in the discussion and adoption of laws and decisions of state-wide significance."[109]

The court's reasoning on the Declaration of Sovereignty seems perfectly sound. A constituent unit of a federation bound to follow federal law cannot unilaterally reject that law, so long as it remains within the federation. Article 81 of the Russian Constitution specifically provides that in conflicts between federal and republic law "the law of the RSFSR shall prevail."[110] The referendum decision seems more problematic. A referendum of this kind, which simply asks whether the people agree on the status of the entity, would not usually have any legal significance. It is not an obvious part of either the constitutional or the legislative process. Indeed, the favorable vote on the referendum appears to have made no legal or other functional difference.

Chairman Zorkin, in subsequent extrajudicial statements, justified the court's involvement on grounds that a positive response to the referendum would have provided "all legal grounds to secede from the Russian Federation," should a more nationalist leadership come to power in Tatarstan.[111] Perhaps this is true under some unusual provisions in either the Russian or Tatarstan Constitution, but this is unlikely since neither Constitution apparently provides for secession by a Russian Federation republic.

It is difficult to grant anything more than political significance to the referendum. Given the ambiguity of the question and the repeated disclaimers as to an intent to secede by both leaders and voters, there may not even be much political significance, though no outsider can accurately evaluate that. The Russian Constitutional Court nevertheless found legal significance. In what seems like an implicit response to this doubt about the appropriateness of treating this matter at this step, the court said:

> The decree . . . serves as a means of stating important legal premises. . . . By putting this definition of the republic status to a general vote, the Tatarstan Republic Supreme Soviet is trying to give it the features of a rule of the highest order—rule established by the people. For this reason, this decree is not only an instrument of law enforcement, but also a legislative instrument, predetermining the direction and content of the legislative process.[112]

Perhaps the referendum does amount to "a legislative instrument, predetermining the direction and content of the legislative process" under Russian law, but to an American lawyer the argument is unpersuasive. Tatarstan is no more a "sovereign state" or a proper "party to international law" after the referendum than before. On the other hand, if a positive answer to the referendum question is indeed of legal significance under Russian or Tatar law and does constitute a legally significant step toward secession, the decision seems correct for the reasons discussed earlier in the comments on the Declaration of Sovereignty.

Chairman Zorkin also criticized Russian Federation officials for not challenging Tatarstan's August 1990 Declaration of Sovereignty when it was first promulgated and asserted that the Tatarstan officials had said that they had interpreted this lack of reaction to the declaration as "a sign of approval" and were thereby emboldened to go further. Then, after chastising Tatarstan officials for not showing up in court, for denying receipt of the decision, and for calling the decision a "judicial travesty," he urged the people of Tatarstan to respect the court, because if they did not respect the Constitutional Court, they could not count on their own court being respected in the future.[113] Mixing the need to obey the court with the social dangers of secession, he warned of "a situation [that] could exceed by a hundred times Yugoslavia and all the other civil war flash points that we have."[114]

In the few days between the decision and the referendum, Chairman Zorkin continued to call for obedience to the court's decision, warning of "a collapse of the constitutional order."[115] Nevertheless, on 21 March the referendum was held. Despite a last-minute plea from President Yeltsin, 61 percent of the 82 percent total turnout voted "yes." Within Kazan, the largely Russian capital, 51 percent, however, voted "no," and there were apparently similar negative results in the other large cities. In the countryside, which is largely Tatar, 75 percent voted "yes."[116] After the referendum, Bakturoshtan, another Russian republic, suspended the operation of the Russian Constitutional Court Act on its territory.

In retrospect, Tatarstan's defiance is not surprising. The issues of judicial supremacy and respect for the court became intertwined with and subordinate to the overriding issue of Tatarstan's adherence to the Russian Federation and its institutions in general. It is now easy to see that, once the forces of nationalism, resentment, and separatism took command in Tatarstan, they would produce defiance of a court decision opposing them. The central authority that the court was trying to assert was the very thing being challenged by Tatarstan in the referendum.

The Tatarstan situation obviously represents a serious challenge to the Constitutional Court. It is difficult to predict both how the court will counteract this defiance, if at all, and how this still-unfolding episode will affect the Russian court's overall impact. Although the court has many difficult issues on its docket, including the aforementioned actions by Yeltsin against the Communist party, few of these cases raise the danger of defiance inherent in a conflict with a national or ethnic group that is already trying to escape from federal authority.

Other Decisions

As of this writing, few details were available about the Russian court's two other decisions. In one case, the court found that age discrimination had prompted the firing of two workers; in the other the court affirmed President Yeltsin's right to reorganize executive agencies. As official translations are unavailable at this time, discussion will be limited to the following brief summaries.

In February 1992, the court responded to an individual complaint by two pensioners. Judge Ernest Ametistov described the case as involving "two pensioners who were dismissed from their jobs because they had reached a pensionable age and [they claimed] were entitled to a pension. Dismissals on such grounds have lately become commonplace. We ruled this practice unconstitutional, because in this case we have age discrimination. And therefore we reinstated the pensioners' rights."[117]

The other case dealt with a former Soviet copyright agency known as VAAP. VAAP had a monopoly on all Soviet publications abroad and was known for political censorship and KGB connections. In February 1992, President Yeltsin created the Russian Agency for Intellectual Property to take over VAAP's functions and property and appointed a liberal lawyer as its director. At about the same time, Supreme Soviet Chairman Ruslan Khasbulatov, a long-time Yeltsin critic, created in the name of the Presidium of the Supreme Soviet an agency named the All Russian Copyright Agency. This was to be the sole heir to VAAP, and Khasbulatov placed a former KGB general in charge.[118]

On 28 April 1992, the Constitutional Court ruled that the resolution of the Supreme Soviet Presidium reviving VAAP was unconstitutional because only the president may reorganize executive agencies, and he had done so by setting up the Russian Agency for Intellectual Property.[119] Khasbulatov had urged the Russian minister of justice, Nikolai Fedorov, to be guided "not just by the laws but by the ideas of reform." Apparently irritated by such statements, Fedorov commented after the Russian court's decision, "I am pleased that there is such a forum as the Russian Constitutional Court which can put in their place—in the good sense of the word—all officials and all state bodies."[120]

Not surprisingly, resort to the Constitutional Court has become a common option for unhappy Russians. The St. Petersburg City Council wants the court to remove Mayor Anatolii Sobchak,[121] the Moscow city councillors want it to annul some of Mayor Gavriil Popov's decrees and its method of electing mayors,[122] and former USSR Prime Minister Valentin Pavlov, one of the coup participants, wants to be reinstated as Russian prime minister.[123] The original Communist challenge to Yeltsin's decrees has produced a counterclaim challenging the legality of the party, and the court has agreed to take evidence in what could turn out to be a lengthy exposé of the Communist party's abuses during the last seventy years.

Summary

In the few months of its existence, the Russian Constitutional Court has established itself as an aggressive tribunal determined to safeguard the emerging Russian democracy. As it proclaimed shortly after its inception,

> the Constitutional Court does not intend to get in [the way of reform] . . . but any changes in the life of the state, even the most beneficial ones, should occur within the framework of the law. . . . [As] the supreme body of the legal authority it intends to take a series of steps to defend the constitutional system in the country and prevent dictatorship and tyranny from setting in, no matter from where they may emanate.[124]

As noted earlier, other European constitutional courts have been equally independent and forceful, such as the Hungarian and German courts. The Russian court is distinguished, however, by the explicit assertiveness of some of the judges, especially Chairman Zorkin. He has given numerous interviews and made many speeches in the Supreme Soviet and on television and other media.[125] He has commented on the implications of the decisions and on the official reactions to them[126] and has threatened some officials with sanctions for their hostile reactions. Zorkin and others have also commented on public issues other than those directly involved in the cases before them and have criticized government officials for what they considered policy mistakes. In short, Zorkin and his colleagues are serious about the court's "plan to actively participate in developing a rule of law strategy."[127]

In the United States and elsewhere, judges have tried to withdraw from public controversy outside the courtroom to maintain an aura of impartiality and objectivity. These considerations do not seem to affect Chairman Zorkin, and this observer, at least, has no idea whether they apply at all in so different and chaotic a society as today's Russia. What is clear is that in Chairman Zorkin the country has not only a skillful jurist but also a powerful personality who, despite differences in style, might well be Russia's John Marshall.

THE BULGARIAN, POLISH, AND CZECHOSLOVAK CONSTITUTIONAL COURTS

It is too soon to predict whether the Russian court's experience will have any impact on the developing courts in other East European nations. Most of the new constitutional courts will probably face issues of ethnic rivalry, human rights, separation of powers, and atonement for the sins of past Communist regimes. This final section will summarize some of the early actions of three other constitutional courts.

The Bulgarian Court

Although the Bulgarian Constitutional Court has existed for about a year and comprises a group of distinguished judges, until April 1992 it dealt only with six relatively minor matters: the status of parliamentary representatives, an effort to dismiss a broadcast executive, and the question of whether a president running for reelection may stay in office during the election campaign.[128] Until then, no human rights cases had come before the court.

In April 1992, however, the court was confronted with one of the most heated issues in Bulgarian life: relations between the Bulgarian majority and the large Turkish Muslim minority, which comprises about 11 percent of the population.[129] The Turkish minority dominates the Movement for Rights and Freedoms (MRF), the political party that came in third in the recent parliamentary elections. Although it agreed not to participate in government in order to avoid exacerbating the situation by giving the now-nationalistic Communists and their allies political ammunition, the MRF is a necessary supporter of the Union of Democratic Forces government.

Bulgaria bans parties based on ethnic ties,[130] but the MRF claims that it is not ethnically based, as it includes non-Turks. Still, some fifty-three members of the current Parliament, joined by ninety-three deputies in the preceding Parliament, petitioned the Constitutional Court to declare the MRF an "anticonstitutional" party and to bar its twenty-three members from the current Parliament, ostensibly because of its ethnic ties. Such a ruling would probably have caused the government to fall. In a decision on 21 April 1992, the court, by a six-to-five vote, rejected the claim and implicitly affirmed the MRF's legal status.[131] As of this writing, details of the Bulgarian court's decision were unavailable.

The Polish Court

Although it is one of the oldest East European constitutional courts, the Polish court's limited jurisdiction over subject matter has prevented it from exercising some of the broad authority enjoyed by the Russian Constitutional Court.[132] Access to the Polish court is quite limited, as are its powers; it may not, for example, review local regulations. As a Polish constitutional expert put it, the tribunal is designed not to supervise Parliament, but to help Parliament maintain its position as the country's supreme legislator.[133] A bill to expand its powers is currently pending in the Sejm and will probably be adopted.

Despite its limitations, the tribunal decided 155 cases from 1986 through 1991.[134] Most of these were brought to the court by Poland's energetic first ombudswoman, Ewa Lętowska, who recently completed a four-year term in that position to widespread approval. In fifty-two of these cases, the governmental authorities altered their behavior in response to the filing of the suit.

Very few cases have been referred to the tribunal by other courts because, according to Vice-President Leonard Lukaszuk, "they do not have such a tradition" and are averse to "risk-taking."[135]

During this period, the Polish court has issued some highly controversial rulings, such as affirming a doctor's right to refuse to perform abortions, allowing religious instruction in schools, permitting border guards to appeal their transfers or dismissals to the Administrative Court, and approving the nationalization of Communist party property. Most of some fifty-six cases referred by the ombudswoman during 1988–91 were resolved in favor of the complainant, although there are sharp differences of opinion on many matters between the former ombudswoman and the tribunal.[136]

As of this writing, the most recent important tribunal decision struck down two laws passed in September 1991 to reduce pensions and freeze salaries for state employees. The decision could add $2.2 billion to the current $4.7 billion deficit, according to the prime minister.[137] Nevertheless, the Sejm has refused to overturn the decision, leading the finance minister to resign and jeopardizing a $2.5 billion loan from the International Monetary Fund.[138]

The tribunal has come under fire from all sides. Composed of judges—half of whom were appointed in the Communist era and half in the post-Communist era—it is considered by some to be too sympathetic to the Sejm and not sufficiently independent. According to one observer, the tribunal allowed religious instruction in the public schools even though it knew this was against the law, prompting accusations that the tribunal wrote to the Sejm about the decision after it was made, suggesting that the Sejm change the law!

The Constitutional Court's vice-president, Lukaszuk, has complained that the tribunal lacks jurisdiction to apply the international law of human rights to Polish domestic legislation,[139] although in the case of the border guards, international law principles were mentioned. The tribunal has pointed out this weakness to the Sejm, and it may soon be changed.

The Polish tribunal will soon confront one of Poland's most wrenching social issues, abortion. There is overwhelming public support for abortion rights, and abortion opponents have failed in their efforts to narrow Poland's very liberal abortion laws. In December 1991, however, the medical association adopted new rules effective 3 May 1992, whereby doctors are allowed to perform abortions only in cases of rape or if the pregnancy threatens the woman's life; it also leaves the decision to conduct prenatal tests for birth defects to the doctor alone.[140] These rules are much narrower than current Polish law allows, and both the former ombudswoman, Lętowska, and her successor have asked the Constitutional Court to strike down the new rules.

The Czechoslovak Court

The key challenges facing the Czechoslovak court include balancing the nationalistic rivalry between Czechs and Slovaks and addressing the abuses of the former Communist government. Both issues have already been brought before the court.

The Czechoslovak Constitutional Court was established in March 1992, over a year after the constitutional act creating the court was passed. The delay resulted from the cumbersome selection process which, in turn, reflected the major problem with which the court will probably have to deal, namely the contentious relationship between the Slovaks and the Czechs. The Constitutional Court Act provides for the twelve members of the court to provide equal representation for the Czechs and the Slovaks. In an effort to promote impartiality, the court was placed in the Moravian city of Brno,[141] rather than either Prague or Bratislava. The judges are selected by the president from three lists of eight nominees each, prepared by each of the Czech, Slovak, and federal Parliaments.[142] The Slovaks delayed preparing their list, which slowed the process. The even number of judges, a not uncommon feature among these new courts,[143] and the equal division of judges between the two nationalities raise a very real danger of deadlocks on issues affecting relations between and among the two republics and the federation.[144] Because of the absence of a clause establishing the supremacy of federal law over republic law, only the federal Constitution and human rights treaties prevail against republic law.[145]

Without federal law supremacy over republic law, there will be no ready means of resolving the inevitable clashes of authority between federal and republic officials, especially since the Czechoslovak governmental structure provides for republic administration under federal legislative guidance. Given the intense Slovak hostility to Prague's centralism, this could derail the economic and environmental reforms that are within the jurisdiction of both federal and republic governments. Although the final comprehensive federal constitution may resolve these problems, many of them seem to be rooted in the Slovak insistence on substantial independence and may be intractable.[146]

The first issue related to federalism came to the court within its first few weeks, and although the result has been reported, a translation of the opinion was not available at the time of this writing in May 1992. The result creates a rather odd amalgam, but may be constitutionally sound.

On 12 December 1990, the Czechoslovak legislature adopted a constitutional act dividing jurisdiction over the economy and other matters between the federal government and the republics.[147] For telecommunications, Article 20 gave the federal government jurisdiction over "the organization *and control* of a uniform system of telecommunications," the "organization of uniform system of posts" and "the issue of postage stamps"; jurisdiction to set "uniform rules for postal, telecommunications and radio-communication traffic and tariffs"; and the authority to "codify matters of posts and telecommunications."[148] On a petition from the Federal Telecommunications Ministry, the court ruled on 15 April 1992 that the federation can operate the telecommunications system; radio and postal system are to be operated by the republics.[149] The result seems consistent with the act's giving the federal government "control" only over telecommunications.[150]

Where human rights are concerned, the Czechoslovak Charter mandates that everybody in Czechoslovakia has the same basic rights.[151] This could enable the court to create some uniformity at least in human rights. The court's first opportunity to do this has already been thrust upon it and in an exceedingly delicate context—the debate over how Czechoslovakia will deal with the misdeeds of its former Communist government. This problem is not unique to Czechoslovakia. One of the most bitter and tragic of the internal struggles erupting throughout the former Communist nations has grown out of their efforts to come to terms with the past. Communist abuses, ranging from murder and blackmail to repression and ostracism, have left a desire for exposure and revenge that has begun to tear these societies apart.[152]

At the same time, Communists and others who held positions of power in the Communist era are still a potent force in the society, either individually or as members of organized groups. The Communists received a substantial number of votes in the

1990 and 1992 Czechoslovak elections, to give but one example. Many people are hostile to the new democratic regimes and are trying to undermine them.[153]

For all these reasons, many of these countries, including Czechoslovakia, have adopted or are considering laws to bar those who held key positions in the prior regimes from occupying important positions today, either for a period of years or indefinitely. Czechoslovakia's statute, called a "lustration law,"[154] bars a wide range of former public officials from a correspondingly wide range of state, state-owned, or state-controlled institutions until 1995.[155] The law, promoted primarily by right-wing members of the Federal Assembly, has come under severe criticism both within and outside of Czechoslovakia,[156] and formed the basis for a Constitutional Court petition filed by ninety-nine members of the Federal Assembly.[157] It will probably be the second major case the court handles.[158]

Conclusions

The outcome of the democratic experiment in these newly liberated countries is far from certain. Economic, ethnic, nationalist, environmental, and religious controversies will trouble these nations for years to come, threatening democracy and the commitment to a rule of law. Almost none of these countries, save Czechoslovakia, has a strong democratic tradition to draw on; indeed, the pre–World War II years, before first Nazi and then Communist dictatorships, saw numerous failures of democracy and a turn to authoritarianism of one kind or another.

In such unfavorable circumstances, the constitutional courts created in these countries may be too frail to block a determined drive to abandon democracy, freedom, and the rule of law. Nevertheless, whatever chance these countries have to continue developing into constitutional democracies depends on strong, independent courts that can repel legislative and executive encroachments on their constitutions.

The performance of some of these courts so far shows that despite the lack of a constitutional court tradition, men and women who don the robe of constitutional court judges can become courageous and vigorous defenders of constitutional principles and human rights, continuing the pattern shown elsewhere in the world. Whether they will be able to continue to do so, and whether the courts in the other former Communist countries will do equally well, will likely depend on forces beyond their control. The record so far—and it is still very early—indicates that these courts will do whatever they can toward maintaining a free constitutional democracy and the rule of law. And this could be a very great contribution indeed.

Notes

This chapter, which was completed in May 1992, is a revised version of an article that was published in the *Michigan Journal of International Law* and is published here with the journal's permission. "The New East European Constitutional Courts," *Michigan Journal of International Law* 13 (1992): 741–85.

[1]For example, the Czechoslovak Constitutional Court, created in 1920 on an Austrian model, did not hear a single case challenging the constitutionality of a statute. See generally Edward Táborský, *Czechoslovak Democracy at Work* (London: Allen & Unwin, 1945).

[2]Even Great Britain has subjected its legislative and executive action to a judicial tribunal, the European Court of Human Rights. For the development of judicial review in the West, see generally Mauro Cappelletti, *The Judicial Process in Comparative Perspective* (Oxford: Clarendon, 1989).

[3]In some countries, such as Ukraine and Estonia, these provisions are parts of draft constitutions that had not been adopted as of May 1992.

[4]For the German experience, see Donald P. Kommers, *Judicial Politics in West Germany: A Study of the Federal Constitutional Court* (New York: Russell Sage, 1976), and Donald P. Kommers, "German Constitutionalism: A Prolegomenon," *Emory Law Journal* 40 (1991): 837; for France, see James Beardsley, "Constitutional Review in France," *Supreme Court Review* (1975): 189; for Italy, see Allan Brewer-Carias, *Judicial Review in Comparative Law* (Cambridge: Cambridge University Press, 1989), 215.

[5]The U.S. Supreme Court also exercises some original jurisdiction. United States Constitution, Article III, Section 2.

[6]The largely empty debate over judicial restraint versus judicial activism is based on the disagreement over the extent to which the courts are authorized to review and annul legislative acts. As is demonstrated by the current Supreme Court, all Supreme Court justices are judicial activists. See generally Herman Schwartz, *Packing the Courts* (New York: Charles Scribner's Sons, 1988).

[7]These courts also perform certain other functions such as supervising elections and banning political parties. See text herein accompanying notes 32–33.

[8]See, for example, Bulgarian Constitution, Chapter 8, Articles 147–51; Hungarian Constitution, Chapters IV (Constitutional Court) and X (Judiciary); Romanian Constitution, Title V, Articles 140–45; Czechoslovakian Con-

stitution (Constitutional Act No. 143, 1968), Chapter 6, Articles 86–101; Spanish Constitution, Titles V (Judiciary), and X (Constitutional Court); but see Federal Republic of Germany Constitution, Chapter IX, Articles 92–104; Russian Soviet Federal Socialist Republic (RSFSR) Constitution (October 1991), Chapter XXI.

[9]Quoted in Louis Favoreu, "Constitutional Review in Europe," in L. Henkin, ed., *Constitutionalism and Rights: The Influence of the United States Constitution Abroad* (New York: Columbia University Press, 1990), 56; see also Favoreu, "Conseil Constitutionnel: Mythes et réalités," *Regards sur l'actualité* (June 1987): 12, 13 ("constitutional judges and ordinary judges do not belong to the same family"—author's translation).

[10]See Cappelletti, *Judicial Process*, 53.

[11]See Beardsley, "Constitutional Review in France"; see also Cynthia Vroom, "Constitutional Protection of Individual Liberties in France: The Conseil Constitutionnel Since 1971," *Tulane Law Review* 63 (1988): 265, 280, but see pp. 303–4 (narrowing the bases for decision).

[12]An English translation of the decision is excerpted in Donald Kommers, *The Constitutional Jurisprudence of the Federal Republic of Germany* (Durham: Duke University Press, 1989), 349–50, 355.

[13]Louis Favoreu, "American and European Models of Constitutional Justice," in David S. Clark, ed., *Comparative and Private International Law* (1990), 105, 109. For a summary of the reasons for this kind of civil law judge, see John H. Merryman, *The Civil Law Tradition*, 2d ed. (Stanford: Stanford University Press, 1985), 34–38.

[14]Vroom, "Constitutional Protection of Individual Liberties in France," 267.

[15]As Merryman notes, "Indeed, a few purists within the civil law tradition suggest that it is wrong to call such constitutional courts 'courts' and their members 'judges.' Because judges cannot make law, the reasoning goes, and because the power to hold statutes illegal is a form of lawmaking, these officials obviously cannot be judges and these institutions cannot be courts," *Civil Law Tradition*, 38.

[16]A good summary of the fundamental characteristics of the European constitutional courts was made in 1987 by Favoreu in discussing the French Conseil Constitutionnel:

> The Conseil Constitutionnel presents the same characteristics as the [European] constitutional courts: [1] "A concentrated control" in the hands of a unique jurisdiction constituted especially for this purpose and independent of the ordinary jurisdictional structure; [2] recruitment of nonprofessional judges by political authorities chosen for political purposes, which, far from being a drawback— as one often believes in France—is a necessity because this assures democratic legitimacy for the constitutional courts when confronting the legislators; [3] abstract control initiated by political authorities and able to issue a decision voiding legislation which has the effect of a final judicial judgment; [and 4] a constitutional statute establishing the court in the constitution itself, its composition and its attributes so that only a constitutional law . . . (which is usually

very difficult and often impossible to enact . . .) can change the constitutional court statute.

"Conseil Constitutionnel," 115–16 (author's translation). For a discussion of a narrowing of the differences between the American and European judiciaries, see Cappelletti, *Judicial Process,* 52–53, and Favoreu, "American and European Models of Constitutional Justice," 115–19.

[17]See "Letter from Thomas Jefferson to James Madison" (15 March 1789), in Julian P. Boyd, ed., *The Papers of Thomas Jefferson* (Princeton: Princeton University Press, 1958), vol. 14, 659.

[18]Learned Hand, address entitled "The Spirit of Liberty" (1944), in Irving Dillard, ed., *The Spirit of Liberty* (New York: Random House, 1959), 144.

[19]Federalist No. 78 (Alexander Hamilton), in Henry B. Dawson, ed., *The Federalist Papers* (1863), 544.

[20]See RSFSR Constitution, Articles 1, 2, 32, 67, 74 (1991); Polish Constitutional Tribunal Act of 29 April 1985, Article 20 [hereinafter Polish Constitutional Tribunal Act].

[21]For purposes of clarity, "federal" will be used to describe the country-wide authority, "state" will be used to describe the next level of relatively autonomous governmental authority, and "local" will be used for the regional and municipal government.

[22]Neither Poland's constitutional act nor Bulgaria's Constitution seem to give their constitutional courts authority to review the constitutionality of state or local law; in Bulgaria, this may be because the constitutionality of Bulgarian local and regional laws is subject to challenge in the administrative court, since these laws are considered administrative acts. Memorandum from Bulgarian Judge Metody Tilev, graduate student at the American University, to the author, April 1992.

[23]Czechoslovak Federal Republic Charter on Human Rights and Freedoms, Section 2.

[24]Romanian Constitution, Article 144 (b); Act No. XXXII of 1989 on the Constitutional Court, Section 1 (a) (Hungary) [hereinafter Hungarian Constitutional Court Act]. The U.S. Constitution explicitly gives each legislative chamber the authority to "determine the Rules of its Proceedings," Article I, Section 5, Clause 2. This would seem to preclude judicial review of such matters, since the first criterion for classifying an issue as a "political question" is that there is "a textually demonstrable commitment of the issue to a coordinate political department." See Baker v. Carr, 369 U.S. 186, 210 (1962).

[25]Deciding intra-agency disputes is one of the few areas where the courts' mandate goes beyond constitutionality, since such issues need not involve any constitutional questions.

[26]The Russian Constitutional Court was also denied the authority to settle interrepublic disputes, another indication of the republics' refusal to give a central authority too much power.

[27]Constitutional Act of 27 February 1991, concerning the Constitutional Court of the Czech and Slovak Federal Republic, Article 2 (c) [hereinafter Czechoslovakian Constitutional Court Act]. Compare with U.S. Constitution, Article VI, Section 2: "the Laws of the United States . . . shall be the supreme Law of the Land."

[28]Czechoslovakian Constitutional Court Act, Article 22 (2).

[29]Czechoslovakian Constitutional Court Act, Article 3 (1), last clause.

[30]Czechoslovakian Constitutional Court Act, Article 22 (2).

[31]Romanian Constitution, Article 145 (i); Bulgarian Constitution, Article 149 (1) 5; Czechoslovakian Constitutional Court Act, Article 7. These extremely dangerous provisions seem to be patterned on the Federal Republic of Germany Constitution, Articles 9 (2) and 21 (1), under which both a Nazi successor party and the Communist party were barred in the 1950s, though attitudes since then have changed in Germany. The two cases involving the Nazi successor party and the Communist party are excerpted in Kommers, *Constitutional Jurisprudence of the Federal Republic of Germany*, 222–31.

[32]Romanian Constitution, Article 144 (e), (g), (h).

[33]The federal courts' role in naturalization proceedings is another example that they are considered impartial.

[34]Only a few judges, notably Justice William O. Douglas, have challenged it. See, for example, Warth v. Seldin, 422 U.S. 490, 519 (Douglas, J., dissenting).

[35]Rescue Army v. Municipal Court, 331 U.S. 549, 571 (1947) (footnote omitted).

[36]For a general discussion of the origins and rationales for these courts, see Brewer-Carias, *Judicial Review in Comparative Law*, 185–96.

[37]See RSFSR Constitutional Court Act, Article 69.1 (14) (the court may refuse to hear the case if "inadvisable").

[38]Bulgarian Constitution, Article 150 (1).

[39]A human rights organization relied successfully on this provision in challenging the Hungarian capital punishment law. According to Péter Paczolay, both this broad standing requirement and the very broad grant of subject-matter jurisdiction were sought by the democratic opposition to the Communists when the two sides were arranging what turned out to be a transfer of power from the Communists. The opposition did not trust any of the established institutions and wanted to give this new center of power, the Constitutional Court, as much authority as possible. The Communists were apparently unaware of the power they were giving the court, with which they were unfamiliar, and did not object. The court has fully met the opposition's expectations, probably to a greater degree than some of those who maneuvered its creation now like. Péter Paczolay, counsel to the Hungarian Constitutional Court's president, address at the American University Washington College of Law, 17 April 1992.

[40]It is not clear from the act what is necessary to challenge such a petition. Does it require a majority vote or just action by the parliamentary leader? See Hungarian Constitutional Court Act, Chapter III.

[41]The Czech and Slovak Federal Republic law, with its broad standing provisions for public officials, is probably a reaction to the very narrow standing provisions in the Constitutional Court's interwar predecessor, under which only a few of the highest federal judicial and legislative officials had standing. The latter had little incentive to challenge legislation they had usually supported, and the judicial officials were probably not eager to have

another court review their rulings. As a result, in some twenty years the interwar court did not handle a single case involving judicial review of legislation. Táborský, *Czechoslovak Democracy at Work,* 77–78.

[42]Ombudsmen are officers of the Polish court system whose duties include the power to appeal to the Constitutional Court matters that involve conflicting practices of administrative bodies. Memorandum to the author from Leonard Lukaszuk, Constitutional Tribunal vice-president, 25 April 1992.

[43]Polish Constitutional Tribunal Act, Article 20.

[44]Romanian Constitution, Article 144 (a), (b).

[45]RSFSR Constitutional Court Act, Article 59.

[46]RSFSR Constitutional Court Act, Articles 66–67.

[47]RSFSR Constitutional Court Act, Article 69.1 (14).

[48]See RSFSR Constitutional Court Act, Article 55; Romanian Constitution, Article 144 (a); Hungarian Constitutional Court Act, Section 21 (7).

[49]RSFSR Constitutional Court Act, article 9.

[50]According to a recent newspaper report:

> In 1991, the number of cases addressed to the Constitutional Court increased considerably over the previous year's figure: 1,625 cases were filed in 1990, while the number for the first ten months of 1991 amounted [to] 2,010. Two-thirds of the cases that have reached the Court so far were found to fall outside its competence. The Court rejected 1,200 appeals, and a further 100 cases were either transferred to other authorities or returned for lack of information. The number of cases that were actually deliberated was 698. Most of the cases (1,620) were brought before the Court by private individuals. Out of the 53 cases in which the Court declared its verdict this year, 40 were found to have violated the Constitution.

Hungarian Observer, January 1992, available in LEXIS, Nexis Library, HUNOBS File.

[51]RSFSR Constitutional Court Act, Article 62.3.

[52]Standing had been limited prior to l974 to the president, prime minister, and presidents of the two legislative chambers. Private parties in France still have no standing before the Conseil Constitutionnel. See Mauro Cappelletti and William Cohen, *Comparative Constitutional Law* (Indianapolis: Bobbs-Merrill, 1979), 47–48.

[53]Brewer-Carias, *Judicial Review in Comparative Law,* 199.

[54]RSFSR Constitutional Court Act, Article 1.3.

[55]See Lawrence H. Tribe, *American Constitutional Law,* 2d ed. (Mineola: Foundation Press, 1991), 152–53 (especially authorities cited in nn. 54–55).

[56]Bulgarian Constitution, Article 150 (2); Hungarian Constitutional Court Act, Section 38 (1). In Poland, Czechoslovakia, Russia, Bulgaria, and Hungary, the highest ordinary and administrative courts can also initiate proceedings in, or refer a case to, the Constitutional Court on a voluntary basis.

[57]In Russia, a private party has only a limited right, subject to the court's discretion. RSFSR Constitutional Court Act, Article 36; in Czechoslovakia, a

private party may go the Constitutional Court only for a human rights violation.

⁵⁸Polish Constitutional Court Act, Article 10.1.

⁵⁹RSFSR Constitutional Court Act, Article 3.1; Polish Constitutional Court Act, Article 13.2; Bulgarian Constitution, Chapter 8, Article 147 (1) (one-third of twelve judges); Romanian Constitution, Title V, Article 140 (2) (three of nine judges by one legislative chamber, three by the other); Hungarian Constitution, Chapter IV, Section 32/A (1) (a judge must be elected by two-thirds majority of the Parliament).

⁶⁰RSFSR Constitutional Court Act, Article 16.1.

⁶¹For Hungary, see Hungarian Constitution, Chapter II, Section 8 (3); for Czechoslovakia, see Czechoslovakian Constitutional Court Act.

⁶²See Cappelletti, *The Judicial Process in Comparative Perspective*, 52; Brewer-Carias, *Judicial Review in Comparative Law.*.

⁶³In Hayburn's Case, 2 U.S. (2 Dall) 409, 410 n. 2 (1792), the Supreme Court refused to accept jurisdiction over pension claims of disabled veterans because the judicial decisions were not final but could have been at least suspended "by the Secretary of War . . . where he [had] cause to suspect imposition or mistake."

⁶⁴Polish Constitutional Tribunal Act, Article 6.

⁶⁵Polish Constitution, Article 106.

⁶⁶The Czechoslovak court was established in March 1992. The Bulgarian court has been in operation about a year. The Polish Constitutional Tribunal, the oldest of the constitutional courts under discussion, has operated since 1985, but has only limited jurisdiction.

⁶⁷The Hungarian court has been the subject of several major articles already and need not be discussed here. See Péter Paczolay, "Judicial Review of the Hungarian Compensation Act," *Michigan Journal of International Law* 13 (1992): 806–31; Ethan Klingsberg, "Judicial Review and Hungary's Transition from Communism to Democracy: The Constitutional Court, the Continuity of Law, and the Redefinition of Property Rights," *Brigham Young University Law Review* 41 (1992): 41–144.

⁶⁸As of June 1992 the Russian court had filled only thirteen seats of its fifteen-judge complement.

⁶⁹For a good survey of Communist law, see Mary Ann Glendon, Michael Wallace Gordon and Christopher Osakwe, *Comparative Legal Traditions* (St. Paul: West Publishing Co., 1985), 672–967.

⁷⁰See "Russian Parliament Tries to Undo 'Mistakes,' " *Current Digest of the Soviet Press* [hereinafter *Soviet Press Digest*], 29 January 1992, 4 (citing *Izvestia*, 25 December 1991, 6), available in LEXIS, Nexis Library, CDSP File. But see Carla Thorson, "Legacy of the USSR Constitutional Court Supervision Committee," *RFE/RL Research Report*, 27 March 1992, 55: "Although it had limited authority, the committee was increasingly seen as an alternative source of political power and as a potential guarantor of human and civil rights. The committee's inadequacy resulted from the illegitimacy of the law it was entrusted to uphold and from the fact that its rulings were treated as rec-

ommendations and as such were not binding on the government. Nevertheless, the committee succeeded on more than one occasion in having legislation overturned."

[71] As of June 1992, the Russian constitution was still far from adoption.

[72] There seems to be no power to mediate disputes between republics in the Russian Federation unless a constitutional question is involved.

[73] Before becoming chairman of the Constitutional Court, Zorkin was the chairman of the Constitutional Commission and almost certainly its dominant figure. He was responsible for tilting the commission's initial recommendations in favor of a strongly presidential government. The recommendation was changed in favor of a parliamentary system after Zorkin left the commission for the court. For how this information bears on the court's decision on the KGB-MVD merger, see the text herein accompanying note 96. Although Zorkin remains a proponent of strong presidential power, I was told by a member of the Russian Parliament that Yeltsin had hoped another candidate, one who was not appointed to the court, would become chairman.

[74] Some judges are well thought of, including a distinguished woman researcher, but doubts have been expressed about the competence of other appointees. Carla Thorson, "RSFSR Forms Constitutional Court," *RFE, Report on the USSR*, 20 December 1991, 13, 15.

[75] I was later told in private conversations that the idea for the merger was actually Barannikov's.

[76] "Russian Parliament Tries to Undo 'Mistakes.' "

[77] There also were other more mundane considerations—many ISS and MVD employees feared they would lose their jobs in the merger, and the ISS members also reportedly were worried that some MVD officials might use their files for blackmail and other corrupt purposes.

[78] Olga Burkaleva, "Parliamentary Vacation: The Deputies Didn't Even Dream of Peace and Quiet," *Soviet Press Digest*, 29 January 1992, 15 (citing *Rossiiskaya Gazeta*, 31 December 1991, 2), available in LEXIS, Nexis Library, CDSP File.

[79] Julia Kozgreva, "Don't Pass Judgment Fellas! Judges Are Not Easy to Scare," *Soviet Press Digest*, 4 January 1992, 1 (citing *Komsomolskaya Pravda*), available in LEXIS, Nexis Library, CDSP File.

[80] See "Russian Parliament Tries to Undo 'Mistakes.' "

[81] The Russian court learned of these plans during the course of the hearing on the decree, 14 January 1992. *Foreign Broadcast Information Service* [hereinafter *FBIS*]-*USR-92-007*, 23 January 1992, 87.

[82] Valery Rudnev, "Constitutional Court Rescinds B. Yeltsin's Decree on the Creation of Security and Internal Affairs," *Soviet Press Digest*, 19 February 1992, p. 13 (citing *Izvestia*, 15 January 1992, 1, 3), available in LEXIS, Nexis Library, CDSP File (ellipsis in original).

[83] Some witnesses did not appear at the hearing, and the ministry concealed some documents from the court. At the close of the argument, Zorkin stated that these two issues would be considered at a later date. As of this writing, it was unclear whether the court had taken any action on them.

[84] The ruling read as follows:

> Having heard in open court the case testing the constitutionality of the Russian President's [merger] decree . . . the court has decided to declare this decree to be not in keeping with the RSFSR Constitution from the standpoint of the separation of legislative, executive and judicial powers established in the republic and . . . codified in the Constitution. This decision is final, cannot be appealed, and enters into force immediately after its proclamation. [T]his means that the Russian President's Decree on the Formation of the Ministry of Security and Internal Affairs and all other . . . acts . . . based on this decree or reproducing it lose their legal force and are to be considered invalid[, and] are to revert to the state existing before the adoption of the unconstitutional decree.

Rudnev, "Constitutional Court Rescinds Yeltsin's Decree."

[85] *FBIS-USR-92-017*, 20 February 1992, 67.

[86] *FBIS-USR-92-017*, 20 February 1992, 68.

[87] The court subsequently imposed a fine of 500 rubles on a newspaper that had printed the decree but not the court's decision.

[88] See Sergei Mostovshchikov, "Will the Constitutional Court Rescind Yeltsin's Decree Creating the Ministry of Security & Internal Affairs," *Soviet Press Digest*, 5 February 1992, 31 (citing *Izvestia*, 9 January 1992, p. 7), available in LEXIS, Nexis Library, CDSP File.

[89] "State Counselor Accepts Court Ruling on Decrees," *FBIS-SOV-92-015*, 23 January 1992, 44–45 (citing *Rossiiskaya Gazeta*, 20 January 1992, 2).

[90] "Security, Internal Ministry Decree Nullified," *FBIS-SOV-92–015*, 15 January 1992, 25 (citing *TASS International Service*, 14 January 1992).

[91] Guy Chazan, "Yeltsin Cancels Order Creating Super-Security Agency," United Press International, 17 January 1992, available in LEXIS, Nexis Library, UPI File. Several weeks later, I asked Chairman Zorkin whether such a threat did not infringe on Shakhrai's right of free speech, especially insofar as it was directed at Shakhrai's comment about the decision's "political and ideological motives." Zorkin replied, "Not where a public servant is concerned. As a private citizen, he can say what he wants to, but as a public servant he is speaking for the president and was, in effect, accusing the court of misconduct." Interview with Valery Zorkin, Russian Constitutional Court chairman, in Moscow, 31 January 1992.

[92] Dmitry Kazutin, "Review of the Press Coverage of the Officers' Assembly, Russian Writers' Protests, and the Constitutional Court Ruling," *Moscow News*, 22 January 1992, available in LEXIS, Nexis Library, CURRNT File.

[93] "By Hook or by Crook," *Soviet Press Digest*, 17 January 1992 (citing *Moskovsky Komsolets*, 17 January 1992, 1), available in LEXIS, Nexis Library, CDSP File.

[94] The day after the decision, Zorkin told a television interviewer that the decision "has been aimed not against the president, but for his protection. The main guarantee that this decision will be observed . . . is the mood of society itself. If society rejects this new option, I think nothing will save either the president, the legislators, or the Constitutional Court." "Constitutional Court on Invalidation Decree" (Moscow Russian Television broadcast, 15 January 1992), *FBIS-SOV-92-011*, 16 January 1992, 38.

95 Conversation with Alexander Blankenagel, professor of law, Würzburg, Germany, in Berlin, 27 January 1992.

96 Interview with Valery Zorkin, 31 January 1992.

97 The "nationalities problem"—the task of bringing together scores of different national, ethnic, and religious groups—has bedeviled Russia for centuries. It remains, according to Oleg Rumyantsev, the Russian Constitutional Commission's Secretary General and its de facto chairman, the major stumbling block to a new constitution. See "Federation: May the Voice of the Law Be More Audible than the Voice of the Legislation," *Soviet Press Digest*, 25 March 1992, 18 (citing *Rossiiskaya Gazeta*, 6 March 1992, 1). See generally Stephan Kux, *Soviet Federalism: A Comparative Perspective* (Boulder, Colo.: Westview Press, 1990).

98 Chechen-Ingushetia, now the self-styled Republic of Chechnya, was one of the first to try to break away. When Yeltsin responded with force, the Russian Parliament stopped him, and the matter simmers. Yeltsin has proposed a treaty among the republics, which eighteen have signed; Tatarstan and Chechnya have refused to sign. See Guy Chazan, "Russian Official Says Tatarstan Referendum Catastrophic," *United Press International*, 18 March 1992, available in LEXIS, Nexis Library, UPI File.

99 Tatarstan, an autonomous republic within the Russian Federation, has been ruled by Russia since 1552, when it was conquered by Ivan the Terrible. Its people, half ethnic Tatars and half Russians, live together peacefully with a good deal of intermarriage. The region is a major oil and gas producer and defense-industry center and has always considered itself exploited and dominated by Moscow. Tatarstan tried unsuccessfully for years to become a Union republic within the USSR, but failed in part because it is completely enclosed by other republics. Stalin reportedly said that the people of Tatarstan had as much chance of becoming a Union republic as they had of seeing their own ears. Ann Sheehy, "Tatarstan Asserts Its Sovereignty," *RFE/RL Daily Report*, 3 April 1992, 1–2.

100 "Constitutional Court Decision on Sovereignty," *FBIS-USR-92-038*, 3 April 1992, 84–90.

101 "Constitutional Court Decision on Sovereignty," 87.

102 The Russian government also felt that the referendum was simply the first step toward secession, even though the question did not explicitly call for that. See "Official Stance Outlined," *FBIS-USR-92-038*, 3 April 1992, 91–92 (citing *Argumenty i Fakty*, 11 March 1992, 4).

103 Interview with Mintimer Shaimiyev, president of the Republic of Tatarstan (Official Kremlin International News Broadcast, 13 March 1992), *Federal News Service*, 13 March 1992, available in LEXIS, Nexis Library, FEDNEW File.

104 Inna Muravgoya, "Notes to the Point: Test of Responsibility," *Soviet Press Digest*, 25 March 1992, 6 (citing *Rossiiskaya Gazeta*, 6 March 1992, 1–2), available in LEXIS, Nexis Library, CDSP File.

105 Steven Erlanger, "Tatar Area in Russia Votes on Sovereignty," *New York Times*, 21 March 1992, A5.

106 See RSFSR Constitution (May 1991), Article 70: "The territory of the RSFSR may not be altered without its consent."

[107]Interview with President Shaimiyev, 13 March 1992. Chairman Zorkin has denied these claims, stating that as early as 3 March 1992 the chairman of Tatarstan's Supreme Soviet had notice of the petition challenging not only the referendum's constitutionality, but also the validity of the sovereignty declarations leading up to the referendum. "Constitutional Court Chairman Presents Ruling on Tatarstan," *BBC Summary of World Broadcasts*, 20 March 1992 (citing Channel 1, Moscow TV television broadcast, 18 March 1992), available in LEXIS, Nexis Library, CURRNT File.

[108]Many other high officials appeared in court, some of whom, including nationalist Vice-President Alexander Rutskoi, testified.

[109]"Constitutional Court Decision on Sovereignty," 85, 87, 88. The court also rejected challenges to several of the laws. Chairman Zorkin later commented at a 19 March 1992 press conference that "a positive response to the referendum question could provoke a surge in nationalistic sentiments and create a threat not only to the state structure, but also to the observance of human rights." "On the Referendum in Tatarstan," *Soviet Press Digest*, 15 April 1992, 21 (citing *Rossiiskaya Gazeta*, 19 March 1992, 1), available in LEXIS, Nexis Library, CDSP File.

[110]RSFSR Constitution (May 1991), Chapter 8, Article 81.

[111]Alexei Tabachnikov, "Russian Parliament to Discuss Tatar Referendum Plans," *TASS*, 18 March 1992, available in LEXIS, Nexis Library, TASS File.

[112]"Constitutional Court Decision on Sovereignty," 87.

[113]"Constitutional Court Chairman Presents Ruling on Tatarstan."

[114]"Constitutional Court Chairman Presents Ruling on Tatarstan."

[115]"Constitutional Court Chairman on Tatarstan," *FBIS-SOV-92-051*, 16 March 1992, 63 (citing Moscow Russian Television Network broadcast, 13 March 1992). Zorkin also raised the possibility that the court might impeach Tatarstan officials who disobeyed the order. "Head of Constitutional Court on Tatar Referendum," *BBC Summary of World Broadcasts*, 20 March 1992 (citing Mayak Radio Moscow broadcast, 18 March 1992), available in LEXIS, Nexis Library, BBCSWB File.

[116]Steven Erlanger, "Tatar Area Vote Backs Autonomy Push," *New York Times*, 23 March 1992, A6.

[117]"Supreme Court Is Impartial" (Official Kremlin News Broadcast), *Federal News Service*, 27 April 1992, available in LEXIS, Nexis Library, FEDNEW File.

[118]Julia Wishnevsky, "Constitutional Court Sides with Yeltsin Against Khasbulatov," *RFE/RL Daily Report*, 29 April 1992, 3.

[119]Compare the KGB-MVB merger decision, discussed here in the text accompanying nn. 85–87. In the merger case, the court held that the Supreme Soviet had constitutional authority to create ministries and jurisdiction over actions involving national security and defense. Wishnevsky, "Constitutional Court Sides with Yeltsin," 3.

[120]Wishnevsky, "Constitutional Court Sides with Yeltsin," 3. After this chapter was written, the court came down with another victory for President Yeltsin against the Russian Parliament. In the first appeal by the president to the court against a parliamentary act, Yeltsin successfully challenged a

law giving Parliament control over an antimonopoly committee that had previously been a part of the government. Telegraph Agency of the Soviet Union, 20 May 1992.

[121]Yury Kukanov, "Soviet and Mayor Part Company," *Soviet Press Digest*, 4 April 1992 (citing *Rossiiskaya Gazeta*), available in LEXIS, Nexis Library, CDSP File.

[122]Yelena Tarasova, "Moscow Government Must Resign!" *Soviet Press Digest*, 26 February 1992, 4 (citing *Kuranty*), available in LEXIS, Nexis Library, CDSP File.

[123]"Valentin Pavlov Still Considers Himself Prime Minister," *Soviet Press Digest*, 26 March 1992 (citing *Nezavisimaya Gazeta*), available in LEXIS, Nexis Library, CDSP File.

[124]"Constitutional Court Pledges to Thwart Dictatorship," *BBC Summary of World Broadcasts*, 8 January 1992 (citing *Sovetskaya Rossiiya*, 27 December 1991), available in LEXIS, Nexis Library, BBCSWB File. The statement first appeared in a Constitutional Court press release issued at the 27 December 1992 session at which the court suspended the ISS-MVD merger decree.

[125]Chairman Zorkin is not the only one to speak up. For example, although the Constitutional Court has not yet ruled in a child custody case, Judge Ernest Ametistov recently said in a news broadcast: "Here is another typical example of an unconstitutional practice. In divorce cases the courts are inclined to give custody of children not to their fathers, but to their mothers, although no such norm is recorded within the Law or in the Constitution[. T]he fundamental principle is the equality of rights of both parents. And the citizens must know this." "Supreme Court Is Impartial." I am told that the Hungarian judges have tried to avoid public attention.

[126]See, for example, D. Muratov, "Life Sentence in Court," translated as "Constitutional Court, Chairman Zorkin Cited," *FBIS-SOV-92-033*, 19 February 1992, 44–45 (citing *Komsomlskaya Pravda*, 8 February 1992, 1) (need for a conservative party). By comparison, when Chief Justice Marshall wanted to defend McCulloch v. Maryland, 17 U.S. (4 Wheat) 316 (1819), extrajudicially, he did so under a pseudonym. See, for example, Gerald Gunther, ed., *John Marshall's Defense of McCulloch v. Maryland* (Stanford: Stanford University Press, 1969).

[127]Dmitry Kazutin, "Review of the Press Coverage of the Officers' Assembly, Russian Writers' Protests, and the Constitutional Court Ruling," *Moscow News*, 22 January 1992, available in LEXIS, Nexis Library, CURRNT File.

[128]Memorandum on the Constitutional Court of Bulgaria prepared by Judge Metody Tilev, April 1992.

[129]For a discussion of these issues, see Kjell Engelbrekt, *RFE/RL Report on Eastern Europe*, 29 November 1991, 7.

[130]Bulgarian Constitution, Article 11 (4).

[131]Rada Nicolaev, *RFE/RL Daily Report*, 22 April 1992, 4–5.

[132]In 1982, a constitutional tribunal was authorized with the very limited subject-matter jurisdiction and standing provisions described earlier, and in 1985 a constitutional act was passed actually establishing the tribunal.

[133]Quoted in Mark F. Brzezinski, "Constitutional Tribunal: Guardian of the Legal System," *The Warsaw Voice*, 19 January 1992, available in LEXIS, Nexis Library, CURRNT File.

[134]Memorandum from Polish Constitutional Court Vice-President Leonard Lukaszuk to the author, 25 April 1992.

[135]Memorandum from Leonard Lukaszuk.

[136]Interview with Leonard Lukaszuk, 25 April 1992.

[137]Linnet Myers, "Polish Wage Hike Sparks Resignation," *Chicago Tribune*, 7 May 1992, C12.

[138]Christopher Bobinski, "Polish IMF Deal in Jeopardy," *Financial Times*, 7 May 1992, 24.

[139]Memorandum from Leonard Lukaszuk.

[140]Stephen Engelberg, "Poland Faces New Battle on Abortion," *New York Times*, 21 April 1992, A3.

[141]Moravia, which is part of the Czech lands, is considered to be more neutral territory than either Prague, the Bohemian capital, or Bratislava, the capital of Slovakia.

[142]Czechoslovakian Constitutional Court Act, Article 10.

[143]The Hungarian court currently has ten judges, although it is ultimately supposed to have fifteen. Bulgaria also has twelve, and Poland has ten. Russia and Romania both have an odd number of judges.

[144]The Hungarians have avoided deadlock by accident. In cases where the full court sits, illness and other absences have resulted in odd-numbered panels. Conversation with Péter Paczolay, counselor to the Hungarian Constitutional Court President.

[145]Czechoslovakian Constitutional Court Act, Article 2.

[146]On these and related problems, see Lloyd Cutler and Herman Schwartz, "Constitutional Reform in Czechoslovakia: E Duobus Unum?," *University of Chicago Law Review* 58 (1991): 511, 542–43. There is also a possibility that Czechs and Slovaks will be unable to agree on a new constitution and will try to get by with amendments to the current Constitution.

[147]Czechoslovak Constitutional Act of 12 December 1990 [hereinafter Division of Powers Act] (amending the Constitutional Act No. 143/1968 on Czechoslovak Federation). For the history of this amendment, see Cutler and Schwartz, "Constitutional Reform in Czechoslovakia," 524–25.

[148]Division of Powers Act, Article 20 (emphasis added).

[149]*FBIS-EEU-92-077,* 21 April 1992, 5–6.

[150]Division of Powers Act, Article 20 (e). For a discussion of this decision, see Eric Stein, "Devolution or Deconstruction Czecho-Slovak Style," *Michigan Journal of International Law* 13 (1992), 786–805.

[151]Czechoslovak Federal Republic Charter of Fundamental Rights and Freedoms, Article 3 (1) (translation on file with the author).

[152]Vera Tolz, "Access to KGB and CPSU Archives in Russia," *RFE/RL Research Report*, 17 April 1992. Opening the secret police files in Germany has revealed husbands informing on wives, doctors poisoning patients, and

betrayals of close friends and family. Stephen Kinzer, "East Germans Face Their Accusers," *New York Times Magazine*, 12 April 1992, 24.

[153]One method is to abandon the traditional Communist disdain for nationalism—only the class struggle counts—and suddenly become intensely nationalistic. This is the case in Slovakia, Bulgaria, Tatarstan, and elsewhere.

[154]"Lustration" means purification.

[155]Act 451/91 (4 October 1991), reprinted in *News from Helsinki Watch: Czechoslovakia*, April 1992, 9–17.

[156]The International Labor Office (ILO) has ruled that the law discriminates on the basis of political belief. Report under Article 24 of the ILO Constitution alleging nonobservance by the Czech and Slovak Federal Republic of the Discrimination (Employment and Occupation) Convention 1958 (No. 111), 5 March 1992; for remarks of Catherine Lalumiere, Secretary General of the Council of Europe, see Barbara Kroulik, "Lalumiere Criticizes Czechoslovak Screening Law," *RFE/RL Daily Report*, 8 April 1992, 5–6 (violates European Convention of Human Rights); see generally Jeri Laber, "Witch Hunt in Prague," *New York Review of Books*, 23 April 1992 (views of Executive Director of Helsinki Watch). Many of these criticisms were aired at the conference "Justice in Times of Transition" convened by the Charter 77 Foundation (New York) in Salzburg, Austria, on 7–10 March 1992, which the author cochaired.

[157]In an obvious effort to avoid entanglement in upcoming parliamentary elections scheduled for 6 June 1992, the court will not deal with the case until after the elections.

[158]There will be a special impartiality problem in the lustration case, for at least two members of the court—including the president, a distinguished and respected lawyer from Slovakia—were members of the Federal Assembly and voted for the law. They should have to recuse themselves, but need not. Since this chapter was written, the possibility that there may not be a Czechoslovak federation has grown to become a high probability. If a split were to occur, obviously the federal Constitutional Court would no longer exist, probably to be replaced by similar courts in the two new states.

Contributors

A. E. DICK HOWARD is the White Burkett Miller Professor of Law and Public Affairs at the University of Virginia. A Rhodes Scholar at Oxford University, he was the chief architect of the current Virginia Constitution. His books include *The Road from Runnymede: Magna Carta and Constitutionalism in America*. He has consulted with drafters of new constitutions in various countries, including Hungary, Poland, Czechoslovakia, Bulgaria, Romania, Albania, and the Russian Republic.

KATARINA MATHERNOVA is an associate at Wilmer, Cutler & Pickering in Washington, D.C. A graduate of Comenius University in Bratislava, she received the LL.M. degree from the University of Michigan. She worked closely with a group of American and West European scholars, judges, and others who consulted with drafters at work on a constitution for the Czech and Slovak Federal Republic.

PÉTER PACZOLAY is Chief Counselor to Hungary's Constitutional Court and a lecturer on political theory and comparative legal systems at Eotvos Lorand University in Budapest. He received his Ph.D. degree from that university and is a former Fellow of the Woodrow Wilson Center.

ANDRZEJ RAPACZYNSKI is Professor of Law at Columbia University. He holds J.D. and Ph.D. degrees from that university. His publications include *Nature and Politics: Liberalism in the Philosophies of Hobbes, Locke and Rousseau*. Professor Rapaczynski has served as an expert adviser to the Subcommittee on Institutions of the Polish Parliament's Constitutional Committee.

JOANNA REGULSKA is Associate Professor of Geography at Rutgers University. A specialist in urban and political geography, she received her Ph.D. degree from the University of Colorado. As director of the Local Democracy in Poland program, Professor

Regulska has worked extensively with political leaders in Central and Eastern Europe, assisting in drafting local government legislation and developing long-term training programs for local government officials.

HERMAN SCHWARTZ is Professor of Law at American University. A graduate of Harvard College and of Harvard Law School, he has worked for human rights in the United States and abroad for more than three decades. A member of the Board of the Charter 77 Foundation (New York), he currently cochairs the project "Justice in Times of Transition." Professor Schwartz has advised over a half-dozen countries in Central and Eastern Europe and the former Soviet Union on constitutional and human rights reforms.

Index

Adams, John, quoted, 21
affirmative rights, in constitutions,
 17–19, 146–48; in Hungary, 47–48;
 in Poland, 107–9
Alliance of Free Democrats (SZDSZ),
 compromise between, and MDF,
 24–25, 37
amendments, constitutional: in
 Czechoslovakia, 67–68, 76; in
 Hungary, 24–25, 32, 47–48; in
 Poland, 109
Ametistov, Ernest, 205n125
anti-Communist coalitions,
 disintegration of, 60–61, 82n26,
 125–26
Aranybulla (Golden Bull) of 1222
 (Hungary), 10, 22–24
aspirational rights, *see* affirmative
 rights
autonomy, Slovaks' goal of, 59–60,
 62–63, 77–78

Badinter, Robert, 10, 12
Barannikov, Victor, 178–80, 181,
 201n75
Bielecki, Krzysztof, 103
bill(s) of rights, 10, 15–19; English, 11;
 Hungarian, 47–48; U.S., 9, 11, 13–
 15
Brazil, 1988 Constitution of, 18
Brno (Moravia), Czechoslovak
 Constitutional Court placed in,
 192
Bulgaria, reform of central-local
 relations in, 138–39
Bulgarian Constitutional Court, 189–
 90; *see also* East European
 constitutional courts
Burke, Edmund, quoted, 23

Catholicism, in Slovak society, 61,
 83n30
CDP (Civic Democratic Party), and
 breakup of the Czechoslovak
 Federation, 78–79
central-local relations: framework for
 comparing, 153–55; reform of,
 137–45
Chamber of Nations
 (Czechoslovakia), 64–65, 69
Chamber of People (Czechoslovakia),
 64–65, 69
Charter of Fundamental Rights and
 Freedoms (1991)
 (Czechoslovakia), 16, 17, 68
church and state, separation of,
 83n30, 128n24
Citizens' Committees (Poland), 115
Civic Democratic Party (CDP), and
 breakup of the Czechoslovak
 Federation, 78–79
Cleveland Agreement (1916), 59
Committee of Delegates (Zbor
 Povereníkov) (Slovakia), 60
Communist Constitution of 1952, in
 Poland, 93–95
Communist regime: in
 Czechoslovakia, 59–60, 72; in
 Poland, 93–98
constitutional amendments, *see*
 amendments, constitutional
Constitutional Committee (Poland),
 99, 104; and electoral law, 110–12,
 117–18; and proportional
 representation, 112–15; as subject
 of controversy, 100–104; *see also*
 Constitutional Subcommittee(s)
 (Poland)